LONG DAY'S
J·O·U·R·N·E·Y
INTO NIGHT

EUGENE O'NEILL

Yale University Press *New Haven & London*

CAUTION: Professionals and amateurs are hereby warned that *Long Day's Journey into Night,* being fully protected under the copyright laws of the United States of America, the British Empire, including the Dominion of Canada, and all other countries of the copyright union, is subject to a royalty. All rights, including professional, amateur, motion picture, television, recitation, public reading, radio broadcasting, and the rights of translation into foreign languages, are strictly reserved. All inquiries regarding this play should be addressed to Cadwalader, Wickersham & Taft, Trustees of C. M. O'Neill, One Wall Street, New York, N.Y. 10005.

THE EUGENE O'NEILL COLLECTION was founded at the Yale University Library in 1931 by Carlotta Monterey O'Neill. It includes notes, photographs, and the manuscripts of plays, among them LONG DAY'S JOURNEY INTO NIGHT. All royalties from the sale of the Yale editions of this book go to Yale University for the benefit of the Eugene O'Neill Collection, for the purchase of books in the field of drama, and for the establishment of Eugene O'Neill Scholarships in the Yale School of Drama.

Frontispiece: Wood engraving by Michael McCurdy

LONG DAY'S

JOURNEY

INTO NIGHT

Publisher's Note, 1989

Since its first publication in February 1956, *Long Day's Journey into Night* has gone through numerous reprintings. With this printing, the sixty-first, we have taken the opportunity to correct several errors recently reported by scholars who have made careful examinations of final typescripts of the play. It has been discovered that Carlotta O'Neill, retyping from a previous version heavily edited by O'Neill, accidentally dropped lines in several places.

We wish to take note first of a correction that was silently made in the fifth printing after Donald Gallup called our attention to missing lines on page 167. The dialogue and stage directions restored were those beginning with "Kid" in line 8 and ending with "old" in line 10.

For the corrections made in this printing, we thank the following: Michael Hinden (for pointing out missing lines on pages 94, 103, and 164 and errors on page 155), Judith E. Barlow (for missing lines on page 95), and Stephen Black (for an error on page 109). On page 94 a sentence ("Anyway, by tonight, what will you care?") has been added to Edmund's dialogue at line 29. On page 95 lines 5–9 are printed for the first time. On page 103 a sentence ("It's a special kind of medicine.") has been restored at line 27. The errors corrected on pages 109 and 155 were minor, although puzzling, misprints (e.g., "fron" for "front," "sibject" for "subject"). On page 164 a sentence ("No one hopes more than I do you'll knock 'em all dead.") has been restored in line 7.

For Carlotta, on our 12th Wedding Anniversary

*Dearest: I give you the original script of this play
of old sorrow, written in tears and blood. A sadly
inappropriate gift, it would seem, for a day
celebrating happiness. But you will understand. I
mean it as a tribute to your love and tenderness which
gave me the faith in love that enabled me to
face my dead at last and write this play—write it
with deep pity and understanding and forgiveness for
all the four haunted Tyrones.*

*These twelve years, Beloved One, have been a
Journey into Light—into love. You know my gratitude.
And my love!*

GENE

*Tao House
July 22, 1941.*

Characters

JAMES TYRONE

MARY CAVAN TYRONE, *his wife*

JAMES TYRONE, JR., *their elder son*

EDMUND TYRONE, *their younger son*

CATHLEEN, *second girl*

Scenes

Act One

SCENE   *Living room of James Tyrone's summer home on a morning in August, 1912.*

At rear are two double doorways with portieres. The one at right leads into a front parlor with the formally arranged, set appearance of a room rarely occupied. The other opens on a dark, windowless back parlor, never used except as a passage from living room to dining room. Against the wall between the doorways is a small bookcase, with a picture of Shakespeare above it, containing novels by Balzac, Zola, Stendhal, philosophical and sociological works by Schopenhauer, Nietzsche, Marx, Engels, Kropotkin, Max Stirner, plays by Ibsen, Shaw, Strindberg, poetry by Swinburne, Rossetti, Wilde, Ernest Dowson, Kipling, etc.

In the right wall, rear, is a screen door leading out on the porch which extends halfway around the house. Farther forward, a series of three windows looks over the front lawn to the harbor and the avenue that runs along the water front. A small wicker table and an ordinary oak desk are against the wall, flanking the windows.

In the left wall, a similar series of windows looks out on the grounds in back of the house. Beneath them is a wicker couch with cushions, its head toward rear. Farther back is a large, glassed-in bookcase with sets of Dumas, Victor Hugo, Charles Lever, three sets of Shakespeare, The World's Best Literature in fifty large volumes, Hume's History of England, Thiers' History of the Consulate and Empire, Smollett's History of England, Gibbon's Roman Empire and miscellaneous volumes of old plays, poetry, and several histories of Ireland. The astonishing thing about these sets is that all the volumes have the look of having been read and reread.

The hardwood floor is nearly covered by a rug, inoffensive in design and color. At center is a round table with a green shaded reading lamp, the cord plugged in one of the four sockets in the chandelier above. Around the table within reading-light range are four chairs, three of them wicker armchairs, the fourth (at right front of table) a varnished oak rocker with leather bottom.

It is around 8.30. Sunshine comes through the windows at right.

As the curtain rises, the family have just finished breakfast. MARY TYRONE and her husband enter together from the back parlor, coming from the dining room.

Mary is fifty-four, about medium height. She still has a young, graceful figure, a trifle plump, but showing little evidence of middle-aged waist and hips, although she is not tightly corseted. Her face is distinctly Irish in type. It must once have been extremely pretty, and is still striking. It does not match her healthy figure but is thin and pale with the bone structure prominent. Her nose is long and straight, her mouth wide with full, sensitive lips. She uses no rouge or any sort of make-up. Her high forehead is framed by thick, pure white hair. Accentuated by her pallor and white hair, her dark brown eyes appear black. They are unusually large and beautiful, with black brows and long curling lashes.

What strikes one immediately is her extreme nervousness. Her hands are never still. They were once beautiful hands, with long, tapering fingers, but rheumatism has knotted the joints and warped the fingers, so that now they have an ugly crippled look. One avoids looking at them, the more so because one is conscious she is sensitive about their appearance and humiliated by her inability to control the nervousness which draws attention to them.

She is dressed simply but with a sure sense of what becomes

her. Her hair is arranged with fastidious care. Her voice is soft and attractive. When she is merry, there is a touch of Irish lilt in it.

Her most appealing quality is the simple, unaffected charm of a shy convent-girl youthfulness she has never lost—an innate unworldly innocence.

JAMES TYRONE *is sixty-five but looks ten years younger. About five feet eight, broad-shouldered and deep-chested, he seems taller and slenderer because of his bearing, which has a soldierly quality of head up, chest out, stomach in, shoulders squared. His face has begun to break down but he is still remarkably good looking—a big, finely shaped head, a handsome profile, deep-set light-brown eyes. His grey hair is thin with a bald spot like a monk's tonsure.*

The stamp of his profession is unmistakably on him. Not that he indulges in any of the deliberate temperamental posturings of the stage star. He is by nature and preference a simple, unpretentious man, whose inclinations are still close to his humble beginnings and his Irish farmer forebears. But the actor shows in all his unconscious habits of speech, movement and gesture. These have the quality of belonging to a studied technique. His voice is remarkably fine, resonant and flexible, and he takes great pride in it.

His clothes, assuredly, do not costume any romantic part. He wears a threadbare, ready-made, grey sack suit and shineless black shoes, a collar-less shirt with a thick white handkerchief knotted loosely around his throat. There is nothing picturesquely careless about this get-up. It is commonplace shabby. He believes in wearing his clothes to the limit of usefulness, is dressed now for gardening, and doesn't give a damn how he looks.

He has never been really sick a day in his life. He has no nerves. There is a lot of stolid, earthy peasant in him, mixed *with streaks of sentimental melancholy and rare flashes of intuitive sensibility.*

Tyrone's arm is around his wife's waist as they appear from the back parlor. Entering the living room he gives her a playful hug.

TYRONE

You're a fine armful now, Mary, with those twenty pounds you've gained.

MARY
Smiles affectionately.
I've gotten too fat, you mean, dear. I really ought to reduce.

TYRONE

None of that, my lady! You're just right. We'll have no talk of reducing. Is that why you ate so little breakfast?

MARY

So little? I thought I ate a lot.

TYRONE

You didn't. Not as much as I'd like to see, anyway.

MARY
Teasingly.
Oh you! You expect everyone to eat the enormous breakfast you do. No one else in the world could without dying of indigestion.
She comes forward to stand by the right of table.

TYRONE
Following her.
I hope I'm not as big a glutton as that sounds.
With hearty satisfaction.
But thank God, I've kept my appetite and I've the digestion of a young man of twenty, if I am sixty-five.

MARY

You surely have, James. No one could deny that.
She laughs and sits in the wicker armchair at right rear of table. He comes around in back of her and selects a cigar

from a box on the table and cuts off the end with a little clipper. From the dining room Jamie's and Edmund's voices are heard. Mary turns her head that way.

Why did the boys stay in the dining room, I wonder? Cathleen must be waiting to clear the table.

TYRONE

Jokingly but with an undercurrent of resentment.

It's a secret confab they don't want me to hear, I suppose. I'll bet they're cooking up some new scheme to touch the Old Man.

She is silent on this, keeping her head turned toward their voices. Her hands appear on the table top, moving restlessly. He lights his cigar and sits down in the rocker at right of table, which is his chair, and puffs contentedly.

There's nothing like the first after-breakfast cigar, if it's a good one, and this new lot have the right mellow flavor. They're a great bargain, too. I got them dead cheap. It was McGuire put me on to them.

MARY

A trifle acidly.

I hope he didn't put you on to any new piece of property at the same time. His real estate bargains don't work out so well.

TYRONE

Defensively.

I wouldn't say that, Mary. After all, he was the one who advised me to buy that place on Chestnut Street and I made a quick turnover on it for a fine profit.

MARY

Smiles now with teasing affection.

I know. The famous one stroke of good luck. I'm sure McGuire never dreamed—

Then she pats his hand.

Never mind, James. I know it's a waste of breath trying to convince you you're not a cunning real estate speculator.

TYRONE

Huffily.

I've no such idea. But land is land, and it's safer than the stocks and bonds of Wall Street swindlers.

15

Then placatingly.
But let's not argue about business this early in the morning.
> *A pause. The boys' voices are again heard and one of them has a fit of coughing. Mary listens worriedly. Her fingers play nervously on the table top.*

MARY

James, it's Edmund you ought to scold for not eating enough. He hardly touched anything except coffee. He needs to eat to keep up his strength. I keep telling him that but he says he simply has no appetite. Of course, there's nothing takes away your appetite like a bad summer cold.

TYRONE

Yes, it's only natural. So don't let yourself get worried—

MARY
> *Quickly.*
Oh, I'm not. I know he'll be all right in a few days if he takes care of himself.
> *As if she wanted to dismiss the subject but can't.*
But it does seem a shame he should have to be sick right now.

TYRONE

Yes, it is bad luck.
> *He gives her a quick, worried look.*
But you mustn't let it upset you, Mary. Remember, you've got to take care of yourself, too.

MARY
> *Quickly.*
I'm not upset. There's nothing to be upset about. What makes you think I'm upset?

TYRONE

Why, nothing, except you've seemed a bit high-strung the past few days.

MARY
> *Forcing a smile.*
I have? Nonsense, dear. It's your imagination.
> *With sudden tenseness.*

You really must not watch me all the time, James. I mean, it makes me self-conscious.

> TYRONE
>
> *Putting a hand over one of her nervously playing ones.*

Now, now, Mary. That's your imagination. If I've watched you it was to admire how fat and beautiful you looked.

> *His voice is suddenly moved by deep feeling.*

I can't tell you the deep happiness it gives me, darling, to see you as you've been since you came back to us, your dear old self again.

> *He leans over and kisses her cheek impulsively—then turning back adds with a constrained air.*

So keep up the good work, Mary.

> MARY
>
> *Has turned her head away.*

I will, dear.

> *She gets up restlessly and goes to the windows at right.*

Thank heavens, the fog is gone.

> *She turns back.*

I do feel out of sorts this morning. I wasn't able to get much sleep with that awful foghorn going all night long.

> TYRONE

Yes, it's like having a sick whale in the back yard. It kept me awake, too.

> MARY
>
> *Affectionately amused.*

Did it? You had a strange way of showing your restlessness. You were snoring so hard I couldn't tell which was the foghorn!

> *She comes to him, laughing, and pats his cheek playfully.*

Ten foghorns couldn't disturb you. You haven't a nerve in you. You've never had.

> TYRONE
>
> *His vanity piqued—testily.*

Nonsense. You always exaggerate about my snoring.

> MARY

I couldn't. If you could only hear yourself once—

A burst of laughter comes from the dining room. She turns her head, smiling.

What's the joke, I wonder?

TYRONE
Grumpily.

It's on me. I'll bet that much. It's always on the Old Man.

MARY
Teasingly.

Yes, it's terrible the way we all pick on you, isn't it? You're so abused!

She laughs—then with a pleased, relieved air.

Well, no matter what the joke is about, it's a relief to hear Edmund laugh. He's been so down in the mouth lately.

TYRONE
Ignoring this—resentfully.

Some joke of Jamie's, I'll wager. He's forever making sneering fun of somebody, that one.

MARY

Now don't start in on poor Jamie, dear.

Without conviction.

He'll turn out all right in the end, you wait and see.

TYRONE

He'd better start soon, then. He's nearly thirty-four.

MARY
Ignoring this.

Good heavens, are they going to stay in the dining room all day?

She goes to the back parlor doorway and calls.

Jamie! Edmund! Come in the living room and give Cathleen a chance to clear the table.

Edmund calls back, "We're coming, Mama." She goes back to the table.

TYRONE
Grumbling.

You'd find excuses for him no matter what he did.

18

MARY

Sitting down beside him, pats his hand.

Shush.

Their sons JAMES, JR., *and* EDMUND *enter together from the back parlor. They are both grinning, still chuckling over what had caused their laughter, and as they come forward they glance at their father and their grins grow broader.*

Jamie, the elder, is thirty-three. He has his father's broad-shouldered, deep-chested physique, is an inch taller and weighs less, but appears shorter and stouter because he lacks Tyrone's bearing and graceful carriage. He also lacks his father's vitality. The signs of premature disintegration are on him. His face is still good looking, despite marks of dissipation, but it has never been handsome like Tyrone's, although Jamie resembles him rather than his mother. He has fine brown eyes, their color midway between his father's lighter and his mother's darker ones. His hair is thinning and already there is indication of a bald spot like Tyrone's. His nose is unlike that of any other member of the family, pronouncedly aquiline. Combined with his habitual expression of cynicism it gives his countenance a Mephistophelian cast. But on the rare occasions when he smiles without sneering, his personality possesses the remnant of a humorous, romantic, irresponsible Irish charm—that of the beguiling ne'er-do-well, with a strain of the sentimentally poetic, attractive to women and popular with men.

He is dressed in an old sack suit, not as shabby as Tyrone's, and wears a collar and tie. His fair skin is sunburned a reddish, freckled tan.

Edmund is ten years younger than his brother, a couple of inches taller, thin and wiry. Where Jamie takes after his father, with little resemblance to his mother, Edmund looks like both his parents, but is more like his mother. Her big, dark eyes are the dominant feature in his long, narrow Irish face. His mouth has the same quality of hypersensitiveness

19

hers possesses. His high forehead is hers accentuated, with dark brown hair, sunbleached to red at the ends, brushed straight back from it. But his nose is his father's and his face in profile recalls Tyrone's. Edmund's hands are noticeably like his mother's, with the same exceptionally long fingers. They even have to a minor degree the same nervousness. It is in the quality of extreme nervous sensibility that the likeness of Edmund to his mother is most marked.

He is plainly in bad health. Much thinner than he should be, his eyes appear feverish and his cheeks are sunken. His skin, in spite of being sunburned a deep brown, has a parched sallowness. He wears a shirt, collar and tie, no coat, old flannel trousers, brown sneakers.

MARY
Turns smilingly to them, in a merry tone that is a bit forced.
I've been teasing your father about his snoring.
To Tyrone.
I'll leave it to the boys, James. They must have heard you. No, not you, Jamie. I could hear you down the hall almost as bad as your father. You're like him. As soon as your head touches the pillow you're off and ten foghorns couldn't wake you.
She stops abruptly, catching Jamie's eyes regarding her with an uneasy, probing look. Her smile vanishes and her manner becomes self-conscious.
Why are you staring, Jamie?
Her hands flutter up to her hair.
Is my hair coming down? It's hard for me to do it up properly now. My eyes are getting so bad and I never can find my glasses.

JAMIE
Looks away guiltily.
Your hair's all right, Mama. I was only thinking how well you look.

TYRONE
Heartily.
Just what I've been telling her, Jamie. She's so fat and sassy, there'll soon be no holding her.

EDMUND

Yes, you certainly look grand, Mama.

> *She is reassured and smiles at him lovingly. He winks with a kidding grin.*

I'll back you up about Papa's snoring. Gosh, what a racket!

JAMIE

I heard him, too.

> *He quotes, putting on a ham-actor manner.*

"The Moor, I know his trumpet."

> *His mother and brother laugh.*

TYRONE

> *Scathingly.*

If it takes my snoring to make you remember Shakespeare instead of the dope sheet on the ponies, I hope I'll keep on with it.

MARY

Now, James! You mustn't be so touchy.

> *Jamie shrugs his shoulders and sits down in the chair on her right.*

EDMUND

> *Irritably.*

Yes, for Pete's sake, Papa! The first thing after breakfast! Give it a rest, can't you?

> *He slumps down in the chair at left of table next to his brother. His father ignores him.*

MARY

> *Reprovingly.*

Your father wasn't finding fault with you. You don't have to always take Jamie's part. You'd think you were the one ten years older.

JAMIE

> *Boredly.*

What's all the fuss about? Let's forget it.

TYRONE

> *Contemptuously.*

Yes, forget! Forget everything and face nothing! It's a convenient philosophy if you've no ambition in life except to—

MARY

James, do be quiet.

She puts an arm around his shoulder—coaxingly.

You must have gotten out of the wrong side of the bed this morning.

To the boys, changing the subject.

What were you two grinning about like Cheshire cats when you came in? What was the joke?

TYRONE

With a painful effort to be a good sport.

Yes, let us in on it, lads. I told your mother I knew damned well it would be one on me, but never mind that, I'm used to it.

JAMIE

Dryly.

Don't look at me. This is the Kid's story.

EDMUND

Grins.

I meant to tell you last night, Papa, and forgot it. Yesterday when I went for a walk I dropped in at the Inn—

MARY

Worriedly.

You shouldn't drink now, Edmund.

EDMUND

Ignoring this.

And who do you think I met there, with a beautiful bun on, but Shaughnessy, the tenant on that farm of yours.

MARY

Smiling.

That dreadful man! But he is funny.

TYRONE

Scowling.

He's not so funny when you're his landlord. He's a wily Shanty Mick, that one. He could hide behind a corkscrew. What's he complaining about now, Edmund—for I'm damned sure he's complaining. I suppose he wants his rent lowered. I let him have the place for

almost nothing, just to keep someone on it, and he never pays that
till I threaten to evict him.

> EDMUND

No, he didn't beef about anything. He was so pleased with life he
even bought a drink, and that's practically unheard of. He was delighted because he'd had a fight with your friend, Harker, the Standard Oil millionaire, and won a glorious victory.

> MARY
> *With amused dismay.*

Oh, Lord! James, you'll really have to do something—

> TYRONE

Bad luck to Shaughnessy, anyway!

> JAMIE
> *Maliciously.*

I'll bet the next time you see Harker at the Club and give him the
old respectful bow, he won't see you.

> EDMUND

Yes. Harker will think you're no gentleman for harboring a tenant
who isn't humble in the presence of a king of America.

> TYRONE

Never mind the Socialist gabble. I don't care to listen—

> MARY
> *Tactfully.*

Go on with your story, Edmund.

> EDMUND
> *Grins at his father provocatively.*

Well, you remember, Papa, the ice pond on Harker's estate is right
next to the farm, and you remember Shaughnessy keeps pigs. Well,
it seems there's a break in the fence and the pigs have been bathing
in the millionaire's ice pond, and Harker's foreman told him he was
sure Shaughnessy had broken the fence on purpose to give his pigs
a free wallow.

> MARY
> *Shocked and amused.*

Good heavens!

TYRONE

Sourly, but with a trace of admiration.

I'm sure he did, too, the dirty scallywag. It's like him.

EDMUND

So Harker came in person to rebuke Shaughnessy.

He chuckles.

A very bonehead play! If I needed any further proof that our ruling plutocrats, especially the ones who inherited their boodle, are not mental giants, that would clinch it.

TYRONE

With appreciation, before he thinks.

Yes, he'd be no match for Shaughnessy.

Then he growls.

Keep your damned anarchist remarks to yourself. I won't have them in my house.

But he is full of eager anticipation.

What happened?

EDMUND

Harker had as much chance as I would with Jack Johnson. Shaughnessy got a few drinks under his belt and was waiting at the gate to welcome him. He told me he never gave Harker a chance to open his mouth. He began by shouting that he was no slave Standard Oil could trample on. He was a King of Ireland, if he had his rights, and scum was scum to him, no matter how much money it had stolen from the poor.

MARY

Oh, Lord!

But she can't help laughing.

EDMUND

Then he accused Harker of making his foreman break down the fence to entice the pigs into the ice pond in order to destroy them. The poor pigs, Shaughnessy yelled, had caught their death of cold. Many of them were dying of pneumonia, and several others had been taken down with cholera from drinking the poisoned water. He told Harker he was hiring a lawyer to sue him for damages. And he wound up by saying that he had to put up with poison ivy, ticks, potato bugs,

24

snakes and skunks on his farm, but he was an honest man who drew the line somewhere, and he'd be damned if he'd stand for a Standard Oil thief trespassing. So would Harker kindly remove his dirty feet from the premises before he sicked the dog on him. And Harker did!
He and Jamie laugh.

MARY
Shocked but giggling.
Heavens, what a terrible tongue that man has!

TYRONE
Admiringly before he thinks.
The damned old scoundrel! By God, you can't beat him!
He laughs—then stops abruptly and scowls.
The dirty blackguard! He'll get me in serious trouble yet. I hope you told him I'd be mad as hell—

EDMUND
I told him you'd be tickled to death over the great Irish victory, and so you are. Stop faking, Papa.

TYRONE
Well, I'm not tickled to death.

MARY
Teasingly.
You are, too, James. You're simply delighted!

TYRONE
No, Mary, a joke is a joke, but—

EDMUND
I told Shaughnessy he should have reminded Harker that a Standard Oil millionaire ought to welcome the flavor of hog in his ice water as an appropriate touch.

TYRONE
The devil you did!
Frowning.
Keep your damned Socialist anarchist sentiments out of my affairs!

EDMUND
Shaughnessy almost wept because he hadn't thought of that one, but

25

he said he'd include it in a letter he's writing to Harker, along with a few other insults he'd overlooked.

He and Jamie laugh.

TYRONE

What are you laughing at? There's nothing funny—A fine son you are to help that blackguard get me into a lawsuit!

MARY

Now, James, don't lose your temper.

TYRONE

Turns on Jamie.

And you're worse than he is, encouraging him. I suppose you're regretting you weren't there to prompt Shaughnessy with a few nastier insults. You've a fine talent for that, if for nothing else.

MARY

James! There's no reason to scold Jamie.

Jamie is about to make some sneering remark to his father, but he shrugs his shoulders.

EDMUND

With sudden nervous exasperation.

Oh, for God's sake, Papa! If you're starting that stuff again, I'll beat it.

He jumps up.

I left my book upstairs, anyway.

He goes to the front parlor, saying disgustedly,

God, Papa, I should think you'd get sick of hearing yourself—

He disappears. Tyrone looks after him angrily.

MARY

You mustn't mind Edmund, James. Remember he isn't well.

Edmund can be heard coughing as he goes upstairs.

She adds nervously.

A summer cold makes anyone irritable.

JAMIE

Genuinely concerned.

It's not just a cold he's got. The Kid is damned sick.

26

His father gives him a sharp warning look but he doesn't see it.

MARY
Turns on him resentfully.
Why do you say that? It *is* just a cold! Anyone can tell that! You always imagine things!

TYRONE
With another warning glance at Jamie—easily.
All Jamie meant was Edmund might have a touch of something else, too, which makes his cold worse.

JAMIE
Sure, Mama. That's all I meant.

TYRONE
Doctor Hardy thinks it might be a bit of malarial fever he caught when he was in the tropics. If it is, quinine will soon cure it.

MARY
A look of contemptuous hostility flashes across her face.
Doctor Hardy! I wouldn't believe a thing he said, if he swore on a stack of Bibles! I know what doctors are. They're all alike. Anything, they don't care what, to keep you coming to them.
She stops short, overcome by a fit of acute self-consciousness as she catches their eyes fixed on her. Her hands jerk nervously to her hair. She forces a smile.
What is it? What are you looking at? Is my hair—?

TYRONE
Puts his arm around her—with guilty heartiness, giving her a playful hug.
There's nothing wrong with your hair. The healthier and fatter you get, the vainer you become. You'll soon spend half the day primping before the mirror.

MARY
Half reassured.
I really should have new glasses. My eyes are so bad now.

TYRONE
With Irish blarney.

Your eyes are beautiful, and well you know it.
> *He gives her a kiss. Her face lights up with a charming, shy embarrassment. Suddenly and startlingly one sees in her face the girl she had once been, not a ghost of the dead, but still a living part of her.*

MARY

You mustn't be so silly, James. Right in front of Jamie!

TYRONE

Oh, he's on to you, too. He knows this fuss about eyes and hair is only fishing for compliments. Eh, Jamie?

JAMIE
> *His face has cleared, too, and there is an old boyish charm in his loving smile at his mother.*

Yes. You can't kid us, Mama.

MARY
> *Laughs and an Irish lilt comes into her voice.*

Go along with both of you!
> *Then she speaks with a girlish gravity.*

But I did truly have beautiful hair once, didn't I, James?

TYRONE

The most beautiful in the world!

MARY

It was a rare shade of reddish brown and so long it came down below my knees. You ought to remember it, too, Jamie. It wasn't until after Edmund was born that I had a single grey hair. Then it began to turn white.
> *The girlishness fades from her face.*

TYRONE
Quickly.

And that made it prettier than ever.

MARY
> *Again embarrassed and pleased.*

28

Will you listen to your father, Jamie—after thirty-five years of marriage! He isn't a great actor for nothing, is he? What's come over you, James? Are you pouring coals of fire on my head for teasing you about snoring? Well then, I take it all back. It must have been only the foghorn I heard.

> *She laughs, and they laugh with her. Then she changes to a brisk businesslike air.*

But I can't stay with you any longer, even to hear compliments. I must see the cook about dinner and the day's marketing.

> *She gets up and sighs with humorous exaggeration.*

Bridget is so lazy. And so sly. She begins telling me about her relatives so I can't get a word in edgeways and scold her. Well, I might as well get it over.

> *She goes to the back-parlor doorway, then turns, her face worried again.*

You mustn't make Edmund work on the grounds with you, James, remember.

> *Again with the strange obstinate set to her face.*

Not that he isn't strong enough, but he'd perspire and he might catch more cold.

> *She disappears through the back parlor. Tyrone turns on Jamie condemningly.*

TYRONE

You're a fine lunkhead! Haven't you any sense? The one thing to avoid is saying anything that would get her more upset over Edmund.

JAMIE

> *Shrugging his shoulders.*

All right. Have it your way. I think it's the wrong idea to let Mama go on kidding herself. It will only make the shock worse when she has to face it. Anyway, you can see she's deliberately fooling herself with that summer cold talk. She knows better.

TYRONE

Knows? Nobody knows yet.

JAMIE

Well, I do. I was with Edmund when he went to Doc Hardy on Monday. I heard him pull that touch of malaria stuff. He was stalling.

29

That isn't what he thinks any more. You know it as well as I do.
You talked to him when you went uptown yesterday, didn't you?

TYRONE

He couldn't say anything for sure yet. He's to phone me today before
Edmund goes to him.

JAMIE

Slowly.

He thinks it's consumption, doesn't he, Papa?

TYRONE

Reluctantly.

He said it might be.

JAMIE

Moved, his love for his brother coming out.

Poor kid! God damn it!

He turns on his father accusingly.

It might never have happened if you'd sent him to a real doctor when
he first got sick.

TYRONE

What's the matter with Hardy? He's always been our doctor up here.

JAMIE

Everything's the matter with him! Even in this hick burg he's rated
third class! He's a cheap old quack!

TYRONE

That's right! Run him down! Run down everybody! Everyone is
a fake to you!

JAMIE

Contemptuously.

Hardy only charges a dollar. That's what makes you think he's a
fine doctor!

TYRONE

Stung.

That's enough! You're not drunk now! There's no excuse—

He controls himself—a bit defensively.

30

If you mean I can't afford one of the fine society doctors who prey on the rich summer people—

JAMIE

Can't afford? You're one of the biggest property owners around here.

TYRONE

That doesn't mean I'm rich. It's all mortgaged—

JAMIE

Because you always buy more instead of paying off mortgages. If Edmund was a lousy acre of land you wanted, the sky would be the limit!

TYRONE

That's a lie! And your sneers against Doctor Hardy are lies! He doesn't put on frills, or have an office in a fashionable location, or drive around in an expensive automobile. That's what you pay for with those other five-dollars-to-look-at-your-tongue fellows, not their skill.

JAMIE

With a scornful shrug of his shoulders.
Oh, all right. I'm a fool to argue. You can't change the leopard's spots.

TYRONE

With rising anger.
No, you can't. You've taught me that lesson only too well. I've lost all hope you will ever change yours. You dare tell me what I can afford? You've never known the value of a dollar and never will! You've never saved a dollar in your life! At the end of each season you're penniless! You've thrown your salary away every week on whores and whiskey!

JAMIE

My salary! Christ!

TYRONE

It's more than you're worth, and you couldn't get that if it wasn't for me. If you weren't my son, there isn't a manager in the business who would give you a part, your reputation stinks so. As it is, I have to humble my pride and beg for you, saying you've turned over a new leaf, although I know it's a lie!

JAMIE

I never wanted to be an actor. You forced me on the stage.

TYRONE

That's a lie! You made no effort to find anything else to do. You left it to me to get you a job and I have no influence except in the theater. Forced you! You never wanted to do anything except loaf in barrooms! You'd have been content to sit back like a lazy lunk and sponge on me for the rest of your life! After all the money I'd wasted on your education, and all you did was get fired in disgrace from every college you went to!

JAMIE

Oh, for God's sake, don't drag up that ancient history!

TYRONE

It's not ancient history that you have to come home every summer to live on me.

JAMIE

I earn my board and lodging working on the grounds. It saves you hiring a man.

TYRONE

Bah! You have to be driven to do even that much!
His anger ebbs into a weary complaint.
I wouldn't give a damn if you ever displayed the slightest sign of gratitude. The only thanks is to have you sneer at me for a dirty miser, sneer at my profession, sneer at every damned thing in the world—except yourself.

JAMIE

Wryly.
That's not true, Papa. You can't hear me talking to myself, that's all.

TYRONE

Stares at him puzzledly, then quotes mechanically.
"Ingratitude, the vilest weed that grows"!

32

JAMIE

I could see that line coming! God, how many thousand times—!

He stops, bored with their quarrel, and shrugs his shoulders.

All right, Papa. I'm a bum. Anything you like, so long as it stops the argument.

TYRONE

With indignant appeal now.

If you'd get ambition in your head instead of folly! You're young yet. You could still make your mark. You had the talent to become a fine actor! You have it still. You're my son—!

JAMIE

Boredly.

Let's forget me. I'm not interested in the subject. Neither are you.

Tyrone gives up. Jamie goes on casually.

What started us on this? Oh, Doc Hardy. When is he going to call you up about Edmund?

TYRONE

Around lunch time.

He pauses—then defensively.

I couldn't have sent Edmund to a better doctor. Hardy's treated him whenever he was sick up here, since he was knee high. He knows his constitution as no other doctor could. It's not a question of my being miserly, as you'd like to make out.

Bitterly.

And what could the finest specialist in America do for Edmund, after he's deliberately ruined his health by the mad life he's led ever since he was fired from college? Even before that when he was in prep school, he began dissipating and playing the Broadway sport to imitate you, when he's never had your constitution to stand it. You're a healthy hulk like me—or you were at his age—but he's always been a bundle of nerves like his mother. I've warned him for years his body couldn't stand it, but he wouldn't heed me, and now it's too late.

JAMIE

Sharply.

What do you mean, too late? You talk as if you thought—

33

TYRONE
Guiltily explosive.

Don't be a damned fool! I meant nothing but what's plain to anyone! His health has broken down and he may be an invalid for a long
time.

JAMIE
Stares at his father, ignoring his explanation.

I know it's an Irish peasant idea consumption is fatal. It probably is
when you live in a hovel on a bog, but over here, with modern
treatment—

TYRONE

Don't I know that! What are you gabbing about, anyway? And keep
your dirty tongue off Ireland, with your sneers about peasants and
bogs and hovels!
Accusingly.

The less you say about Edmund's sickness, the better for your con-
science! You're more responsible than anyone!

JAMIE
Stung.

That's a lie! I won't stand for that, Papa!

TYRONE

It's the truth! You've been the worst influence for him. He grew up
admiring you as a hero! A fine example you set him! If you ever
gave him advice except in the ways of rottenness, I've never heard
of it! You made him old before his time, pumping him full of what
you consider worldly wisdom, when he was too young to see that
your mind was so poisoned by your own failure in life, you wanted
to believe every man was a knave with his soul for sale, and every
woman who wasn't a whore was a fool!

JAMIE
With a defensive air of weary indifference again.

All right. I did put Edmund wise to things, but not until I saw he'd
started to raise hell, and knew he'd laugh at me if I tried the good advice, older brother stuff. All I did was make a pal of him and be absolutely frank so he'd learn from my mistakes that—

34

He shrugs his shoulders—cynically.

Well, that if you can't be good you can at least be careful.

> *His father snorts contemptuously. Suddenly Jamie becomes*
> *really moved.*

That's a rotten accusation, Papa. You know how much the Kid means to me, and how close we've always been—not like the usual brothers! I'd do anything for him.

TYRONE

Impressed—mollifyingly.

I know you may have thought it was for the best, Jamie. I didn't say you did it deliberately to harm him.

JAMIE

Besides it's damned rot! I'd like to see anyone influence Edmund more than he wants to be. His quietness fools people into thinking they can do what they like with him. But he's stubborn as hell inside and what he does is what he wants to do, and to hell with anyone else! What had I to do with all the crazy stunts he's pulled in the last few years—working his way all over the map as a sailor and all that stuff. I thought that was a damned fool idea, and I told him so. You can't imagine me getting fun out of being on the beach in South America, or living in filthy dives, drinking rotgut, can you? No, thanks! I'll stick to Broadway, and a room with a bath, and bars that serve bonded Bourbon.

TYRONE

You and Broadway! It's made you what you are!

> *With a touch of pride.*

Whatever Edmund's done, he's had the guts to go off on his own, where he couldn't come whining to me the minute he was broke.

JAMIE

Stung into sneering jealousy.

He's always come home broke finally, hasn't he? And what did his going away get him? Look at him now!

> *He is suddenly shamefaced.*

Christ! That's a lousy thing to say. I don't mean that.

TYRONE

Decides to ignore this.

He's been doing well on the paper. I was hoping he'd found the work he wants to do at last.

JAMIE

Sneering jealously again.

A hick town rag! Whatever bull they hand you, they tell me he's a pretty bum reporter. If he weren't your son—

Ashamed again.

No, that's not true! They're glad to have him, but it's the special stuff that gets him by. Some of the poems and parodies he's written are damned good.

Grudgingly again.

Not that they'd ever get him anywhere on the big time.

Hastily.

But he's certainly made a damned good start.

TYRONE

Yes. He's made a start. You used to talk about wanting to become a newspaper man but you were never willing to start at the bottom. You expected—

JAMIE

Oh, for Christ's sake, Papa! Can't you lay off me!

TYRONE

Stares at him—then looks away—after a pause.

It's damnable luck Edmund should be sick right now. It couldn't have come at a worse time for him.

He adds, unable to conceal an almost furtive uneasiness.

Or for your mother. It's damnable she should have this to upset her, just when she needs peace and freedom from worry. She's been so well in the two months since she came home.

His voice grows husky and trembles a little.

It's been heaven to me. This home has been a home again. But I needn't tell you, Jamie.

His son looks at him, for the first time with an understanding sympathy. It is as if suddenly a deep bond of common feeling existed between them in which their antagonisms could be forgotten.

36

JAMIE
Almost gently.
I've felt the same way, Papa.

TYRONE
Yes, this time you can see how strong and sure of herself she is. She's a different woman entirely from the other times. She has control of her nerves—or she had until Edmund got sick. Now you can feel her growing tense and frightened underneath. I wish to God we could keep the truth from her, but we can't if he has to be sent to a sanatorium. What makes it worse is her father died of consumption. She worshiped him and she's never forgotten. Yes, it will be hard for her. But she can do it! She has the will power now! We must help her, Jamie, in every way we can! *Mother common ground*

JAMIE
Moved.
Of course, Papa.
Hesitantly.
Outside of nerves, she seems perfectly all right this morning.

TYRONE
With hearty confidence now.
Never better. She's full of fun and mischief.
Suddenly he frowns at Jamie suspiciously.
Why do you say, seems? Why shouldn't she be all right? What the hell do you mean?

JAMIE
Don't start jumping down my throat! God, Papa, this ought to be one thing we can talk over frankly without a battle.

TYRONE
I'm sorry, Jamie.
Tensely.
But go on and tell me—

JAMIE
There's nothing to tell. I was all wrong. It's just that last night—Well, you know how it is, I can't forget the past. I can't help being suspicious. Any more than you can.

37

Bitterly.

That's the hell of it. And it makes it hell for Mama! She watches us watching her—

TYRONE

Sadly.

I know.

Tensely.

Well, what was it? Can't you speak out?

JAMIE

Nothing, I tell you. Just my damned foolishness. Around three o'clock this morning, I woke up and heard her moving around in the spare room. Then she went to the bathroom. I pretended to be asleep. She stopped in the hall to listen, as if she wanted to make sure I was.

TYRONE

With forced scorn.

For God's sake, is that all? She told me herself the foghorn kept her awake all night, and every night since Edmund's been sick she's been up and down, going to his room to see how he was.

JAMIE

Eagerly.

Yes, that's right, she did stop to listen outside his room.

Hesitantly again.

It was her being in the spare room that scared me. I couldn't help remembering that when she starts sleeping alone in there, it has always been a sign—

TYRONE

It isn't this time! It's easily explained. Where else could she go last night to get away from my snoring?

He gives way to a burst of resentful anger.

By God, how you can live with a mind that sees nothing but the worst motives behind everything is beyond me!

JAMIE

Stung.

Don't pull that! I've just said I was all wrong. Don't you suppose I'm as glad of that as you are!

TYRONE
Mollifyingly.
I'm sure you are, Jamie.
> *A pause. His expression becomes somber. He speaks slowly with a superstitious dread.*

It would be like a curse she can't escape if worry over Edmund—
It was in her long sickness after bringing him into the world that she
first—

JAMIE
She didn't have anything to do with it!

TYRONE
I'm not blaming her.

JAMIE
Bitingly.
Then who are you blaming? Edmund, for being born?

TYRONE
You damned fool! No one was to blame.

JAMIE
The bastard of a doctor was! From what Mama's said, he was another
cheap quack like Hardy! You wouldn't pay for a first-rate—

TYRONE
That's a lie!
> *Furiously.*

So I'm to blame! That's what you're driving at, is it? You evil-
minded loafer!

JAMIE
Warningly as he hears his mother in the dining room.
Ssh!

> *Tyrone gets hastily to his feet and goes to look out the win-
> dows at right. Jamie speaks with a complete change of tone.*

Well, if we're going to cut the front hedge today, we'd better go
to work.

> *Mary comes in from the back parlor. She gives a quick,
> suspicious glance from one to the other, her manner nervously
> self-conscious.*

TYRONE
Turns from the window—with an actor's heartiness.
Yes, it's too fine a morning to waste indoors arguing. Take a look
out the window, Mary. There's no fog in the harbor. I'm sure the
spell of it we've had is over now.

MARY
Going to him.
I hope so, dear.
To Jamie, forcing a smile.
Did I actually hear you suggesting work on the front hedge, Jamie?
Wonders will never cease! You must want pocket money badly.

JAMIE
Kiddingly.
When don't I?
He winks at her, with a derisive glance at his father.
I expect a salary of at least one large iron man at the end of the week
—to carouse on!

MARY
*Does not respond to his humor—her hands fluttering over
the front of her dress.*
What were you two arguing about?

JAMIE
Shrugs his shoulders.
The same old stuff.

MARY
I heard you say something about a doctor, and your father accusing
you of being evil-minded.

JAMIE
Quickly.
Oh, that. I was saying again Doc Hardy isn't my idea of the world's
greatest physician.

MARY
Knows he is lying—vaguely.
Oh. No, I wouldn't say he was, either.
Changing the subject—forcing a smile.

40

That Bridget! I thought I'd never get away. She told me all about
her second cousin on the police force in St. Louis.

Then with nervous irritation.

Well, if you're going to work on the hedge why don't you go?

Hastily.

I mean, take advantage of the sunshine before the fog comes back.

Strangely, as if talking aloud to herself.

Because I know it will.

*Suddenly she is self-consciously aware that they are both
staring fixedly at her—flurriedly, raising her hands.*

Or I should say, the rheumatism in my hands knows. It's a better
weather prophet than you are, James.

She stares at her hands with fascinated repulsion.

Ugh! How ugly they are! Who'd ever believe they were once beautiful?

They stare at her with a growing dread.

TYRONE

Takes her hands and gently pushes them down.

Now, now, Mary. None of that foolishness. They're the sweetest
hands in the world.

*She smiles, her face lighting up, and kisses him gratefully.
He turns to his son.*

Come on Jamie. Your mother's right to scold us. The way to start
work is to start work. The hot sun will sweat some of that booze
fat off your middle.

*He opens the screen door and goes out on the porch and dis-
appears down a flight of steps leading to the ground. Jamie
rises from his chair and, taking off his coat, goes to the door.
At the door he turns back but avoids looking at her, and she
does not look at him.*

JAMIE

With an awkward, uneasy tenderness.

We're all so proud of you, Mama, so darned happy.

*She stiffens and stares at him with a frightened defiance. He
flounders on.*

But you've still got to be careful. You mustn't worry so much about
Edmund. He'll be all right.

41

MARY

With a stubborn, bitterly resentful look.

Of course, he'll be all right. And I don't know what you mean,
warning me to be careful.

JAMIE

Rebuffed and hurt, shrugs his shoulders.

All right, Mama. I'm sorry I spoke.

> *He goes out on the porch. She waits rigidly until he dis-
> appears down the steps. Then she sinks down in the chair
> he had occupied, her face betraying a frightened, furtive des-
> peration, her hands roving over the table top, aimlessly
> moving objects around. She hears Edmund descending the
> stairs in the front hall. As he nears the bottom he has a fit of
> coughing. She springs to her feet, as if she wanted to run
> away from the sound, and goes quickly to the windows at
> right. She is looking out, apparently calm, as he enters from
> the front parlor, a book in one hand. She turns to him, her
> lips set in a welcoming, motherly smile.*

MARY

Here you are. I was just going upstairs to look for you.

EDMUND

I waited until they went out. I don't want to mix up in any argu-
ments. I feel too rotten.

MARY

Almost resentfully.

Oh, I'm sure you don't feel half as badly as you make out. You're
such a baby. You like to get us worried so we'll make a fuss over you.

> *Hastily.*

I'm only teasing, dear. I know how miserably uncomfortable you
must be. But you feel better today, don't you?

> *Worriedly, taking his arm.*

All the same, you've grown much too thin. You need to rest all you
can. Sit down and I'll make you comfortable.

> *He sits down in the rocking chair and she puts a pillow be-
> hind his back.*

There. How's that?

42

EDMUND

Grand. Thanks, Mama.

MARY

Kisses him—tenderly.

All you need is your mother to nurse you. Big as you are, you're still the baby of the family to me, you know.

EDMUND

Takes her hand—with deep seriousness.

Never mind me. You take care of yourself. That's all that counts.

MARY

Evading his eyes.

But I am, dear.

Forcing a laugh.

Heavens, don't you see how fat I've grown! I'll have to have all my dresses let out.

She turns away and goes to the windows at right. She attempts a light, amused tone.

They've started clipping the hedge. Poor Jamie! How he hates working in front where everyone passing can see him. There go the Chatfields in their new Mercedes. It's a beautiful car, isn't it? Not like our secondhand Packard. Poor Jamie! He bent almost under the hedge so they wouldn't notice him. They bowed to your father and he bowed back as if he were taking a curtain call. In that filthy old suit I've tried to make him throw away.

Her voice has grown bitter.

Really, he ought to have more pride than to make such a show of himself.

EDMUND

He's right not to give a damn what anyone thinks. Jamie's a fool to care about the Chatfields. For Pete's sake, who ever heard of them outside this hick burg?

MARY

With satisfaction.

No one. You're quite right, Edmund. Big frogs in a small puddle. It is stupid of Jamie.

She pauses, looking out the window—then with an under-current of lonely yearning.

Still, the Chatfields and people like them stand for something. I mean they have decent, presentable homes they don't have to be ashamed of. They have friends who entertain them and whom they entertain. They're not cut off from everyone.

She turns back from the window.

Not that I want anything to do with them. I've always hated this town and everyone in it. You know that. I never wanted to live here in the first place, but your father liked it and insisted on building this house, and I've had to come here every summer.

EDMUND

Well, it's better than spending the summer in a New York hotel, isn't it? And this town's not so bad. I like it well enough. I suppose because it's the only home we've had.

MARY

I've never felt it was my home. It was wrong from the start. Every-thing was done in the cheapest way. Your father would never spend the money to make it right. It's just as well we haven't any friends here. I'd be ashamed to have them step in the door. But he's never wanted family friends. He hates calling on people, or receiving them. All he likes is to hobnob with men at the Club or in a barroom. Jamie and you are the same way, but you're not to blame. You've never had a chance to meet decent people here. I know you both would have been so different if you'd been able to associate with nice girls instead of— You'd never have disgraced yourselves as you have, so that now no respectable parents will let their daughters be seen with you.

EDMUND

Irritably.

Oh, Mama, forget it! Who cares? Jamie and I would be bored stiff. And about the Old Man, what's the use of talking? You can't change him.

MARY

Mechanically rebuking.

Don't call your father the Old Man. You should have more respect.

44

Then dully.

I know it's useless to talk. But sometimes I feel so lonely.
> *Her lips quiver and she keeps her head turned away.*

EDMUND

Anyway, you've got to be fair, Mama. It may have been all his fault in the beginning, but you know that later on, even if he'd wanted to, we couldn't have had people here—
> *He flounders guiltily.*

I mean, you wouldn't have wanted them.

MARY
> *Wincing—her lips quivering pitifully.*

Don't. I can't bear having you remind me.

EDMUND

Don't take it that way! Please, Mama! I'm trying to help. Because it's bad for you to forget. The right way is to remember. So you'll always be on your guard. You know what's happened before.
> *Miserably.*

God, Mama, you know I hate to remind you. I'm doing it because it's been so wonderful having you home the way you've been, and it would be terrible—

MARY
> *Strickenly.*

Please, dear. I know you mean it for the best, but—
> *A defensive uneasiness comes into her voice again.*

I don't understand why you should suddenly say such things. What put it in your mind this morning?

EDMUND
> *Evasively.*

Nothing. Just because I feel rotten and blue, I suppose.

MARY

Tell me the truth. Why are you so suspicious all of a sudden?

EDMUND

I'm not!

MARY

Oh, yes you are. I can feel it. Your father and Jamie, too—particularly Jamie.

45

EDMUND

Now don't start imagining things, Mama.

MARY

Her hands fluttering.

It makes it so much harder, living in this atmosphere of constant suspicion, knowing everyone is spying on me, and none of you believe in me, or trust me.

EDMUND

That's crazy, Mama. We do trust you.

MARY

If there was only some place I could go to get away for a day, or even an afternoon, some woman friend I could talk to—not about anything serious, simply laugh and gossip and forget for a while—someone besides the servants—that stupid Cathleen!

EDMUND

Gets up worriedly and puts his arm around her.

Stop it, Mama. You're getting yourself worked up over nothing.

MARY

Your father goes out. He meets his friends in barrooms or at the Club. You and Jamie have the boys you know. You go out. But I am alone. I've always been alone.

EDMUND

Soothingly.

Come now! You know that's a fib. One of us always stays around to keep you company, or goes with you in the automobile when you take a drive.

MARY

Bitterly.

Because you're afraid to trust me alone!

She turns on him—sharply.

I insist you tell me why you act so differently this morning—why you felt you had to remind me—

EDMUND

Hesitates—then blurts out guiltily.

46

It's stupid. It's just that I wasn't asleep when you came in my room last night. You didn't go back to your and Papa's room. You went in the spare room for the rest of the night.

MARY

Because your father's snoring was driving me crazy! For heaven's sake, haven't I often used the spare room as my bedroom?
>   *Bitterly.*
But I see what you thought. That was when—

EDMUND
>   *Too vehemently.*
I didn't think anything!

MARY

So you pretended to be asleep in order to spy on me!

EDMUND

No! I did it because I knew if you found out I was feverish and couldn't sleep, it would upset you.

MARY

Jamie was pretending to be asleep, too, I'm sure, and I suppose your father—

EDMUND

Stop it, Mama!

MARY

Oh, I can't bear it, Edmund, when even you—!
>   *Her hands flutter up to pat her hair in their aimless, dis-*
>   *tracted way. Suddenly a strange undercurrent of revenge-*
>   *fulness comes into her voice.*
It would serve all of you right if it was true!

EDMUND

Mama! Don't say that! That's the way you talk when—

MARY

Stop suspecting me! Please, dear! You hurt me! I couldn't sleep because I was thinking about you. That's the real reason! I've been so worried ever since you've been sick.

She puts her arms around him and hugs him with a frightened, protective tenderness.

EDMUND
Soothingly.
That's foolishness. You know it's only a bad cold.

MARY
Yes, of course, I know that!

EDMUND
But listen, Mama. I want you to promise me that even if it should turn out to be something worse, you'll know I'll soon be all right again, anyway, and you won't worry yourself sick, and you'll keep on taking care of yourself—

MARY
Frightenedly.
I won't listen when you're so silly! There's absolutely no reason to talk as if you expected something dreadful! Of course, I promise you. I give you my sacred word of honor!
Then with a sad bitterness.
But I suppose you're remembering I've promised before on my word of honor.

EDMUND
No!

MARY
Her bitterness receding into a resigned helplessness.
I'm not blaming you, dear. How can you help it? How can any one of us forget?
Strangely.
That's what makes it so hard—for all of us. We can't forget.

EDMUND
Grabs her shoulder.
Mama! Stop it!

MARY
Forcing a smile.
All right, dear. I didn't mean to be so gloomy. Don't mind me. Here.

Let me feel your head. Why, it's nice and cool. You certainly haven't any fever now.

MARY

EDMUND

Forget! It's you—

MARY

But I'm quite all right, dear.

With a quick, strange, calculating, almost sly glance at him.
Except I naturally feel tired and nervous this morning, after such a bad night. I really ought to go upstairs and lie down until lunch time and take a nap.

He gives her an instinctive look of suspicion—then, ashamed of himself, looks quickly away. She hurries on nervously.
What are you going to do? Read here? It would be much better for you to go out in the fresh air and sunshine. But don't get overheated, remember. Be sure and wear a hat.

She stops, looking straight at him now. He avoids her eyes.
There is a tense pause. Then she speaks jeeringly.
Or are you afraid to trust me alone?

EDMUND

Tormentedly.
No! Can't you stop talking like that! I think you ought to take a nap.

He goes to the screen door—forcing a joking tone.
I'll go down and help Jamie bear up. I love to lie in the shade and watch him work.

He forces a laugh in which she makes herself join. Then he goes out on the porch and disappears down the steps. Her first reaction is one of relief. She appears to relax. She sinks down in one of the wicker armchairs at rear of table and leans her head back, closing her eyes. But suddenly she grows terribly tense again. Her eyes open and she strains forward, seized by a fit of nervous panic. She begins a desperate battle with herself. Her long fingers, warped and knotted by rheumatism, drum on the arms of the chair, driven by an insistent life of their own, without her consent.

CURTAIN

Act Two, Scene One

SCENE *The same. It is around quarter to one. No sunlight comes into the room now through the windows at right. Outside the day is still fine but increasingly sultry, with a faint haziness in the air which softens the glare of the sun.*

Edmund sits in the armchair at left of table, reading a book. Or rather he is trying to concentrate on it but cannot. He seems to be listening for some sound from upstairs. His manner is nervously apprehensive and he looks more sickly than in the previous act.

The second girl, CATHLEEN, *enters from the back parlor. She carries a tray on which is a bottle of bonded Bourbon, several whiskey glasses, and a pitcher of ice water. She is a buxom Irish peasant, in her early twenties, with a red-cheeked comely face, black hair and blue eyes—amiable, ignorant, clumsy, and possessed by a dense, well-meaning stupidity. She puts the tray on the table. Edmund pretends to be so absorbed in his book he does not notice her, but she ignores this.*

CATHLEEN
With garrulous familiarity.
Here's the whiskey. It'll be lunch time soon. Will I call your father and Mister Jamie, or will you?

EDMUND
Without looking up from his book.
You do it.

CATHLEEN
It's a wonder your father wouldn't look at his watch once in a while. He's a divil for making the meals late, and then Bridget curses me as if I was to blame. But he's a grand handsome man, if he is old. You'll never see the day you're as good looking—nor Mister Jamie, either.

She chuckles.

I'll wager Mister Jamie wouldn't miss the time to stop work and have his drop of whiskey if he had a watch to his name!

EDMUND
Gives up trying to ignore her and grins.
You win that one.

CATHLEEN
And here's another I'd win, that you're making me call them so you can sneak a drink before they come.

EDMUND
Well, I hadn't thought of that—

CATHLEEN
Oh no, not you! Butter wouldn't melt in your mouth, I suppose.

EDMUND
But now you suggest it—

CATHLEEN
Suddenly primly virtuous.
I'd never suggest a man or a woman touch drink, Mister Edmund. Sure, didn't it kill an uncle of mine in the old country.
Relenting.
Still, a drop now and then is no harm when you're in low spirits, or have a bad cold.

EDMUND
Thanks for handing me a good excuse.
Then with forced casualness.
You'd better call my mother, too.

CATHLEEN
What for? She's always on time without any calling. God bless her, she has some consideration for the help.

EDMUND
She's been taking a nap.

CATHLEEN
She wasn't asleep when I finished my work upstairs a while back.

She was lying down in the spare room with her eyes wide open.
She'd a terrible headache, she said.

>EDMUND
>
>*His casualness more forced.*

Oh well then, just call my father.

>CATHLEEN
>
>*Goes to the screen door, grumbling good-naturedly.*

No wonder my feet kill me each night. I won't walk out in this heat
and get sunstroke. I'll call from the porch.

>*She goes out on the side porch, letting the screen door slam
>behind her, and disappears on her way to the front porch. A
>moment later she is heard shouting.*

Mister Tyrone! Mister Jamie! It's time!

>*Edmund, who has been staring frightenedly before him, for-
>getting his book, springs to his feet nervously.*

>EDMUND

God, what a wench!

>*He grabs the bottle and pours a drink, adds ice water and
>drinks. As he does so, he hears someone coming in the front
>door. He puts the glass hastily on the tray and sits down
>again, opening his book. Jamie comes in from the front parlor,
>his coat over his arm. He has taken off collar and tie and
>carries them in his hand. He is wiping sweat from his fore-
>head with a handkerchief. Edmund looks up as if his reading
>was interrupted. Jamie takes one look at the bottle and glasses
>and smiles cynically.*

>JAMIE

Sneaking one, eh? Cut out the bluff, Kid. You're a rottener actor
than I am.

>EDMUND
>
>*Grins.*

Yes, I grabbed one while the going was good.

>JAMIE
>
>*Puts a hand affectionately on his shoulder.*

That's better. Why kid me? We're pals, aren't we?

EDMUND

I wasn't sure it was you coming.

JAMIE

I made the Old Man look at his watch. I was halfway up the walk when Cathleen burst into song. Our wild Irish lark! She ought to be a train announcer.

EDMUND

That's what drove me to drink. Why don't you sneak one while you've got a chance?

JAMIE

I was thinking of that little thing.
          He goes quickly to the window at right.
The Old Man was talking to old Captain Turner. Yes, he's still at it.
          He comes back and takes a drink.
And now to cover up from his eagle eye. He memorizes the level in the bottle after every drink.
          He measures two drinks of water and pours them in the whiskey bottle and shakes it up.
There. That fixes it.
          He pours water in the glass and sets it on the table by Edmund.
And here's the water you've been drinking.

EDMUND

Fine! You don't think it will fool him, do you?

JAMIE

Maybe not, but he can't prove it.
          Putting on his collar and tie.
I hope he doesn't forget lunch listening to himself talk. I'm hungry.
          He sits across the table from Edmund—irritably.
That's what I hate about working down in front. He puts on an act for every damned fool that comes along.

EDMUND

          Gloomily.
You're in luck to be hungry. The way I feel I don't care if I ever eat again.

54

JAMIE

Gives him a glance of concern.

Listen, Kid. You know me. I've never lectured you, but Doctor Hardy was right when he told you to cut out the redeye.

EDMUND

Oh, I'm going to after he hands me the bad news this afternoon. A few before then won't make any difference.

JAMIE

Hesitates—then slowly.

I'm glad you've got your mind prepared for bad news. It won't be such a jolt.

He catches Edmund staring at him.

I mean, it's a cinch you're really sick, and it would be wrong dope to kid yourself.

EDMUND

Disturbed.

I'm not. I know how rotten I feel, and the fever and chills I get at night are no joke. I think Doctor Hardy's last guess was right. It must be the damned malaria come back on me.

JAMIE

Maybe, but don't be too sure.

EDMUND

Why? What do you think it is?

JAMIE

Hell, how would I know? I'm no Doc.

Abruptly.

Where's Mama?

EDMUND

Upstairs.

JAMIE

Looks at him sharply.

When did she go up?

EDMUND

Oh, about the time I came down to the hedge, I guess. She said she was going to take a nap.

JAMIE

You didn't tell me—

EDMUND

Defensively.

Why should I? What about it? She was tired out. She didn't get much sleep last night.

JAMIE

I know she didn't.

A pause. The brothers avoid looking at each other.

EDMUND

That damned foghorn kept me awake, too.

Another pause.

JAMIE

She's been upstairs alone all morning, eh? You haven't seen her?

EDMUND

No. I've been reading here. I wanted to give her a chance to sleep.

JAMIE

Is she coming down to lunch?

EDMUND

Of course.

JAMIE

Dryly.

No of course about it. She might not want any lunch. Or she might start having most of her meals alone upstairs. That's happened, hasn't it?

EDMUND

With frightened resentment.

Cut it out, Jamie! Can't you think anything but—?

Persuasively.

You're all wrong to suspect anything. Cathleen saw her not long ago. Mama didn't tell her she wouldn't be down to lunch.

JAMIE

Then she wasn't taking a nap?

EDMUND

Not right then, but she was lying down, Cathleen said.

JAMIE

In the spare room?

EDMUND

Yes. For Pete's sake, what of it?

JAMIE
Bursts out.
You damned fool! Why did you leave her alone so long? Why didn't you stick around?

EDMUND

Because she accused me—and you and Papa—of spying on her all the time and not trusting her. She made me feel ashamed. I know how rotten it must be for her. And she promised on her sacred word of honor—

JAMIE
With a bitter weariness.
You ought to know that doesn't mean anything.

EDMUND

It does this time!

JAMIE

That's what we thought the other times.
He leans over the table to give his brother's arm an affection-ate grasp.
Listen, Kid, I know you think I'm a cynical bastard, but remember I've seen a lot more of this game than you have. You never knew what was really wrong until you were in prep school. Papa and I kept it from you. But I was wise ten years or more before we had to tell you. I know the game backwards and I've been thinking all morning of the way she acted last night when she thought we were asleep. I haven't been able to think of anything else. And now you tell me she got you to leave her alone upstairs all morning.

EDMUND

She didn't! You're crazy!

JAMIE
Placatingly.

All right, Kid. Don't start a battle with me. I hope as much as you do I'm crazy. I've been as happy as hell because I'd really begun to believe that this time—

He stops—looking through the front parlor toward the hall —lowering his voice, hurriedly.

She's coming downstairs. You win on that. I guess I'm a damned suspicious louse.

They grow tense with a hopeful, fearful expectancy. Jamie mutters.

Damn! I wish I'd grabbed another drink.

EDMUND

Me, too.

He coughs nervously and this brings on a real fit of coughing. Jamie glances at him with worried pity. Mary enters from the front parlor. At first one notices no change except that she appears to be less nervous, to be more as she was when we first saw her after breakfast, but then one becomes aware that her eyes are brighter, and there is a peculiar detachment in her voice and manner, as if she were a little withdrawn from her words and actions.

MARY

Goes worriedly to Edmund and puts her arm around him.

You mustn't cough like that. It's bad for your throat. You don't want to get a sore throat on top of your cold.

She kisses him. He stops coughing and gives her a quick apprehensive glance, but if his suspicions are aroused her tenderness makes him renounce them and he believes what he wants to believe for the moment. On the other hand, Jamie knows after one probing look at her that his suspicions are justified. His eyes fall to stare at the floor, his face sets in an expression of embittered, defensive cynicism. Mary goes on, half sitting on the arm of Edmund's chair, her arm around him, so her face is above and behind his and he cannot look into her eyes.

But I seem to be always picking on you, telling you don't do this and don't do that. Forgive me, dear. It's just that I want to take care of you.

EDMUND

I know, Mama. How about you? Do you feel rested?

MARY

Yes, ever so much better. I've been lying down ever since you went out. It's what I needed after such a restless night. I don't feel nervous now.

EDMUND

That's fine.

He pats her hand on his shoulder. Jamie gives him a strange, almost contemptuous glance, wondering if his brother can really mean this. Edmund does not notice but his mother does.

MARY

In a forced teasing tone.

Good heavens, how down in the mouth you look, Jamie. What's the matter now?

JAMIE

Without looking at her.

Nothing.

MARY

Oh, I'd forgotten you've been working on the front hedge. That accounts for your sinking into the dumps, doesn't it?

JAMIE

If you want to think so, Mama.

MARY

Keeping her tone.

Well, that's the effect it always has, isn't it? What a big baby you are! Isn't he, Edmund?

EDMUND

He's certainly a fool to care what anyone thinks.

MARY

Strangely.

Yes, the only way is to make yourself not care.
>
> *She catches Jamie giving her a bitter glance and changes the subject.*

Where is your father? I heard Cathleen call him.

EDMUND

Gabbing with old Captain Turner, Jamie says. He'll be late, as usual.
>
> *Jamie gets up and goes to the windows at right, glad of an excuse to turn his back.*

MARY

I've told Cathleen time and again she must go wherever he is and tell him. The idea of screaming as if this were a cheap boardinghouse!

JAMIE

Looking out the window.

She's down there now.

Sneeringly.

Interrupting the famous Beautiful Voice! She should have more respect.

MARY

Sharply—letting her resentment toward him come out.

It's you who should have more respect! Stop sneering at your father! I won't have it! You ought to be proud you're his son! He may have his faults. Who hasn't? But he's worked hard all his life. He made his way up from ignorance and poverty to the top of his profession! Everyone else admires him and you should be the last one to sneer— you, who, thanks to him, have never had to work hard in your life!

Stung, Jamie has turned to stare at her with accusing antagonism. Her eyes waver guiltily and she adds in a tone which begins to placate.

Remember your father is getting old, Jamie. You really ought to show more consideration.

JAMIE

I ought to?

EDMUND

Uneasily.

Oh, dry up, Jamie!

60

Jamie looks out the window again.
And, for Pete's sake, Mama, why jump on Jamie all of a sudden?

MARY
Bitterly.
Because he's always sneering at someone else, always looking for the worst weakness in everyone.
Then with a strange, abrupt change to a detached, impersonal tone.
But I suppose life has made him like that, and he can't help it. None of us can help the things life has done to us. They're done before you realize it, and once they're done they make you do other things until at last everything comes between you and what you'd like to be, and you've lost your true self forever.
Edmund is made apprehensive by her strangeness. He tries to look up in her eyes but she keeps them averted. Jamie turns to her—then looks quickly out of the window again.

JAMIE
Dully.
I'm hungry. I wish the Old Man would get a move on. It's a rotten trick the way he keeps meals waiting, and then beefs because they're spoiled.

MARY
With a resentment that has a quality of being automatic and on the surface while inwardly she is indifferent.
Yes, it's very trying, Jamie. You don't know how trying. You don't have to keep house with summer servants who don't care because they know it isn't a permanent position. The really good servants are all with people who have homes and not merely summer places. And your father won't even pay the wages the best summer help ask. So every year I have stupid, lazy greenhorns to deal with. But you've heard me say this a thousand times. So has he, but it goes in one ear and out the other. He thinks money spent on a home is money wasted. He's lived too much in hotels. Never the best hotels, of course. Second-rate hotels. He doesn't understand a home. He doesn't feel at home in it. And yet, he wants a home. He's even proud of having this shabby place. He loves it here.

She laughs—a hopeless and yet amused laugh.
It's really funny, when you come to think of it. He's a peculiar man.

EDMUND
Again attempting uneasily to look up in her eyes.
What makes you ramble on like that, Mama?

MARY
Quickly casual—patting his cheek.
Why, nothing in particular, dear. It *is* foolish.
As she speaks, Cathleen enters from the back parlor.

CATHLEEN
Volubly.
Lunch is ready, Ma'am, I went down to Mister Tyrone, like you ordered, and he said he'd come right away, but he kept on talking to that man, telling him of the time when—

MARY
Indifferently.
All right, Cathleen. Tell Bridget I'm sorry but she'll have to wait a few minutes until Mister Tyrone is here.
Cathleen mutters, "Yes, Ma'am," and goes off through the back parlor, grumbling to herself.

JAMIE
Damn it! Why don't you go ahead without him? He's told us to.

MARY
With a remote, amused smile.
He doesn't mean it. Don't you know your father yet? He'd be so terribly hurt.

EDMUND
Jumps up—as if he was glad of an excuse to leave.
I'll make him get a move on.
He goes out on the side porch. A moment later he is heard calling from the porch exasperatedly.
Hey! Papa! Come on! We can't wait all day!
Mary has risen from the arm of the chair. Her hands play restlessly over the table top. She does not look at Jamie but

she feels the cynically appraising glance he gives her face and hands.

MARY
Tensely.
Why do you stare like that?

JAMIE
You know.
He turns back to the window.

MARY
I don't know.

JAMIE
Oh, for God's sake, do you think you can fool me, Mama? I'm not blind.

MARY
Looks directly at him now, her face set again in an expression of blank, stubborn denial.
I don't know what you're talking about.

JAMIE
No? Take a look at your eyes in the mirror!

EDMUND
Coming in from the porch.
I got Papa moving. He'll be here in a minute.
With a glance from one to the other, which his mother avoids —uneasily.
What's happened? What's the matter, Mama?

MARY
Disturbed by his coming, gives way to a flurry of guilty, nervous excitement.
Your brother ought to be ashamed of himself. He's been insinuating I don't know what.

EDMUND
Turns on Jamie.
God damn you!

*He takes a threatening step toward him. Jamie turns his back
with a shrug and looks out the window.*

MARY
More upset, grabs Edmund's arm—excitedly.
Stop this at once, do you hear me? How dare you use such language
before me!

*Abruptly her tone and manner change to the strange detach-
ment she has shown before.*
It's wrong to blame your brother. He can't help being what the past
has made him. Any more than your father can. Or you. Or I.

EDMUND
Frightenedly—with a desperate hoping against hope.
He's a liar! It's a lie, isn't it, Mama?

MARY
Keeping her eyes averted.
What is a lie? Now you're talking in riddles like Jamie.
*Then her eyes meet his stricken, accusing look. She stam-
mers.*
Edmund! Don't!
*She looks away and her manner instantly regains the quality
of strange detachment—calmly.*
There's your father coming up the steps now. I must tell Bridget.
*She goes through the back parlor. Edmund moves slowly to
his chair. He looks sick and hopeless.*

JAMIE
From the window, without looking around.
Well?

EDMUND
*Refusing to admit anything to his brother yet—weakly de-
fiant.*
Well, what? You're a liar.
*Jamie again shrugs his shoulders. The screen door on the
front porch is heard closing. Edmund says dully.*
Here's Papa. I hope he loosens up with the old bottle.
*Tyrone comes in through the front parlor. He is putting on
his coat.*

TYRONE

Sorry I'm late. Captain Turner stopped to talk and once he starts gabbing you can't get away from him.

JAMIE

Without turning—dryly.

You mean once he starts listening.

His father regards him with dislike. He comes to the table with a quick measuring look at the bottle of whiskey. Without turning, Jamie senses this.

It's all right. The level in the bottle hasn't changed.

TYRONE

I wasn't noticing that.

He adds caustically.

As if it proved anything with you around. I'm on to your tricks.

EDMUND

Dully.

Did I hear you say, let's all have a drink?

TYRONE

Frowns at him.

Jamie is welcome after his hard morning's work, but I won't invite you. Doctor Hardy—

EDMUND

To hell with Doctor Hardy! One isn't going to kill me. I feel—all in, Papa.

TYRONE

With a worried look at him—putting on a fake heartiness.

Come along, then. It's before a meal and I've always found that good whiskey, taken in moderation as an appetizer, is the best of tonics.

Edmund gets up as his father passes the bottle to him. He pours a big drink. Tyrone frowns admonishingly.

I said, in moderation.

He pours his own drink and passes the bottle to Jamie, grumbling.

It'd be a waste of breath mentioning moderation to you.

Ignoring the hint, Jamie pours a big drink. His father

65

scowls—then, giving it up, resumes his hearty air, raising his glass.

Well, here's health and happiness!
Edmund gives a bitter laugh.

EDMUND

That's a joke!

TYRONE

What is?

EDMUND

Nothing. Here's how.
They drink.

TYRONE
Becoming aware of the atmosphere.
What's the matter here? There's gloom in the air you could cut with a knife.
Turns on Jamie resentfully.
You got the drink you were after, didn't you? Why are you wearing that gloomy look on your mug?

JAMIE
Shrugging his shoulders.
You won't be singing a song yourself soon.

EDMUND

Shut up, Jamie.

TYRONE
Uneasy now—changing the subject.
I thought lunch was ready. I'm hungry as a hunter. Where is your mother?

MARY
Returning through the back parlor, calls.
Here I am.
She comes in. She is excited and self-conscious. As she talks, she glances everywhere except at any of their faces.
I've had to calm down Bridget. She's in a tantrum over your being late again, and I don't blame her. If your lunch is dried up from

waiting in the oven, she said it served you right, you could like it or leave it for all she cared.

> *With increasing excitement.*

Oh, I'm so sick and tired of pretending this is a home! You won't help me! You won't put yourself out the least bit! You don't know how to act in a home! You don't really want one! You never have wanted one—never since the day we were married! You should have remained a bachelor and lived in second-rate hotels and entertained your friends in barrooms!

> *She adds strangely, as if she were now talking aloud to herself rather than to Tyrone.*

Then nothing would ever have happened.

> *They stare at her. Tyrone knows now. He suddenly looks a tired, bitterly sad old man. Edmund glances at his father and sees that he knows, but he still cannot help trying to warn his mother.*

EDMUND

Mama! Stop talking. Why don't we go in to lunch.

MARY

> *Starts and at once the quality of unnatural detachment settles on her face again. She even smiles with an ironical amusement to herself.*

Yes, it is inconsiderate of me to dig up the past, when I know your father and Jamie must be hungry.

> *Putting her arm around Edmund's shoulder—with a fond solicitude which is at the same time remote.*

I do hope you have an appetite, dear. You really must eat more.

> *Her eyes become fixed on the whiskey glass on the table beside him—sharply.*

Why is that glass there? Did you take a drink? Oh, how can you be such a fool? Don't you know it's the worst thing?

> *She turns on Tyrone.*

You're to blame, James. How could you let him? Do you want to kill him? Don't you remember my father? He wouldn't stop after he was stricken. He said doctors were fools! He thought, like you, that whiskey is a good tonic!

> *A look of terror comes into her eyes and she stammers.*

But, of course, there's no comparison at all. I don't know why I— Forgive me for scolding you, James. One small drink won't hurt Edmund. It might be good for him, if it gives him an appetite.

> *She pats Edmund's cheek playfully, the strange detachment again in her manner. He jerks his head away. She seems not to notice, but she moves instinctively away.*

JAMIE
> *Roughly, to hide his tense nerves.*

For God's sake, let's eat. I've been working in the damned dirt under the hedge all morning. I've earned my grub.

> *He comes around in back of his father, not looking at his mother, and grabs Edmund's shoulder.*

Come on, Kid. Let's put on the feed bag.

> *Edmund gets up, keeping his eyes averted from his mother. They pass her, heading for the back parlor.*

TYRONE
> *Dully.*

Yes, you go in with your mother, lads. I'll join you in a second.

> *But they keep on without waiting for her. She looks at their backs with a helpless hurt and, as they enter the back parlor, starts to follow them. Tyrone's eyes are on her, sad and condemning. She feels them and turns sharply without meeting his stare.*

MARY

Why do you look at me like that?

> *Her hands flutter up to pat her hair.*

Is it my hair coming down? I was so worn out from last night. I thought I'd better lie down this morning. I drowsed off and had a nice refreshing nap. But I'm sure I fixed my hair again when I woke up.

> *Forcing a laugh.*

Although, as usual, I couldn't find my glasses.

> *Sharply.*

Please stop staring! One would think you were accusing me—

> *Then pleadingly.*

James! You don't understand!

TYRONE

With dull anger.

I understand that I've been a God-damned fool to believe in you!

He walks away from her to pour himself a big drink.

MARY

Her face again sets in stubborn defiance.

I don't know what you mean by "believing in me." All I've felt was
distrust and spying and suspicion.

Then accusingly.

Why are you having another drink? You never have more than one
before lunch.

Bitterly.

I know what to expect. You will be drunk tonight. Well, it won't
be the first time, will it—or the thousandth?

Again she bursts out pleadingly.

Oh, James, please! You don't understand! I'm so worried about Edmund! I'm so afraid he—

TYRONE

I don't want to listen to your excuses, Mary.

MARY

Strickenly.

Excuses? You mean— ? Oh, you can't believe that of me! You
mustn't believe that, James!

*Then slipping away into her strange detachment—quite
casually.*

Shall we not go into lunch, dear? I don't want anything but I know
you're hungry.

*He walks slowly to where she stands in the doorway. He
walks like an old man. As he reaches her she bursts out
piteously.*

James! I tried so hard! I tried so hard! Please believe—!

TYRONE

Moved in spite of himself—helplessly.

I suppose you did, Mary.

Then grief-strickenly.

For the love of God, why couldn't you have the strength to keep on?

MARY

Her face setting into that stubborn denial again.

I don't know what you're talking about. Have the strength to keep on what?

TYRONE

Hopelessly.

Never mind. It's no use now.

He moves on and she keeps beside him as they disappear in the back parlor.

CURTAIN

Act Two, Scene Two

SCENE   *The same, about a half hour later. The tray with the bottle of whiskey has been removed from the table. The family are returning from lunch as the curtain rises. Mary is the first to enter from the back parlor. Her husband follows. He is not with her as he was in the similar entrance after breakfast at the opening of Act One. He avoids touching her or looking at her. There is condemnation in his face, mingled now with the beginning of an old weary, helpless resignation. Jamie and Edmund follow their father. Jamie's face is hard with defensive cynicism. Edmund tries to copy this defense but without success. He plainly shows he is heartsick as well as physically ill.*

Mary is terribly nervous again, as if the strain of sitting through lunch with them had been too much for her. Yet at the same time, in contrast to this, her expression shows more of that strange aloofness which seems to stand apart from her nerves and the anxieties which harry them.

She is talking as she enters—a stream of words that issues casually, in a routine of family conversation, from her mouth. She appears indifferent to the fact that their thoughts are not on what she is saying any more than her own are. As she talks, she comes to the left of the table and stands, facing front, one hand fumbling with the bosom of her dress, the other playing over the table top. Tyrone lights a cigar and goes to the screen door, staring out. Jamie fills a pipe from a jar on top of the bookcase at rear. He lights it as he goes to look out the window at right. Edmund sits in a chair by the table, turned half away from his mother so he does not have to watch her.

MARY

It's no use finding fault with Bridget. She doesn't listen. I can't threaten her, or she'd threaten she'd leave. And she does do her best

71

at times. It's too bad they seem to be just the times you're sure to be late, James. Well, there's this consolation: it's difficult to tell from her cooking whether she's doing her best or her worst.

She gives a little laugh of detached amusement—indifferently.
Never mind. The summer will soon be over, thank goodness. Your season will open again and we can go back to second-rate hotels and trains. I hate them, too, but at least I don't expect them to be like a home, and there's no housekeeping to worry about. It's unreasonable to expect Bridget or Cathleen to act as if this was a home. They know it isn't as well as we know it. It never has been and it never will be.

TYRONE
Bitterly without turning around.
No, it never can be now. But it was once, before you—

MARY
Her face instantly set in blank denial.
Before I what?
There is a dead silence. She goes on with a return of her detached air.
No, no. Whatever you mean, it isn't true, dear. It was never a home. You've always preferred the Club or a barroom. And for me it's always been as lonely as a dirty room in a one-night stand hotel. In a real home one is never lonely. You forget I know from experience what a home is like. I gave up one to marry you—my father's home.
At once, through an association of ideas she turns to Edmund. Her manner becomes tenderly solicitous, but there is the strange quality of detachment in it.
I'm worried about you, Edmund. You hardly touched a thing at lunch. That's no way to take care of yourself. It's all right for me not to have an appetite. I've been growing too fat. But you must eat.
Coaxingly maternal.
Promise me you will, dear, for my sake.

EDMUND
Dully.
Yes, Mama.

MARY

Pats his cheek as he tries not to shrink away.

That's a good boy.

There is another pause of dead silence. Then the telephone in the front hall rings and all of them stiffen startledly.

TYRONE

Hastily.

I'll answer. McGuire said he'd call me.

He goes out through the front parlor.

MARY

Indifferently.

McGuire. He must have another piece of property on his list that no one would think of buying except your father. It doesn't matter any more, but it's always seemed to me your father could afford to keep on buying property but never to give me a home.

She stops to listen as Tyrone's voice is heard from the hall.

TYRONE

Hello.

With forced heartiness.

Oh, how are you, Doctor?

Jamie turns from the window. Mary's fingers play more rapidly on the table top. Tyrone's voice, trying to conceal, reveals that he is hearing bad news.

I see—

Hurriedly.

Well, you'll explain all about it when you see him this afternoon. Yes, he'll be in without fail. Four o'clock. I'll drop in myself and have a talk with you before that. I have to go uptown on business, anyway. Goodbye, Doctor.

EDMUND

Dully.

That didn't sound like glad tidings.

Jamie gives him a pitying glance—then looks out the window again. Mary's face is terrified and her hands flutter distractedly. Tyrone comes in. The strain is obvious in his casualness as he addresses Edmund.

73

TYRONE

It was Doctor Hardy. He wants you to be sure and see him at four.

EDMUND

Dully.

What did he say? Not that I give a damn now.

MARY

Bursts out excitedly.

I wouldn't believe him if he swore on a stack of Bibles. You mustn't pay attention to a word he says, Edmund.

TYRONE

Sharply.

Mary!

MARY

More excitedly.

Oh, we all realize why you like him, James! Because he's cheap! But please don't try to tell me! I know all about Doctor Hardy. Heaven knows I ought to after all these years. He's an ignorant fool! There should be a law to keep men like him from practicing. He hasn't the slightest idea— When you're in agony and half insane, he sits and holds your hand and delivers sermons on will power!

> *Her face is drawn in an expression of intense suffering by the memory. For the moment, she loses all caution. With bitter hatred.*

He deliberately humiliates you! He makes you beg and plead! He treats you like a criminal! He understands nothing! And yet it was exactly the same type of cheap quack who first gave you the medicine—and you never knew what it was until too late!

> *Passionately.*

I hate doctors! They'll do anything—anything to keep you coming to them. They'll sell their souls! What's worse, they'll sell yours, and you never know it till one day you find yourself in hell!

EDMUND

Mama! For God's sake, stop talking.

TYRONE

Shakenly.

Yes, Mary, it's no time—

74

MARY

Suddenly is overcome by guilty confusion—stammers.

I— Forgive me, dear. You're right. It's useless to be angry now.

There is again a pause of dead silence. When she speaks again, her face has cleared and is calm, and the quality of uncanny detachment is in her voice and manner.

I'm going upstairs for a moment, if you'll excuse me. I have to fix my hair.

She adds smilingly.

That is if I can find my glasses. I'll be right down.

TYRONE

As she starts through the doorway—pleading and rebuking.

Mary!

MARY

Turns to stare at him calmly.

Yes, dear? What is it?

TYRONE

Helplessly.

Nothing.

MARY

With a strange derisive smile.

You're welcome to come up and watch me if you're so suspicious.

TYRONE

As if that could do any good! You'd only postpone it. And I'm not your jailor. This isn't a prison.

MARY

No. I know you can't help thinking it's a home.

She adds quickly with a detached contrition.

I'm sorry, dear. I don't mean to be bitter. It's not your fault.

She turns and disappears through the back parlor. The three in the room remain silent. It is as if they were waiting until she got upstairs before speaking.

JAMIE

Cynically brutal.

Another shot in the arm!

75

EDMUND

Angrily.

Cut out that kind of talk!

TYRONE

Yes! Hold your foul tongue and your rotten Broadway loafer's lingo! Have you no pity or decency?

Losing his temper.

You ought to be kicked out in the gutter! But if I did it, you know damned well who'd weep and plead for you, and excuse you and complain till I let you come back.

JAMIE

A spasm of pain crosses his face.

Christ, don't I know that? No pity? I have all the pity in the world for her. I understand what a hard game to beat she's up against—which is more than you ever have! My lingo didn't mean I had no feeling. I was merely putting bluntly what we all know, and have to live with now, again.

Bitterly.

The cures are no damned good except for a while. The truth is there is no cure and we've been saps to hope—

Cynically.

They never come back!

EDMUND

Scornfully parodying his brother's cynicism.

They never come back! Everything is in the bag! It's all a frame-up! We're all fall guys and suckers and we can't beat the game!

Disdainfully.

Christ, if I felt the way you do—!

JAMIE

Stung for a moment—then shrugging his shoulders, dryly.

I thought you did. Your poetry isn't very cheery. Nor the stuff you read and claim you admire.

He indicates the small bookcase at rear.

Your pet with the unpronounceable name, for example.

EDMUND

Nietzsche. You don't know what you're talking about. You haven't read him.

JAMIE

Enough to know it's a lot of bunk!

TYRONE

Shut up, both of you! There's little choice between the philosophy you learned from Broadway loafers, and the one Edmund got from his books. They're both rotten to the core. You've both flouted the faith you were born and brought up in—the one true faith of the Catholic Church—and your denial has brought nothing but self-destruction!

His two sons stare at him contemptuously. They forget their quarrel and are as one against him on this issue.

EDMUND

That's the bunk, Papa!

JAMIE

We don't pretend, at any rate.
Caustically.
I don't notice you've worn any holes in the knees of your pants going to Mass.

TYRONE

It's true I'm a bad Catholic in the observance, God forgive me. But I believe!
Angrily.
And you're a liar! I may not go to church but every night and morning of my life I get on my knees and pray!

EDMUND

Bitingly.
Did you pray for Mama?

TYRONE

I did. I've prayed to God these many years for her.

EDMUND

Then Nietzsche must be right.

He quotes from Thus Spake Zarathustra.
"God is dead: of His pity for man hath God died."

TYRONE
Ignores this.
If your mother had prayed, too— She hasn't denied her faith, but she's forgotten it, until now there's no strength of the spirit left in her to fight against her curse.
Then dully resigned.
But what's the good of talk? We've lived with this before and now we must again. There's no help for it.
Bitterly.
Only I wish she hadn't led me to hope this time. By God, I never will again!

EDMUND
That's a rotten thing to say, Papa!
Defiantly.
Well, I'll hope! She's just started. It can't have got a hold on her yet. She can still stop. I'm going to talk to her.

JAMIE
Shrugs his shoulders.
You can't talk to her now. She'll listen but she won't listen. She'll be here but she won't be here. You know the way she gets.

TYRONE
Yes, that's the way the poison acts on her always. Every day from now on, there'll be the same drifting away from us until by the end of each night—

EDMUND
Miserably.
Cut it out, Papa!
He jumps up from his chair.
I'm going to get dressed.
Bitterly, as he goes.
I'll make so much noise she can't suspect I've come to spy on her.
He disappears through the front parlor and can be heard stamping noisily upstairs.

78

JAMIE
After a pause.
What did Doc Hardy say about the Kid?

TYRONE
Dully.
It's what you thought. He's got consumption.

JAMIE
God damn it!

TYRONE
There is no possible doubt, he said.

JAMIE
He'll have to go to a sanatorium.

TYRONE
Yes, and the sooner the better, Hardy said, for him and everyone around him. He claims that in six months to a year Edmund will be cured, if he obeys orders.
He sighs—gloomily and resentfully.
I never thought a child of mine— It doesn't come from my side of the family. There wasn't one of us that didn't have lungs as strong as an ox.

JAMIE
Who gives a damn about that part of it! Where does Hardy want to send him?

TYRONE
That's what I'm to see him about.

JAMIE
Well, for God's sake, pick out a good place and not some cheap dump!

TYRONE
Stung.
I'll send him wherever Hardy thinks best!

JAMIE
Well, don't give Hardy your old over-the-hills-to-the-poorhouse song about taxes and mortgages.

TYRONE

I'm no millionaire who can throw money away! Why shouldn't I tell Hardy the truth?

JAMIE

Because he'll think you want him to pick a cheap dump, and because he'll know it isn't the truth—especially if he hears afterwards you've seen McGuire and let that flannel-mouth, gold-brick merchant sting you with another piece of bum property!

TYRONE

Furiously.

Keep your nose out of my business!

JAMIE

This is Edmund's business. What I'm afraid of is, with your Irish bog-trotter idea that consumption is fatal, you'll figure it would be a waste of money to spend any more than you can help.

TYRONE

You liar!

JAMIE

All right. Prove I'm a liar. That's what I want. That's why I brought it up.

TYRONE

His rage still smouldering.

I have every hope Edmund will be cured. And keep your dirty tongue off Ireland! You're a fine one to sneer, with the map of it on your face!

JAMIE

Not after I wash my face.

Then before his father can react to this insult to the Old Sod, he adds dryly, shrugging his shoulders.

Well, I've said all I have to say. It's up to you.

Abruptly.

What do you want me to do this afternoon, now you're going up-town? I've done all I can do on the hedge until you cut more of it. You don't want me to go ahead with your clipping, I know that.

80

TYRONE

No. You'd get it crooked, as you get everything else.

JAMIE

Then I'd better go uptown with Edmund. The bad news coming on
top of what's happened to Mama may hit him hard.

TYRONE

Forgetting his quarrel.

Yes, go with him, Jamie. Keep up his spirits, if you can.

He adds caustically.

If you can without making it an excuse to get drunk!

JAMIE

What would I use for money? The last I heard they were still selling
booze, not giving it away.

He starts for the front-parlor doorway.

I'll get dressed.

*He stops in the doorway as he sees his mother approaching
from the hall, and moves aside to let her come in. Her eyes
look brighter, and her manner is more detached. This change
becomes more marked as the scene goes on.*

MARY

Vaguely.

You haven't seen my glasses anywhere, have you, Jamie?

*She doesn't look at him. He glances away, ignoring her
question but she doesn't seem to expect an answer. She comes
forward, addressing her husband without looking at him.*

You haven't seen them, have you, James?

Behind her Jamie disappears through the front parlor.

TYRONE

Turns to look out the screen door.

No, Mary.

MARY

What's the matter with Jamie? Have you been nagging at him again?
You shouldn't treat him with such contempt all the time. He's not
to blame. If he'd been brought up in a real home, I'm sure he would
have been different.

She comes to the windows at right—lightly.
You're not much of a weather prophet, dear. See how hazy it's getting. I can hardly see the other shore.

TYRONE
Trying to speak naturally.
Yes, I spoke too soon. We're in for another night of fog, I'm afraid.

MARY
Oh, well, I won't mind it tonight.

TYRONE
No, I don't imagine you will, **Mary.**

MARY
Flashes a glance at him—after a pause.
I don't see Jamie going down to the hedge. Where did he go?

TYRONE
He's going with Edmund to the Doctor's. He went up to change his clothes.
Then, glad of an excuse to leave her.
I'd better do the same or I'll be late for my appointment at the Club.
He makes a move toward the front-parlor doorway, but with a swift impulsive movement she reaches out and clasps his arm.

MARY
A note of pleading in her voice.
Don't go yet, dear. I don't want to be alone.
Hastily.
I mean, you have plenty of time. You know you boast you can dress in one-tenth the time it takes the boys.
Vaguely.
There is something I wanted to say. What is it? I've forgotten. I'm glad Jamie is going uptown. You didn't give him any money, I hope.

TYRONE
I did not.

MARY
He'd only spend it on drink and you know what a vile, poisonous

tongue he has when he's drunk. Not that I would mind anything he said tonight, but he always manages to drive you into a rage, especially if you're drunk, too, as you will be.

TYRONE
Resentfully.
I won't. I never get drunk.

MARY
Teasing indifferently.
Oh, I'm sure you'll hold it well. You always have. It's hard for a stranger to tell, but after thirty-five years of marriage—

TYRONE
I've never missed a performance in my life. That's the proof!
Then bitterly.
If I did get drunk it is not you who should blame me. No man has ever had a better reason.

MARY
Reason? What reason? You always drink too much when you go to the Club, don't you? Particularly when you meet McGuire. He sees to that. Don't think I'm finding fault, dear. You must do as you please. I won't mind.

TYRONE
I know you won't.
He turns toward the front parlor, anxious to escape.
I've got to get dressed.

MARY
Again she reaches out and grasps his arm—pleadingly.
No, please wait a little while, dear. At least, until one of the boys comes down. You will all be leaving me so soon.

TYRONE
With bitter sadness.
It's you who are leaving us, Mary.

MARY
I? That's a silly thing to say, James. How could I leave? There is nowhere I could go. Who would I go to see? I have no friends.

TYRONE

It's your own fault—

He stops and sighs helplessly—persuasively.

There's surely one thing you can do this afternoon that will be good for you, Mary. Take a drive in the automobile. Get away from the house. Get a little sun and fresh air.

Injuredly.

I bought the automobile for you. You know I don't like the damned things. I'd rather walk any day, or take a trolley.

With growing resentment.

I had it here waiting for you when you came back from the sanatorium. I hoped it would give you pleasure and distract your mind. You used to ride in it every day, but you've hardly used it at all lately. I paid a lot of money I couldn't afford, and there's the chauffeur I have to board and lodge and pay high wages whether he drives you or not.

Bitterly.

Waste! The same old waste that will land me in the poorhouse in my old age! What good did it do you? I might as well have thrown the money out the window.

MARY

With detached calm.

Yes, it was a waste of money, James. You shouldn't have bought a secondhand automobile. You were swindled again as you always are, because you insist on secondhand bargains in everything.

TYRONE

It's one of the best makes! Everyone says it's better than any of the new ones!

MARY

Ignoring this.

It was another waste to hire Smythe, who was only a helper in a garage and had never been a chauffeur. Oh, I realize his wages are less than a real chauffeur's, but he more than makes up for that, I'm sure, by the graft he gets from the garage on repair bills. Something is always wrong. Smythe sees to that, I'm afraid.

84

TYRONE

I don't believe it! He may not be a fancy millionaire's flunky but
he's honest! You're as bad as Jamie, suspecting everyone!

MARY

You mustn't be offended, dear. I wasn't offended when you gave me
the automobile. I knew you didn't mean to humiliate me. I knew
that was the way you had to do everything. I was grateful and
touched. I knew buying the car was a hard thing for you to do, and
it proved how much you loved me, in your way, especially when
you couldn't really believe it would do me any good.

TYRONE

Mary!

He suddenly hugs her to him—brokenly.

Dear Mary! For the love of God, for my sake and the boys' sake and
your own, won't you stop now?

MARY

Stammers in guilty confusion for a second.

I— James! Please!

Her strange, stubborn defense comes back instantly.

Stop what? What are you talking about?

*He lets his arm fall to his side brokenly. She impulsively
puts her arm around him.*

James! We've loved each other! We always will! Let's remember
only that, and not try to understand what we cannot understand, or
help things that cannot be helped—the things life has done to us we
cannot excuse or explain.

TYRONE

As if he hadn't heard—bitterly.

You won't even try?

MARY

*Her arms drop hopelessly and she turns away—with de-
tachment.*

Try to go for a drive this afternoon, you mean? Why, yes, if you
wish me to, although it makes me feel lonelier than if I stayed here.
There is no one I can invite to drive with me, and I never know where
to tell Smythe to go. If there was a friend's house where I could drop

85

in and laugh and gossip awhile. But, of course, there isn't. There never has been.

Her manner becoming more and more remote.

At the Convent I had so many friends. Girls whose families lived in lovely homes. I used to visit them and they'd visit me in my father's home. But, naturally, after I married an actor—you know how actors were considered in those days—a lot of them gave me the cold shoulder. And then, right after we were married, there was the scandal of that woman who had been your mistress, suing you. From then on, all my old friends either pitied me or cut me dead. I hated the ones who cut me much less than the pitiers.

TYRONE

With guilty resentment.

For God's sake, don't dig up what's long forgotten. If you're that far gone in the past already, when it's only the beginning of the afternoon, what will you be tonight?

MARY

Stares at him defiantly now.

Come to think of it, I do have to drive uptown. There's something I must get at the drugstore.

TYRONE

Bitterly scornful.

Leave it to you to have some of the stuff hidden, and prescriptions for more! I hope you'll lay in a good stock ahead so we'll never have another night like the one when you screamed for it, and ran out of the house in your nightdress half crazy, to try and throw yourself off the dock!

MARY

Tries to ignore this.

I have to get tooth powder and toilet soap and cold cream—

She breaks down pitiably.

James! You mustn't remember! You mustn't humiliate me so!

TYRONE

Ashamed.

I'm sorry. Forgive me, Mary!

MARY

Defensively detached again.

It doesn't matter. Nothing like that ever happened. You must have dreamed it.

He stares at her hopelessly. Her voice seems to drift farther and farther away.

I was so healthy before Edmund was born. You remember, James. There wasn't a nerve in my body. Even traveling with you season after season, with week after week of one-night stands, in trains without Pullmans, in dirty rooms of filthy hotels, eating bad food, bearing children in hotel rooms, I still kept healthy. But bearing Edmund was the last straw. I was so sick afterwards, and that ignorant quack of a cheap hotel doctor— All he knew was I was in pain. It was easy for him to stop the pain.

TYRONE

Mary! For God's sake, forget the past!

MARY

With strange objective calm.

Why? How can I? The past is the present, isn't it? It's the future, too. We all try to lie out of that but life won't let us.

Going on.

I blame only myself. I swore after Eugene died I would never have another baby. I was to blame for his death. If I hadn't left him with my mother to join you on the road, because you wrote telling me you missed me and were so lonely, Jamie would never have been allowed, when he still had measles, to go in the baby's room.

Her face hardening.

I've always believed Jamie did it on purpose. He was jealous of the baby. He hated him.

As Tyrone starts to protest.

Oh, I know Jamie was only seven, but he was never stupid. He'd been warned it might kill the baby. He knew. I've never been able to forgive him for that.

TYRONE

With bitter sadness.

Are you back with Eugene now? Can't you let our dead baby rest in peace?

87

As if she hadn't heard him.

It was my fault. I should have insisted on staying with Eugene and not have let you persuade me to join you, just because I loved you. Above all, I shouldn't have let you insist I have another baby to take Eugene's place, because you thought that would make me forget his death. I knew from experience by then that children should have homes to be born in, if they are to be good children, and women need homes, if they are to be good mothers. I was afraid all the time I carried Edmund. I knew something terrible would happen. I knew I'd proved by the way I'd left Eugene that I wasn't worthy to have another baby, and that God would punish me if I did. I never should have borne Edmund.

TYRONE

With an uneasy glance through the front parlor.

Mary! Be careful with your talk. If he heard you he might think you never wanted him. He's feeling bad enough already without—

MARY

Violently.

It's a lie! I did want him! More than anything in the world! You don't understand! I meant, for his sake. He has never been happy. He never will be. Nor healthy. He was born nervous and too sensitive, and that's my fault. And now, ever since he's been so sick I've kept remembering Eugene and my father and I've been so frightened and guilty—

Then, catching herself, with an instant change to stubborn denial.

Oh, I know it's foolish to imagine dreadful things when there's no reason for it. After all, everyone has colds and gets over them.

Tyrone stares at her and sighs helplessly. He turns away toward the front parlor and sees Edmund coming down the stairs in the hall.

TYRONE

Sharply, in a low voice.

Here's Edmund. For God's sake try and be yourself—at least until he goes! You can do that much for him!

*He waits, forcing his face into a pleasantly paternal ex-
pression. She waits frightenedly, seized again by a nervous
panic, her hands fluttering over the bosom of her dress, up
to her throat and hair, with a distracted aimlessness. Then,
as Edmund approaches the doorway, she cannot face him.
She goes swiftly away to the windows at left and stares out
with her back to the front parlor. Edmund enters. He has
changed to a ready-made blue serge suit, high stiff collar and
tie, black shoes.*

With an actor's heartiness.
Well! You look spic and span. I'm on my way up to change, too.
He starts to pass him.

EDMUND
Dryly.
Wait a minute, Papa. I hate to bring up disagreeable topics, but
there's the matter of carfare. I'm broke.

TYRONE
Starts automatically on a customary lecture.
You'll always be broke until you learn the value—
*Checks himself guiltily, looking at his son's sick face with
worried pity.*
But you've been learning, lad. You worked hard before you took
ill. You've done splendidly. I'm proud of you.
*He pulls out a small roll of bills from his pants pocket and
carefully selects one. Edmund takes it. He glances at it and
his face expresses astonishment. His father again reacts cus-
tomarily—sarcastically.*

Thank you.
He quotes.
"How sharper than a serpent's tooth it is—"

EDMUND
"To have a thankless child." I know. Give me a chance, Papa. I'm
knocked speechless. This isn't a dollar. It's a ten spot.

TYRONE
Embarrassed by his generosity.

Put it in your pocket. You'll probably meet some of your friends uptown and you can't hold your end up and be sociable with nothing in your jeans.

> EDMUND

You meant it? Gosh, thank you, Papa.
>> *He is genuinely pleased and grateful for a moment—then he stares at his father's face with uneasy suspicion.*

But why all of a sudden—?
>> *Cynically.*

Did Doc Hardy tell you I was going to die?
>> *Then he sees his father is bitterly hurt.*

No! That's a rotten crack. I was only kidding, Papa.
>> *He puts an arm around his father impulsively and gives him an affectionate hug.*

I'm very grateful. Honest, Papa.

> TYRONE
>> *Touched, returns his hug.*

You're welcome, lad.

> MARY
>> *Suddenly turns to them in a confused panic of frightened anger.*

I won't have it!
>> *She stamps her foot.*

Do you hear, Edmund! Such morbid nonsense! Saying you're going to die! It's the books you read! Nothing but sadness and death! Your father shouldn't allow you to have them. And some of the poems you've written yourself are even worse! You'd think you didn't want to live! A boy of your age with everything before him! It's just a pose you get out of books! You're not really sick at all!

> TYRONE

Mary! Hold your tongue!

> MARY
>> *Instantly changing to a detached tone.*

But, James, it's absurd of Edmund to be so gloomy and make such a great to-do about nothing.

> *Turning to Edmund but avoiding his eyes—teasingly af-*
> *fectionate.*

Never mind, dear. I'm on to you.

> *She comes to him.*

You want to be petted and spoiled and made a fuss over, isn't that it? You're still such a baby.

> *She puts her arm around him and hugs him. He remains*
> *rigid and unyielding. Her voice begins to tremble.*

But please don't carry it too far, dear. Don't say horrible things. I know it's foolish to take them seriously but I can't help it. You've got me—so frightened.

> *She breaks and hides her face on his shoulder, sobbing. Ed-*
> *mund is moved in spite of himself. He pats her shoulder with*
> *an awkward tenderness.*

EDMUND

Don't, mother.

> *His eyes meet his father's.*

TYRONE

> *Huskily—clutching at hopeless hope.*

Maybe if you asked your mother now what you said you were going to

> *He fumbles with his watch.*

By God, look at the time! I'll have to shake a leg.

> *He hurries away through the front parlor. Mary lifts her*
> *head. Her manner is again one of detached motherly solici-*
> *tude. She seems to have forgotten the tears which are still in*
> *her eyes.*

MARY

How do you feel, dear?

> *She feels his forehead.*

Your head is a little hot, but that's just from going out in the sun. You look ever so much better than you did this morning.

> *Taking his hand.*

Come and sit down. You mustn't stand on your feet so much. You must learn to husband your strength.

> *She gets him to sit and she sits sideways on the arm of his*

*chair, an arm around his shoulder, so he cannot meet her
eyes.*

EDMUND

Starts to blurt out the appeal he now feels is quite hopeless.

Listen, Mama—

MARY

Interrupting quickly.

Now, now! Don't talk. Lean back and rest.

Persuasively.

You know, I think it would be much better for you if you stayed
home this afternoon and let me take care of you. It's such a tiring
trip uptown in the dirty old trolley on a hot day like this. I'm sure
you'd be much better off here with me.

EDMUND

Dully.

You forget I have an appointment with Hardy.

Trying again to get his appeal started.

Listen, Mama—

MARY

Quickly.

You can telephone and say you don't feel well enough.

Excitedly.

It's simply a waste of time and money seeing him. He'll only tell you
some lie. He'll pretend he's found something serious the matter because that's his bread and butter.

She gives a hard sneering little laugh.

The old idiot! All he knows about medicine is to look solemn and
preach will power!

EDMUND

Trying to catch her eyes.

Mama! Please listen! I want to ask you something! You— You're
only just started. You can still stop. You've got the will power!
We'll all help you. I'll do anything! Won't you, Mama?

MARY

Stammers pleadingly.

Please don't—talk about things you don't understand!

92

EDMUND
Dully.
All right, I give up. I knew it was no use. /

MARY
In blank denial now.
Anyway, I don't know what you're referring to. But I do know you should be the last one— Right after I returned from the sanatorium, you began to be ill. The doctor there had warned me I must have peace at home with nothing to upset me, and all I've done is worry about you.
Then distractedly.
But that's no excuse! I'm only trying to explain. It's not an excuse!
She hugs him to her—pleadingly.
Promise me, dear, you won't believe I made you an excuse.

EDMUND
Bitterly.
What else can I believe?

MARY
Slowly takes her arm away—her manner remote and objective again.
Yes, I suppose you can't help suspecting that.

EDMUND
Ashamed but still bitter.
What do you expect?

MARY
Nothing, I don't blame you. How could you believe me—when I can't believe myself? I've become such a liar. I never lied about anything once upon a time. Now I have to lie, especially to myself. But how can you understand, when I don't myself. I've never understood anything about it, except that one day long ago I found I could no longer call my soul my own.
She pauses—then lowering her voice to a strange tone of whispered confidence.
But some day, dear, I will find it again—some day when you're all well, and I see you healthy and happy and successful, and I don't

have to feel guilty any more—some day when the Blessed Virgin Mary forgives me and gives me back the faith in Her love and pity I used to have in my convent days, and I can pray to Her again— when She sees no one in the world can believe in me even for a moment any more, then She will believe in me, and with Her help it will be so easy. I will hear myself scream with agony, and at the same time I will laugh because I will be so sure of myself.

Then as Edmund remains hopelessly silent, she adds sadly.
Of course, you can't believe that, either.

She rises from the arm of his chair and goes to stare out the windows at right with her back to him—casually.
Now I think of it, you might as well go uptown. I forgot I'm taking a drive. I have to go to the drugstore. You would hardly want to go there with me. You'd be so ashamed.

EDMUND
Brokenly.
Mama! Don't!

MARY
I suppose you'll divide that ten dollars your father gave you with Jamie. You always divide with each other, don't you? Like good sports. Well, I know what he'll do with his share. Get drunk some-place where he can be with the only kind of woman he understands or likes.

She turns to him, pleading frightenedly.
Edmund! Promise me you won't drink! It's so dangerous! You know Doctor Hardy told you—

EDMUND
Bitterly.
I thought he was an old idiot. Anyway, by tonight, what will you care?

MARY
Pitifully.
Edmund!

Jamie's voice is heard from the front hall,
"Come on, Kid, let's beat it."
Mary's manner at once becomes detached again.
Go on, Edmund. Jamie's waiting.

She goes to the front-parlor doorway.
There comes your father downstairs, too.
Tyrone's voice calls,
"Come on, Edmund."

EDMUND
Jumping up from his chair.
I'm coming.
He stops beside her—without looking at her.
Goodbye, Mama.

MARY
Kisses him with detached affection.
Goodbye, dear. If you're coming home for dinner, try not to be late.
And tell your father. You know what Bridget is.
He turns and hurries away. Tyrone calls from the hall,
"Goodbye, Mary," *and then Jamie,* "Goodbye, Mama."
She calls back.
Goodbye.

*The front screen door is heard closing after them. She comes
and stands by the table, one hand drumming on it, the other
fluttering up to pat her hair. She stares about the room with
frightened, forsaken eyes and whispers to herself.*
It's so lonely here.
Then her face hardens into bitter self-contempt.
You're lying to yourself again. You wanted to get rid of them. Their
contempt and disgust aren't pleasant company. You're glad they're
gone.
She gives a little despairing laugh.
Then Mother of God, why do I feel so lonely?

CURTAIN

Act Three

SCENE *The same. It is around half past six in the evening. Dusk is gathering in the living room, an early dusk due to the fog which has rolled in from the Sound and is like a white curtain drawn down outside the windows. From a lighthouse beyond the harbor's mouth, a foghorn is heard at regular intervals, moaning like a mournful whale in labor, and from the harbor itself, intermittently, comes the warning ringing of bells on yachts at anchor.*

The tray with the bottle of whiskey, glasses, and pitcher of ice water is on the table, as it was in the pre-luncheon scene of the previous act.

Mary and the second girl, Cathleen, are discovered. The latter is standing at left of table. She holds an empty whiskey glass in her hand as if she'd forgotten she had it. She shows the effects of drink. Her stupid, good-humored face wears a pleased and flattered simper.

Mary is paler than before and her eyes shine with unnatural brilliance. The strange detachment in her manner has intensified. She has hidden deeper within herself and found refuge and release in a dream where present reality is but an appearance to be accepted and dismissed unfeelingly—even with a hard cynicism—or entirely ignored. There is at times an uncanny gay, free youthfulness in her manner, as if in spirit she were released to become again, simply and without self-consciousness, the naive, happy, chattering schoolgirl of her convent days. She wears the dress into which she had changed for her drive to town, a simple, fairly expensive affair, which would be extremely becoming if it were not for the careless, almost slovenly way she wears it. Her hair is no longer fastidiously in place. It has a slightly disheveled, lopsided look. She talks to Cathleen with a confiding fa-

97

miliarity, as if the second girl were an old, intimate friend. As the curtain rises, she is standing by the screen door looking out. A moan of the foghorn is heard.

MARY
Amused—girlishly.
That foghorn! Isn't it awful, Cathleen?

CATHLEEN
Talks more familiarly than usual but never with intentional impertinence because she sincerely likes her mistress.
It is indeed, Ma'am. It's like a banshee.

MARY
Goes on as if she hadn't heard. In nearly all the following dialogue there is the feeling that she has Cathleen with her merely as an excuse to keep talking.
I don't mind it tonight. Last night it drove me crazy. I lay awake worrying until I couldn't stand it any more.

CATHLEEN
Bad cess to it. I was scared out of my wits riding back from town. I thought that ugly monkey, Smythe, would drive us in a ditch or against a tree. You couldn't see your hand in front of you. I'm glad you had me sit in back with you, Ma'am. If I'd been in front with that monkey— He can't keep his dirty hands to himself. Give him half a chance and he's pinching me on the leg or you-know-where— asking your pardon, Ma'am, but it's true.

MARY
Dreamily.
It wasn't the fog I minded, Cathleen. I really love fog.

CATHLEEN
They say it's good for the complexion.

MARY
It hides you from the world and the world from you. You feel that everything has changed, and nothing is what it seemed to be. No one can find or touch you any more.

98

CATHLEEN

I wouldn't care so much if Smythe was a fine, handsome man like some chauffeurs I've seen—I mean, if it was all in fun, for I'm a decent girl. But for a shriveled runt like Smythe—! I've told him, you must think I'm hard up that I'd notice a monkey like you. I've warned him, one day I'll give a clout that'll knock him into next week. And so I will!

MARY

It's the foghorn I hate. It won't let you alone. It keeps reminding you, and warning you, and calling you back.
She smiles strangely.
But it can't tonight. It's just an ugly sound. It doesn't remind me of anything.
She gives a teasing, girlish laugh.
Except, perhaps, Mr. Tyrone's snores. I've always had such fun teasing him about it. He has snored ever since I can remember, especially when he's had too much to drink, and yet he's like a child, he hates to admit it.
She laughs, coming to the table.
Well, I suppose I snore at times, too, and I don't like to admit it. So I have no right to make fun of him, have I?
She sits in the rocker at right of table.

CATHLEEN

Ah, sure, everybody healthy snores. It's a sign of sanity, they say.
Then, worriedly.
What time is it, Ma'am? I ought to go back in the kitchen. The damp is in Bridget's rheumatism and she's like a raging divil. She'll bite my head off.
She puts her glass on the table and makes a movement toward the back parlor.

MARY
With a flash of apprehension.
No, don't go, Cathleen. I don't want to be alone, yet.

CATHLEEN

You won't be for long. The Master and the boys will be home soon.

MARY

I doubt if they'll come back for dinner. They have too good an excuse to remain in the barrooms where they feel at home.

> *Cathleen stares at her, stupidly puzzled. Mary goes on smilingly.*

Don't worry about Bridget. I'll tell her I kept you with me, and you can take a big drink of whiskey to her when you go. She won't mind then.

CATHLEEN

> *Grins—at her ease again.*

No, Ma'am. That's the one thing can make her cheerful. She loves her drop.

MARY

Have another drink yourself, if you wish, Cathleen.

CATHLEEN

I don't know if I'd better, Ma'am. I can feel what I've had already.
> *Reaching for the bottle.*

Well, maybe one more won't harm.
> *She pours a drink.*

Here's your good health, Ma'am.
> *She drinks without bothering about a chaser.*

MARY

> *Dreamily.*

I really did have good health once, Cathleen. But that was long ago.

CATHLEEN

> *Worried again.*

The Master's sure to notice what's gone from the bottle. He has the eye of a hawk for that.

MARY

> *Amusedly.*

Oh, we'll play Jamie's trick on him. Just measure a few drinks of water and pour them in.

CATHLEEN

> *Does this—with a silly giggle.*

God save me, it'll be half water. He'll know by the taste.

MARY

Indifferently.

No, by the time he comes home he'll be too drunk to tell the difference. He has such a good excuse, he believes, to drown his sorrows.

CATHLEEN

Philosophically.

Well, it's a good man's failing. I wouldn't give a trauneen for a teetotaler. They've no high spirits.

Then, stupidly puzzled.

Good excuse? You mean Master Edmund, Ma'am? I can tell the Master is worried about him.

MARY

Stiffens defensively—but in a strange way the reaction has a mechanical quality, as if it did not penetrate to real emotion.

Don't be silly, Cathleen. Why should he be? A touch of grippe is nothing. And Mr. Tyrone never is worried about anything, except money and property and the fear he'll end his days in poverty. I mean, deeply worried. Because he cannot really understand anything else.

She gives a little laugh of detached, affectionate amusement.

My husband is a very peculiar man, Cathleen.

CATHLEEN

Vaguely resentful.

Well, he's a fine, handsome, kind gentleman just the same, Ma'am. Never mind his weakness.

MARY

Oh, I don't mind. I've loved him dearly for thirty-six years. That proves I know he's lovable at heart and can't help being what he is, doesn't it?

CATHLEEN

Hazily reassured.

That's right, Ma'am. Love him dearly, for any fool can see he worships the ground you walk on.

Fighting the effect of her last drink and trying to be soberly conversational.

Speaking of acting, Ma'am, how is it you never went on the stage?

MARY

Resentfully.

I? What put that absurd notion in your head? I was brought up in a respectable home and educated in the best convent in the Middle West. Before I met Mr. Tyrone I hardly knew there was such a thing as a theater. I was a very pious girl. I even dreamed of becoming a nun. I've never had the slightest desire to be an actress.

CATHLEEN

Bluntly.

Well, I can't imagine you a holy nun, Ma'am. Sure, you never darken the door of a church, God forgive you.

MARY

Ignores this.

I've never felt at home in the theater. Even though Mr. Tyrone has made me go with him on all his tours, I've had little to do with the people in his company, or with anyone on the stage. Not that I have anything against them. They have always been kind to me, and I to them. But I've never felt at home with them. Their life is not my life. It has always stood between me and—

She gets up—abruptly.

But let's not talk of old things that couldn't be helped.

She goes to the porch door and stares out.

How thick the fog is. I can't see the road. All the people in the world could pass by and I would never know. I wish it was always that way. It's getting dark already. It will soon be night, thank goodness.

She turns back—vaguely.

It was kind of you to keep me company this afternoon, Cathleen. I would have been lonely driving uptown alone.

CATHLEEN

Sure, wouldn't I rather ride in a fine automobile than stay here and listen to Bridget's lies about her relations? It was like a vacation, Ma'am.

She pauses—then stupidly.

There was only one thing I didn't like.

MARY

Vaguely.

What was that, Cathleen?

CATHLEEN

The way the man in the drugstore acted when I took in the prescription for you.
Indignantly.
The impidence of him!

MARY

With stubborn blankness.
What are you talking about? What drugstore? What prescription?
Then hastily, as Cathleen stares in stupid amazement.
Oh, of course, I'd forgotten. The medicine for the rheumatism in my hands. What did the man say?
Then with indifference.
Not that it matters, as long as he filled the prescription.

CATHLEEN

It mattered to me, then! I'm not used to being treated like a thief. He gave me a long look and says insultingly, "Where did you get hold of this?" and I says, "It's none of your damned business, but if you must know, it's for the lady I work for, Mrs. Tyrone, who's sitting out in the automobile." That shut him up quick. He gave a look out at you and said, "Oh," and went to get the medicine.

MARY

Vaguely.
Yes, he knows me.
She sits in the armchair at right rear of table. She adds in a calm, detached voice.
It's a special kind of medicine. I have to take it because there is no other that can stop the pain—*all* the pain—I mean, in my hands.
She raises her hands and regards them with melancholy sympathy. There is no tremor in them now.
Poor hands! You'd never believe it, but they were once one of my good points, along with my hair and eyes, and I had a fine figure, too.
Her tone has become more and more far-off and dreamy.
They were a musician's hands. I used to love the piano. I worked so hard at my music in the Convent—if you can call it work when you do something you love. Mother Elizabeth and my music teacher

both said I had more talent than any student they remembered. My father paid for special lessons. He spoiled me. He would do anything I asked. He would have sent me to Europe to study after I graduated from the Convent. I might have gone—if I hadn't fallen in love with Mr. Tyrone. Or I might have become a nun. I had two dreams. To be a nun, that was the more beautiful one. To become a concert pianist, that was the other.

> *She pauses, regarding her hands fixedly. Cathleen blinks her eyes to fight off drowsiness and a tipsy feeling.*

I haven't touched a piano in so many years. I couldn't play with such crippled fingers, even if I wanted to. For a time after my marriage I tried to keep up my music. But it was hopeless. One-night stands, cheap hotels, dirty trains, leaving children, never having a home—

> *She stares at her hands with fascinated disgust.*

See, Cathleen, how ugly they are! So maimed and crippled! You would think they'd been through some horrible accident!

> *She gives a strange little laugh.*

So they have, come to think of it.

> *She suddenly thrusts her hands behind her back.*

I won't look at them. They're worse than the foghorn for reminding me—

> *Then with defiant self-assurance.*

But even they can't touch me now.

> *She brings her hands from behind her back and deliberately stares at them—calmly.*

They're far away. I see them, but the pain has gone.

CATHLEEN
Stupidly puzzled.

You've taken some of the medicine? It made you act funny, Ma'am. If I didn't know better, I'd think you'd a drop taken.

MARY
Dreamily.

It kills the pain. You go back until at last you are beyond its reach. Only the past when you were happy is real.

> *She pauses—then as if her words had been an evocation which called back happiness she changes in her whole manner*

and facial expression. She looks younger. There is a quality
of an innocent convent girl about her, and she smiles shyly.
If you think Mr. Tyrone is handsome now, Cathleen, you should
have seen him when I first met him. He had the reputation of being
one of the best looking men in the country. The girls in the Convent
who had seen him act, or seen his photographs, used to rave about
him. He was a great matinee idol then, you know. Women used to
wait at the stage door just to see him come out. You can imagine how
excited I was when my father wrote me he and James Tyrone had
become friends, and that I was to meet him when I came home for
Easter vacation. I showed the letter to all the girls, and how envious
they were! My father took me to see him act first. It was a play about
the French Revolution and the leading part was a nobleman. I
couldn't take my eyes off him. I wept when he was thrown in prison
—and then was so mad at myself because I was afraid my eyes and
nose would be red. My father had said we'd go backstage to his
dressing room right after the play, and so we did.
      She gives a little excited, shy laugh.
I was so bashful all I could do was stammer and blush like a little fool.
But he didn't seem to think I was a fool. I know he liked me the first
moment we were introduced.
      Coquettishly.
I guess my eyes and nose couldn't have been red, after all. I was
really very pretty then, Cathleen. And he was handsomer than my
wildest dream, in his make-up and his nobleman's costume that was
so becoming to him. He was different from all ordinary men, like
someone from another world. At the same time he was simple, and
kind, and unassuming, not a bit stuck-up or vain. I fell in love right
then. So did he, he told me afterwards. I forgot all about becoming
a nun or a concert pianist. All I wanted was to be his wife.
      She pauses, staring before her with unnaturally bright,
      dreamy eyes, and a rapt, tender, girlish smile.
Thirty-six years ago, but I can see it as clearly as if it were tonight!
We've loved each other ever since. And in all those thirty-six years,
there has never been a breath of scandal about him. I mean, with any
other woman. Never since he met me. That has made me very happy,
Cathleen. It has made me forgive so many other things.

CATHLEEN

Fighting tipsy drowsiness—sentimentally.

He's a fine gentleman and you're a lucky woman.

Then, fidgeting.

Can I take the drink to Bridget, Ma'am? It must be near dinnertime and I ought to be in the kitchen helping her. If she don't get something to quiet her temper, she'll be after me with the cleaver.

MARY

With a vague exasperation at being brought back from her dream.

Yes, yes, go. I don't need you now.

CATHLEEN

With relief.

Thank you, Ma'am.

She pours out a big drink and starts for the back parlor with it.

You won't be alone long. The Master and the boys—

MARY

Impatiently.

No, no, they won't come. Tell Bridget I won't wait. You can serve dinner promptly at half past six. I'm not hungry but I'll sit at the table and we'll get it over with.

CATHLEEN

You ought to eat something, Ma'am. It's a queer medicine if it takes away your appetite.

MARY

Has begun to drift into dreams again—reacts mechanically.

What medicine? I don't know what you mean.

In dismissal.

You better take the drink to Bridget.

CATHLEEN

Yes, Ma'am.

She disappears through the back parlor. Mary waits until she hears the pantry door close behind her. Then she settles back in relaxed dreaminess, staring fixedly at nothing. Her

*arms rest limply along the arms of the chair, her hands with
long, warped, swollen-knuckled, sensitive fingers drooping
in complete calm. It is growing dark in the room. There is a
pause of dead quiet. Then from the world outside comes the
melancholy moan of the foghorn, followed by a chorus of
bells, muffled by the fog, from the anchored craft in the harbor. Mary's face gives no sign she has heard, but her hands
jerk and the fingers automatically play for a moment on the
air. She frowns and shakes her head mechanically as if a fly
had walked across her mind. She suddenly loses all the
girlish quality and is an aging, cynically sad, embittered
woman.*

MARY
Bitterly.

You're a sentimental fool. What is so wonderful about that first
meeting between a silly romantic schoolgirl and a matinee idol? You
were much happier before you knew he existed, in the Convent
when you used to pray to the Blessed Virgin.

Longingly.

If I could only find the faith I lost, so I could pray again!

*She pauses—then begins to recite the Hail Mary in a flat,
empty tone.*

"Hail, Mary, full of grace! The Lord is with Thee; blessed art Thou
among women."

Sneeringly.

You expect the Blessed Virgin to be fooled by a lying dope fiend
reciting words! You can't hide from her!

*She springs to her feet. Her hands fly up to pat her hair dis-
tractedly.*

I must go upstairs. I haven't taken enough. When you start again you
never know exactly how much you need.

*She goes toward the front parlor—then stops in the doorway
as she hears the sound of voices from the front path. She
starts guiltily.*

That must be them—

*She hurries back to sit down. Her face sets in stubborn de-
fensiveness—resentfully.*

Why are they coming back? They don't want to. And I'd much rather be alone.

> *Suddenly her whole manner changes. She becomes pathetically relieved and eager.*

Oh, I'm so glad they've come! I've been so horribly lonely!

> *The front door is heard closing and Tyrone calls uneasily from the hall.*

TYRONE

Are you there, Mary?

> *The light in the hall is turned on and shines through the front parlor to fall on Mary.*

MARY

> *Rises from her chair, her face lighting up lovingly—with excited eagerness.*

I'm here, dear. In the living room. I've been waiting for you.

> *Tyrone comes in through the front parlor. Edmund is behind him. Tyrone has had a lot to drink but beyond a slightly glazed look in his eyes and a trace of blur in his speech, he does not show it. Edmund has also had more than a few drinks without much apparent effect, except that his sunken cheeks are flushed and his eyes look bright and feverish. They stop in the doorway to stare appraisingly at her. What they see fulfills their worst expectations. But for the moment Mary is unconscious of their condemning eyes. She kisses her husband and then Edmund. Her manner is unnaturally effusive. They submit shrinkingly. She talks excitedly.*

I'm so happy you've come. I had given up hope. I was afraid you wouldn't come home. It's such a dismal, foggy evening. It must be much more cheerful in the barrooms uptown, where there are people you can talk and joke with. No, don't deny it. I know how you feel. I don't blame you a bit. I'm all the more grateful to you for coming home. I was sitting here so lonely and blue. Come and sit down.

> *She sits at left rear of table, Edmund at left of table, and Tyrone in the rocker at right of it.*

Dinner won't be ready for a minute. You're actually a little early. Will wonders never cease. Here's the whiskey, dear. Shall I pour a drink for you?

Without waiting for a reply she does so.
And you, Edmund? I don't want to encourage you, but one before dinner, as an appetizer, can't do any harm.

She pours a drink for him. They make no move to take the drinks. She talks on as if unaware of their silence.

Where's Jamie? But, of course, he'll never come home so long as he has the price of a drink left.

She reaches out and clasps her husband's hand—sadly.

I'm afraid Jamie has been lost to us for a long time, dear.

Her face hardens.

But we mustn't allow him to drag Edmund down with him, as he'd like to do. He's jealous because Edmund has always been the baby— just as he used to be of Eugene. He'll never be content until he makes Edmund as hopeless a failure as he is.

EDMUND
Miserably.
Stop talking, Mama.

TYRONE
Dully.
Yes, Mary, the less you say now—

Then to Edmund, a bit tipsily.

All the same there's truth in your mother's warning. Beware of that brother of yours, or he'll poison life for you with his damned sneering serpent's tongue!

EDMUND
As before.
Oh, cut it out, Papa.

MARY
Goes on as if nothing had been said.
It's hard to believe, seeing Jamie as he is now, that he was ever my baby. Do you remember what a healthy, happy baby he was, James? The one-night stands and filthy trains and cheap hotels and bad food never made him cross or sick. He was always smiling or laughing. He hardly ever cried. Eugene was the same, too, happy and healthy, during the two years he lived before I let him die through my neglect.

TYRONE

Oh, for the love of God! I'm a fool for coming home!

EDMUND

Papa! Shut up!

MARY

Smiles with detached tenderness at Edmund.
It was Edmund who was the crosspatch when he was little, always getting upset and frightened about nothing at all.
She pats his hand—teasingly.
Everyone used to say, dear, you'd cry at the drop of a hat.

EDMUND

Cannot control his bitterness.
Maybe I guessed there was a good reason not to laugh.

TYRONE

Reproving and pitying.
Now, now, lad. You know better than to pay attention—

MARY

As if she hadn't heard—sadly again.
Who would have thought Jamie would grow up to disgrace us. You remember, James, for years after he went to boarding school, we received such glowing reports. Everyone liked him. All his teachers told us what a fine brain he had, and how easily he learned his lessons. Even after he began to drink and they had to expel him, they wrote us how sorry they were, because he was so likable and such a brilliant student. They predicted a wonderful future for him if he would only learn to take life seriously.
She pauses—then adds with a strange, sad detachment.
It's such a pity. Poor Jamie! It's hard to understand—
Abruptly a change comes over her. Her face hardens and she stares at her husband with accusing hostility.
No, it isn't at all. You brought him up to be a boozer. Since he first opened his eyes, he's seen you drinking. Always a bottle on the bureau in the cheap hotel rooms! And if he had a nightmare when he was little, or a stomach-ache, your remedy was to give him a teaspoonful of whiskey to quiet him.

TYRONE
Stung.
So I'm to blame because that lazy hulk has made a drunken loafer of
himself? Is that what I came home to listen to? I might have known!
When you have the poison in you, you want to blame everyone but
yourself!

EDMUND
Papa! You told me not to pay attention.
Then, resentfully.
Anyway it's true. You did the same thing with me. I can remember
that teaspoonful of booze every time I woke up with a nightmare.

MARY
In a detached reminiscent tone.
Yes, you were continually having nightmares as a child. You were
born afraid. Because I was so afraid to bring you into the world.
She pauses—then goes on with the same detachment.
Please don't think I blame your father, Edmund. He didn't know any
better. He never went to school after he was ten. His people were the
most ignorant kind of poverty-stricken Irish. I'm sure they honestly
believed whiskey is the healthiest medicine for a child who is sick
or frightened.
*Tyrone is about to burst out in angry defense of his family
but Edmund intervenes.*

EDMUND
Sharply.
Papa!
Changing the subject.
Are we going to have this drink, or aren't we?

TYRONE
Controlling himself—dully.
You're right. I'm a fool to take notice.
He picks up his glass listlessly.
Drink hearty, lad.
*Edmund drinks but Tyrone remains staring at the glass in
in his hand. Edmund at once realizes how much the whiskey*

has been watered. He frowns, glancing from the bottle to his mother—starts to say something but stops.

MARY
In a changed tone—repentently.

I'm sorry if I sounded bitter, James. I'm not. It's all so far away. But I did feel a little hurt when you wished you hadn't come home. I was so relieved and happy when you came, and grateful to you. It's very dreary and sad to be here alone in the fog with night falling.

TYRONE
Moved.

I'm glad I came, Mary, when you act like your real self.

MARY

I was so lonesome I kept Cathleen with me just to have someone to talk to.

Her manner and quality drift back to the shy convent girl again.

Do you know what I was telling her, dear? About the night my father took me to your dressing room and I first fell in love with you. Do you remember?

TYRONE
Deeply moved—his voice husky.

Can you think I'd ever forget, Mary?

Edmund looks away from them, sad and embarrassed.

MARY
Tenderly.

No. I know you still love me, James, in spite of everything.

TYRONE
His face works and he blinks back tears—with quiet intensity.

Yes! As God is my judge! Always and forever, Mary!

MARY

And I love you, dear, in spite of everything.

There is a pause in which Edmund moves embarrassedly. The strange detachment comes over her manner again as if she were speaking impersonally of people seen from a distance.

But I must confess, James, although I couldn't help loving you, I would never have married you if I'd known you drank so much. I remember the first night your barroom friends had to help you up to the door of our hotel room, and knocked and then ran away before I came to the door. We were still on our honeymoon, do you remember?

> TYRONE
> *With guilty vehemence.*

I don't remember! It wasn't on our honeymoon! And I never in my life had to be helped to bed, or missed a performance!

> MARY
> *As though he hadn't spoken.*

I had waited in that ugly hotel room hour after hour. I kept making excuses for you. I told myself it must be some business connected with the theater. I knew so little about the theater. Then I became terrified. I imagined all sorts of horrible accidents. I got on my knees and prayed that nothing had happened to you—and then they brought you up and left you outside the door.

> *She gives a little, sad sigh.*

I didn't know how often that was to happen in the years to come, how many times I was to wait in ugly hotel rooms. I became quite used to it.

> EDMUND
> *Bursts out with a look of accusing hate at his father.*

Christ! No wonder— !

> *He controls himself—gruffly.*

When is dinner, Mama? It must be time.

> TYRONE
> *Overwhelmed by shame which he tries to hide, fumbles with his watch.*

Yes. It must be. Let's see.

> *He stares at his watch without seeing it. Pleadingly.*

Mary! Can't you forget—?

MARY
With detached pity.

No, dear. But I forgive. I always forgive you. So don't look so guilty. I'm sorry I remembered out loud. I don't want to be sad, or to make you sad. I want to remember only the happy part of the past.

Her manner drifts back to the shy, gay convent girl.

Do you remember our wedding, dear? I'm sure you've completely forgotten what my wedding gown looked like. Men don't notice such things. They don't think they're important. But it was important to me, I can tell you! How I fussed and worried! I was so excited and happy! My father told me to buy anything I wanted and never mind what it cost. The best is none too good, he said. I'm afraid he spoiled me dreadfully. My mother didn't. She was very pious and strict. I think she was a little jealous. She didn't approve of my marrying—especially an actor. I think she hoped I would become a nun. She used to scold my father. She'd grumble, "You never tell me, never mind what it costs, when I buy anything! You've spoiled that girl so, I pity her husband if she ever marries. She'll expect him to give her the moon. She'll never make a good wife."

She laughs affectionately.

Poor mother!

She smiles at Tyrone with a strange, incongruous coquetry.

But she was mistaken, wasn't she, James? I haven't been such a bad wife, have I?

TYRONE
Huskily, trying to force a smile.

I'm not complaining, Mary.

MARY
A shadow of vague guilt crosses her face.

At least, I've loved you dearly, and done the best I could—under the circumstances.

The shadow vanishes and her shy, girlish expression returns.

That wedding gown was nearly the death of me and the dressmaker, too!

She laughs.

114

I was so particular. It was never quite good enough. At last she said she refused to touch it any more or she might spoil it, and I made her leave so I could be alone to examine myself in the mirror. I was so pleased and vain. I thought to myself, "Even if your nose and mouth and ears are a trifle too large, your eyes and hair and figure, and your hands, make up for it. You're just as pretty as any actress he's ever met, and you don't have to use paint."

She pauses, wrinkling her brow in an effort of memory.
Where is my wedding gown now, I wonder? I kept it wrapped up in tissue paper in my trunk. I used to hope I would have a daughter and when it came time for her to marry— She couldn't have bought a lovelier gown, and I knew, James, you'd never tell her, never mind the cost. You'd want her to pick up something at a bargain. It was made of soft, shimmering satin, trimmed with wonderful old duchesse lace, in tiny ruffles around the neck and sleeves, and worked in with the folds that were draped round in a bustle effect at the back. The basque was boned and very tight. I remember I held my breath when it was fitted, so my waist would be as small as possible. My father even let me have duchesse lace on my white satin slippers, and lace with the orange blossoms in my veil. Oh, how I loved that gown! It was so beautiful! Where is it now, I wonder? I used to take it out from time to time when I was lonely, but it always made me cry, so finally a long while ago—

She wrinkles her forehead again.
I wonder where I hid it? Probably in one of the old trunks in the attic. Some day I'll have to look.

> *She stops, staring before her. Tyrone sighs, shaking his head hopelessly, and attempts to catch his son's eye, looking for sympathy, but Edmund is staring at the floor.*

TYRONE
Forces a casual tone.
Isn't it dinner time, dear?
With a feeble attempt at teasing.
You're forever scolding me for being late, but now I'm on time for once, it's dinner that's late.
She doesn't appear to hear him. He adds, still pleasantly.
Well, if I can't eat yet, I can drink. I'd forgotten I had this.

115

He drinks his drink. Edmund watches him. Tyrone scowls and looks at his wife with sharp suspicion—roughly.

Who's been tampering with my whiskey? The damned stuff is half water! Jamie's been away and he wouldn't overdo his trick like this, anyway. Any fool could tell— Mary, answer me!

With angry disgust.

I hope to God you haven't taken to drink on top of—

 EDMUND

Shut up, Papa!

To his mother, without looking at her.

You treated Cathleen and Bridget, isn't that it, Mama?

MARY

With indifferent casualness.

Yes, of course. They work hard for poor wages. And I'm the house-keeper, I have to keep them from leaving. Besides, I wanted to treat Cathleen because I had her drive uptown with me, and sent her to get my prescription filled.

EDMUND

For God's sake, Mama! You can't trust her! Do you want everyone on earth to know?

MARY

Her face hardening stubbornly.

Know what? That I suffer from rheumatism in my hands and have to take medicine to kill the pain? Why should I be ashamed of that?

Turns on Edmund with a hard, accusing antagonism—almost a revengeful enmity.

I never knew what rheumatism was before you were born! Ask your father!

Edmund looks away, shrinking into himself.

TYRONE

Don't mind her, lad. It doesn't mean anything. When she gets to the stage where she gives the old crazy excuse about her hands she's gone far away from us.

MARY

Turns on him—with a strangely triumphant, taunting smile.

I'm glad you realize that, James! Now perhaps you'll give up trying to remind me, you and Edmund!

> *Abruptly, in a detached, matter-of-fact tone.*

Why don't you light the light, James? It's getting dark. I know you hate to, but Edmund has proved to you that one bulb burning doesn't cost much. There's no sense letting your fear of the poorhouse make you too stingy.

TYRONE
> *Reacts mechanically.*

I never claimed one bulb cost much! It's having them on, one here and one there, that makes the Electric Light Company rich.

> *He gets up and turns on the reading lamp—roughly.*

But I'm a fool to talk reason to you.

> *To Edmund.*

I'll get a fresh bottle of whiskey, lad, and we'll have a real drink.

> *He goes through the back parlor.*

MARY
> *With detached amusement.*

He'll sneak around to the outside cellar door so the servants won't see him. He's really ashamed of keeping his whiskey padlocked in the cellar. Your father is a strange man, Edmund. It took many years before I understood him. You must try to understand and forgive him, too, and not feel contempt because he's close-fisted. His father deserted his mother and their six children a year or so after they came to America. He told them he had a premonition he would die soon, and he was homesick for Ireland, and wanted to go back there to die. So he went and he did die. He must have been a peculiar man, too. Your father had to go to work in a machine shop when he was only ten years old.

EDMUND
> *Protests dully.*

Oh, for Pete's sake, Mama. I've heard Papa tell that machine shop story ten thousand times.

MARY
Yes, dear, you've had to listen, but I don't think you've ever tried to understand.

EDMUND

Ignoring this—miserably.

Listen, Mama! You're not so far gone yet you've forgotten everything. You haven't asked me what I found out this afternoon. Don't
you care a damn?

MARY

Shakenly.

Don't say that! You hurt me, dear!

EDMUND

What I've got is serious, Mama. Doc Hardy knows for sure now.

MARY

Stiffens into scornful, defensive stubbornness.

That lying old quack! I warned you he'd invent— !

EDMUND

Miserably dogged.

He called in a specialist to examine me, so he'd be absolutely sure.

MARY

Ignoring this.

Don't tell me about Hardy! If you heard what the doctor at the sanatorium, who really knows something, said about how he'd treated
me! He said he ought to be locked up! He said it was a wonder I
hadn't gone mad! I told him I had once, that time I ran down in my
nightdress to throw myself off the dock. You remember that, don't
you? And yet you want me to pay attention to what Doctor Hardy
says. Oh, no!

EDMUND

Bitterly.

I remember, all right. It was right after that Papa and Jamie decided
they couldn't hide it from me any more. Jamie told me. I called him
a liar! I tried to punch him in the nose. But I knew he wasn't lying.

His voice trembles, his eyes begin to fill with tears.

God, it made everything in life seem rotten!

MARY

Pitiably.

Oh, don't. My baby! You hurt me so dreadfully!

118

EDMUND

Dully.

I'm sorry, Mama. It was you who brought it up.

Then with a bitter, stubborn persistence.

Listen, Mama. I'm going to tell you whether you want to hear or not. I've got to go to a sanatorium.

MARY

Dazedly, as if this was something that had never occurred to her.

Go away?

Violently.

No! I won't have it! How dare Doctor Hardy advise such a thing without consulting me! How dare your father allow him! What right has he? You are my baby! Let him attend to Jamie!

More and more excited and bitter.

I know why he wants you sent to a sanatorium. To take you from me! He's always tried to do that. He's been jealous of every one of my babies! He kept finding ways to make me leave them. That's what caused Eugene's death. He's been jealous of you most of all. He knew I loved you most because—

EDMUND

Miserably.

Oh, stop talking crazy, can't you, Mama! Stop trying to blame him. And why are you so against my going away now? I've been away a lot, and I've never noticed it broke your heart!

MARY

Bitterly.

I'm afraid you're not very sensitive, after all.

Sadly.

You might have guessed, dear, that after I knew you knew—about me—I had to be glad whenever you were where you couldn't see me.

EDMUND

Brokenly.

Mama! Don't!

He reaches out blindly and takes her hand—but he drops it immediately, overcome by bitterness again.

All this talk about loving me—and you won't even listen when I try
to tell you how sick—

> MARY
> *With an abrupt transformation into a detached bullying
> motherliness.*

Now, now. That's enough! I don't care to hear because I know it's
nothing but Hardy's ignorant lies.

> *He shrinks back into himself. She keeps on in a forced, teas-
> ing tone but with an increasing undercurrent of resentment.*

You're so like your father, dear. You love to make a scene out of
nothing so you can be dramatic and tragic.

> *With a belittling laugh.*

If I gave you the slightest encouragement, you'd tell me next you
were going to die—

> EDMUND

People do die of it. Your own father—

> MARY
> *Sharply.*

Why do you mention him? There's no comparison at all with you.
He had consumption.

> *Angrily.*

I hate you when you become gloomy and morbid! I forbid you to
remind me of my father's death, do you hear me?

> EDMUND
> *His face hard—grimly.*

Yes, I hear you, Mama. I wish to God I didn't!

> *He gets up from his chair and stands staring condemningly
> at her—bitterly.*

It's pretty hard to take at times, having a dope fiend for a mother!

> *She winces—all life seeming to drain from her face, leaving
> it with the appearance of a plaster cast. Instantly Edmund
> wishes he could take back what he has said. He stammers
> miserably.*

Forgive me, Mama. I was angry. You hurt me.

> *There is a pause in which the foghorn and the ships' bells
> are heard.*

120

MARY

*Goes slowly to the windows at right like an automaton—
looking out, a blank, far-off quality in her voice.*

Just listen to that awful foghorn. And the bells. Why is it fog makes
everything sound so sad and lost, I wonder?

EDMUND

Brokenly.

I—I can't stay here. I don't want any dinner.

*He hurries away through the front parlor. She keeps staring
out the window until she hears the front door close behind
him. Then she comes back and sits in her chair, the same
blank look on her face.*

MARY

Vaguely.

I must go upstairs. I haven't taken enough.

She pauses—then longingly.

I hope, sometime, without meaning it, I will take an overdose. I
never could do it deliberately. The Blessed Virgin would never forgive me, then.

*She hears Tyrone returning and turns as he comes in,
through the back parlor, with a bottle of whiskey he has
just uncorked. He is fuming.*

TYRONE

Wrathfully.

The padlock is all scratched. That drunken loafer has tried to pick
the lock with a piece of wire, the way he's done before.

*With satisfaction, as if this was a perpetual battle of wits
with his elder son.*

But I've fooled him this time. It's a special padlock a professional
burglar couldn't pick.

*He puts the bottle on the tray and suddenly is aware of Ed-
mund's absence.*

Where's Edmund?

MARY

With a vague far-away air.

He went out. Perhaps he's going uptown again to find Jamie. He still has some money left, I suppose, and it's burning a hole in his pocket. He said he didn't want any dinner. He doesn't seem to have any appetite these days.

> *Then stubbornly.*

But it's just a summer cold.

> *Tyrone stares at her and shakes his head helplessly and pours himself a big drink and drinks it. Suddenly it is too much for her and she breaks out and sobs.*

Oh, James, I'm so frightened!

> *She gets up and throws her arms around him and hides her face on his shoulder—sobbingly.*

I know he's going to die!

TYRONE

Don't say that! It's not true! They promised me in six months he'd be cured.

MARY

You don't believe that! I can tell when you're acting! And it will be my fault. I should never have borne him. It would have been better for his sake. I could never hurt him then. He wouldn't have had to know his mother was a dope fiend—and hate her!

TYRONE

> *His voice quivering.*

Hush, Mary, for the love of God! He loves you. He knows it was a curse put on you without your knowing or willing it. He's proud you're his mother!

> *Abruptly as he hears the pantry door opening.*

Hush, now! Here comes Cathleen. You don't want her to see you crying.

> *She turns quickly away from him to the windows at right, hastily wiping her eyes. A moment later Cathleen appears in the back-parlor doorway. She is uncertain in her walk and grinning woozily.*

CATHLEEN

> *Starts guiltily when she sees Tyrone—with dignity.*

Dinner is served, Sir.

> *Raising her voice unnecessarily.*

Dinner is served, Ma'am.

> *She forgets her dignity and addresses Tyrone with good-natured familiarity.*

So you're here, are you? Well, well. Won't Bridget be in a rage! I told her the Madame said you wouldn't be home.

> *Then reading accusation in his eye.*

Don't be looking at me that way. If I've a drop taken, I didn't steal it. I was invited.

> *She turns with huffy dignity and disappears through the back parlor.*

TYRONE

> *Sighs—then summoning his actor's heartiness.*

Come along, dear. Let's have our dinner. I'm hungry as a hunter.

MARY

> *Comes to him—her face is composed in plaster again and her tone is remote.*

I'm afraid you'll have to excuse me, James. I couldn't possibly eat anything. My hands pain me dreadfully. I think the best thing for me is to go to bed and rest. Good night, dear.

> *She kisses him mechanically and turns toward the front parlor.*

TYRONE

> *Harshly.*

Up to take more of that God-damned poison, is that it? You'll be like a mad ghost before the night's over!

MARY

> *Starts to walk away—blankly.*

I don't know what you're talking about, James. You say such mean, bitter things when you've drunk too much. You're as bad as Jamie or Edmund.

> *She moves off through the front parlor. He stands a second as if not knowing what to do. He is a sad, bewildered, broken old man. He walks wearily off through the back parlor toward the dining room.*

CURTAIN

Act Four

SCENE   *The same. It is around midnight. The lamp in the front hall
has been turned out, so that now no light shines through the
front parlor. In the living room only the reading lamp on the
table is lighted. Outside the windows the wall of fog appears
denser than ever. As the curtain rises, the foghorn is heard,
followed by the ships' bells from the harbor.*

*Tyrone is seated at the table. He wears his pince-nez, and
is playing solitaire. He has taken off his coat and has on an
old brown dressing gown. The whiskey bottle on the tray
is three-quarters empty. There is a fresh full bottle on the
table, which he has brought from the cellar so there will be
an ample reserve at hand. He is drunk and shows it by the
owlish, deliberate manner in which he peers at each card to
make certain of its identity, and then plays it as if he wasn't
certain of his aim. His eyes have a misted, oily look and his
mouth is slack. But despite all the whiskey in him, he has
not escaped, and he looks as he appeared at the close of the
preceding act, a sad, defeated old man, possessed by hopeless resignation.*

*As the curtain rises, he finishes a game and sweeps the cards
together. He shuffles them clumsily, dropping a couple on
the floor. He retrieves them with difficulty, and starts to
shuffle again, when he hears someone entering the front door.
He peers over his pince-nez through the front parlor.*

TYRONE
His voice thick.
Who's that? Is it you, Edmund?
*Edmund's voice answers curtly, "Yes." Then he evidently
collides with something in the dark hall and can be heard
cursing. A moment later the hall lamp is turned on. Tyrone
frowns and calls.*

Turn that light out before you come in.

> *But Edmund doesn't. He comes in through the front parlor. He is drunk now, too, but like his father he carries it well, and gives little physical sign of it except in his eyes and a chip-on-the-shoulder aggressiveness in his manner. Tyrone speaks, at first with a warm, relieved welcome.*

I'm glad you've come, lad. I've been damned lonely.

> *Then resentfully.*

You're a fine one to run away and leave me to sit alone here all night when you know—

> *With sharp irritation.*

I told you to turn out that light! We're not giving a ball. There's no reason to have the house ablaze with electricity at this time of night, burning up money!

EDMUND

Angrily.

Ablaze with electricity! One bulb! Hell, everyone keeps a light on in the front hall until they go to bed.

> *He rubs his knee.*

I damned near busted my knee on the hat stand.

TYRONE

The light from here shows in the hall. You could see your way well enough if you were sober.

EDMUND

If *I* was sober? I like that!

TYRONE

I don't give a damn what other people do. If they want to be wasteful fools, for the sake of show, let them be!

EDMUND

One bulb! Christ, don't be such a cheap skate! I've proved by figures if you left the light bulb on all night it wouldn't be as much as one drink!

TYRONE

To hell with your figures! The proof is in the bills I have to pay!

EDMUND

Sits down opposite his father—contemptuously.

Yes, facts don't mean a thing, do they? What you want to believe,
that's the only truth!

Derisively.

Shakespeare was an Irish Catholic, for example.

TYRONE

Stubbornly.

So he was. The proof is in his plays.

EDMUND

Well he wasn't, and there's no proof of it in his plays, except to you!

Jeeringly.

The Duke of Wellington, there was another good Irish Catholic!

TYRONE

I never said he was a good one. He was a renegade but a Catholic just
the same.

EDMUND

Well, he wasn't. You just want to believe no one but an Irish Catholic
general could beat Napoleon.

TYRONE

I'm not going to argue with you. I asked you to turn out that light
in the hall.

EDMUND

I heard you, and as far as I'm concerned it stays on.

TYRONE

None of your damned insolence! Are you going to obey me or not?

EDMUND

Not! If you want to be a crazy miser put it out yourself!

TYRONE

With threatening anger.

Listen to me! I've put up with a lot from you because from the mad
things you've done at times I've thought you weren't quite right in
your head. I've excused you and never lifted my hand to you. But
there's a straw that breaks the camel's back. You'll obey me and

127

put out that light or, big as you are, I'll give you a thrashing that'll teach you— !

> *Suddenly he remembers Edmund's illness and instantly becomes guilty and shamefaced.*

Forgive me, lad. I forgot— You shouldn't goad me into losing my temper.

EDMUND
> *Ashamed himself now.*

Forget it, Papa. I apologize, too. I had no right being nasty about nothing. I am a bit soused, I guess. I'll put out the damned light.

> *He starts to get up.*

TYRONE

No, stay where you are. Let it burn.

> *He stands up abruptly—and a bit drunkenly—and begins turning on the three bulbs in the chandelier, with a childish, bitterly dramatic self-pity.*

We'll have them all on! Let them burn! To hell with them! The poorhouse is the end of the road, and it might as well be sooner as later!

> *He finishes turning on the lights.*

EDMUND
> *Has watched this proceeding with an awakened sense of humor—now he grins, teasing affectionately.*

That's a grand curtain.

> *He laughs.*

You're a wonder, Papa.

TYRONE
> *Sits down sheepishly—grumbles pathetically.*

That's right, laugh at the old fool! The poor old ham! But the final curtain will be in the poorhouse just the same, and that's not comedy!

> *Then as Edmund is still grinning, he changes the subject.*

Well, well, let's not argue. You've got brains in that head of yours, though you do your best to deny them. You'll live to learn the value of a dollar. You're not like your damned tramp of a brother. I've given up hope he'll ever get sense. Where is he, by the way?

128

EDMUND

How would I know?

TYRONE

I thought you'd gone back uptown to meet him.

EDMUND

No. I walked out to the beach. I haven't seen him since this afternoon.

TYRONE

Well, if you split the money I gave you with him, like a fool—

EDMUND

Sure I did. He's always staked me when he had anything.

TYRONE

Then it doesn't take a soothsayer to tell he's probably in the whore-house.

EDMUND

What of it if he is? Why not?

TYRONE

Contemptuously.

Why not, indeed. It's the fit place for him. If he's ever had a loftier dream than whores and whiskey, he's never shown it.

EDMUND

Oh, for Pete's sake, Papa! If you're going to start that stuff, I'll beat it.

He starts to get up.

TYRONE

Placatingly.

All right, all right, I'll stop. God knows, I don't like the subject either. Will you join me in a drink?

EDMUND

Ah! Now you're talking!

TYRONE

Passes the bottle to him—mechanically.

I'm wrong to treat you. You've had enough already.

EDMUND

Pouring a big drink—a bit drunkenly.

Enough is *not* as good as a feast.
He hands back the bottle.

TYRONE

It's too much in your condition.

EDMUND

Forget my condition!
He raises his glass.
Here's how.

TYRONE

Drink hearty.
They drink.
If you walked all the way to the beach you must be damp and chilled.

EDMUND

Oh, I dropped in at the Inn on the way out and back.

TYRONE

It's not a night I'd pick for a long walk.

EDMUND

I loved the fog. It was what I needed.
He sounds more tipsy and looks it.

TYRONE

You should have more sense than to risk—

EDMUND

To hell with sense! We're all crazy. What do we want with sense?
He quotes from Dowson sardonically.
"They are not long, the weeping and the laughter,
Love and desire and hate:
I think they have no portion in us after
We pass the gate.

They are not long, the days of wine and roses:
Out of a misty dream
Our path emerges for a while, then closes
Within a dream."

Staring before him.

The fog was where I wanted to be. Halfway down the path you can't see this house. You'd never know it was here. Or any of the other places down the avenue. I couldn't see but a few feet ahead. I didn't meet a soul. Everything looked and sounded unreal. Nothing was what it is. That's what I wanted—to be alone with myself in another world where truth is untrue and life can hide from itself. Out beyond the harbor, where the road runs along the beach, I even lost the feeling of being on land. The fog and the sea seemed part of each other. It was like walking on the bottom of the sea. As if I had drowned long ago. As if I was a ghost belonging to the fog, and the fog was the ghost of the sea. It felt damned peaceful to be nothing more than a ghost within a ghost.

He sees his father staring at him with mingled worry and irritated disapproval. He grins mockingly.

Don't look at me as if I'd gone nutty. I'm talking sense. Who wants to see life as it is, if they can help it? It's the three Gorgons in one. You look in their faces and turn to stone. Or it's Pan. You see him and you die—that is, inside you—and have to go on living as a ghost.

TYRONE

Impressed and at the same time revolted.

You have a poet in you but it's a damned morbid one!

Forcing a smile.

Devil take your pessimism. I feel low-spirited enough.

He sighs.

Why can't you remember your Shakespeare and forget the third-raters. You'll find what you're trying to say in him—as you'll find everything else worth saying.

He quotes, using his fine voice.

"We are such stuff as dreams are made on, and our little life is rounded with a sleep."

EDMUND

Ironically.

Fine! That's beautiful. But I wasn't trying to say that. We are such stuff as manure is made on, so let's drink up and forget it. That's more my idea.

TYRONE
Disgustedly.

Ach! Keep such sentiments to yourself. I shouldn't have given you
that drink.

EDMUND

It did pack a wallop, all right. On you, too.
He grins with affectionate teasing.
Even if you've never missed a performance!
Aggressively.
Well, what's wrong with being drunk? It's what we're after, isn't it?
Let's not kid each other, Papa. Not tonight. We know what we're
trying to forget.
Hurriedly.
But let's not talk about it. It's no use now.

TYRONE
Dully.

No. All we can do is try to be resigned—again.

EDMUND

Or be so drunk you can forget.
*He recites, and recites well, with bitter, ironical passion,
the Symons' translation of Baudelaire's prose poem.*
"Be always drunken. Nothing else matters: that is the only question.
If you would not feel the horrible burden of Time weighing on your
shoulders and crushing you to the earth, be drunken continually.

Drunken with what? With wine, with poetry, or with virtue, as
you will. But be drunken.

And if sometimes, on the stairs of a palace, or on the green side of
a ditch, or in the dreary solitude of your own room, you should
awaken and the drunkenness be half or wholly slipped away from
you, ask of the wind, or of the wave, or of the star, or of the bird,
or of the clock, of whatever flies, or sighs, or rocks, or sings, or speaks,
ask what hour it is; and the wind, wave, star, bird, clock, will answer
you: 'It is the hour to be drunken! Be drunken, if you would not
be martyred slaves of Time; be drunken continually! With wine,
with poetry, or with virtue, as you will.' "
He grins at his father provocatively.

132

TYRONE

Thickly humorous.

I wouldn't worry about the virtue part of it, if I were you.

Then disgustedly.

Pah! It's morbid nonsense! What little truth is in it you'll find nobly said in Shakespeare.

Then appreciatively.

But you recited it well, lad. Who wrote it?

EDMUND

Baudelaire.

TYRONE

Never heard of him.

EDMUND

Grins provocatively.

He also wrote a poem about Jamie and the Great White Way.

TYRONE

That loafer! I hope to God he misses the last car and has to stay uptown!

EDMUND

Goes on, ignoring this.

Although he was French and never saw Broadway and died before Jamie was born. He knew him and Little Old New York just the same.

He recites the Symons' translation of Baudelaire's "Epilogue."

"With heart at rest I climbed the citadel's
Steep height, and saw the city as from a tower,
Hospital, brothel, prison, and such hells,

Where evil comes up softly like a flower.
Thou knowest, O Satan, patron of my pain,
Not for vain tears I went up at that hour;

But like an old sad faithful lecher, fain
To drink delight of that enormous trull
Whose hellish beauty makes me young again.

Whether thou sleep, with heavy vapours full,
Sodden with day, or, new apparelled, stand
In gold-laced veils of evening beautiful,

I love thee, infamous city! Harlots and
Hunted have pleasures of their own to give,
The vulgar herd can never understand."

TYRONE

With irritable disgust.

Morbid filth! Where the hell do you get your taste in literature?
Filth and despair and pessimism! Another atheist, I suppose. When
you deny God, you deny hope. That's the trouble with you. If you'd
get down on your knees—

EDMUND

As if he hadn't heard—sardonically.

It's a good likeness of Jamie, don't you think, hunted by himself and
whiskey, hiding in a Broadway hotel room with some fat tart—he
likes them fat—reciting Dowson's Cynara to her.

He recites derisively, but with deep feeling.

"All night upon mine heart I felt her warm heart beat,
Night-long within mine arms in love and sleep she lay;
Surely the kisses of her bought red mouth were sweet;
But I was desolate and sick of an old passion,
When I awoke and found the dawn was gray:
I have been faithful to thee, Cynara! in my fashion."

Jeeringly.

And the poor fat burlesque queen doesn't get a word of it, but sus-
pects she's being insulted! And Jamie never loved any Cynara, and
was never faithful to a woman in his life, even in his fashion! But he
lies there, kidding himself he is superior and enjoys pleasures "the
vulgar herd can never understand"!

He laughs.

It's nuts—completely nuts!

TYRONE

Vaguely—his voice thick.

It's madness, yes. If you'd get on your knees and pray. When you
deny God, you deny sanity.

134

EDMUND
Ignoring this.
But who am I to feel superior? I've done the same damned thing.
And it's no more crazy than Dowson himself, inspired by an absinthe
hangover, writing it to a dumb barmaid, who thought he was a poor
crazy souse, and gave him the gate to marry a waiter!
He laughs—then soberly, with genuine sympathy.
Poor Dowson. Booze and consumption got him.
He starts and for a second looks miserable and frightened.
Then with defensive irony.
Perhaps it would be tactful of me to change the subject.

TYRONE
Thickly.
Where you get your taste in authors— That damned library of yours!
He indicates the small bookcase at rear.
Voltaire, Rousseau, Schopenhauer, Nietzsche, Ibsen! Atheists, fools,
and madmen! And your poets! This Dowson, and this Baudelaire,
and Swinburne and Oscar Wilde, and Whitman and Poe! Whore-
mongers and degenerates! Pah! When I've three good sets of Shakespeare there (*he nods at the large bookcase*) you could read.

EDMUND
Provocatively.
They say he was a souse, too.

TYRONE
They lie! I don't doubt he liked his glass—it's a good man's failing—
but he knew how to drink so it didn't poison his brain with morbidness and filth. Don't compare him with the pack you've got in
there.
He indicates the small bookcase again.
Your dirty Zola! And your Dante Gabriel Rossetti who was a dope
fiend!
He starts and looks guilty.

EDMUND
With defensive dryness.
Perhaps it would be wise to change the subject.
A pause.

135

You can't accuse me of not knowing Shakespeare. Didn't I win five dollars from you once when you bet me I couldn't learn a leading part of his in a week, as you used to do in stock in the old days. I learned Macbeth and recited it letter perfect, with you giving me the cues.

TYRONE
Approvingly.
That's true. So you did.
He smiles teasingly and sighs.
It was a terrible ordeal, I remember, hearing you murder the lines. I kept wishing I'd paid over the bet without making you prove it.
He chuckles and Edmund grins. Then he starts as he hears a sound from upstairs—with dread.
Did you hear? She's moving around. I was hoping she'd gone to sleep.

EDMUND
Forget it! How about another drink?
He reaches out and gets the bottle, pours a drink and hands it back. Then with a strained casualness, as his father pours a drink.
When did Mama go to bed?

TYRONE
Right after you left. She wouldn't eat any dinner. What made you run away?

EDMUND
Nothing.
Abruptly raising his glass.
Well, here's how.

TYRONE
Mechanically.
Drink hearty, lad.
They drink. Tyrone again listens to sounds upstairs—with dread.
She's moving around a lot. I hope to God she doesn't come down.

EDMUND

Dully.

Yes. She'll be nothing but a ghost haunting the past by this time.

He pauses—then miserably.

Back before I was born—

TYRONE

Doesn't she do the same with me? Back before she ever knew me.
You'd think the only happy days she's ever known were in her
father's home, or at the Convent, praying and playing the piano.

Jealous resentment in his bitterness.

As I've told you before, you must take her memories with a grain
of salt. Her wonderful home was ordinary enough. Her father
wasn't the great, generous, noble Irish gentleman she makes out. He
was a nice enough man, good company and a good talker. I liked
him and he liked me. He was prosperous enough, too, in his whole-
sale grocery business, an able man. But he had his weakness. She con-
demns my drinking but she forgets his. It's true he never touched a
drop till he was forty, but after that he made up for lost time. He
became a steady champagne drinker, the worst kind. That was his
grand pose, to drink only champagne. Well, it finished him quick—
that and the consumption—

He stops with a guilty glance at his son.

EDMUND

Sardonically.

We don't seem able to avoid unpleasant topics, do we?

TYRONE

Sighs sadly.

No.

Then with a pathetic attempt at heartiness.

What do you say to a game or two of Casino, lad?

EDMUND

All right.

TYRONE

Shuffling the cards clumsily.

We can't lock up and go to bed till Jamie comes on the last trolley—

137

which I hope he won't—and I don't want to go upstairs, anyway, till she's asleep.

> EDMUND

Neither do I.

> TYRONE
> *Keeps shuffling the cards fumblingly, forgetting to deal them.*

As I was saying, you must take her tales of the past with a grain of salt. The piano playing and her dream of becoming a concert pianist. That was put in her head by the nuns flattering her. She was their pet. They loved her for being so devout. They're innocent women, anyway, when it comes to the world. They don't know that not one in a million who shows promise ever rises to concert playing. Not that your mother didn't play well for a schoolgirl, but that's no reason to take it for granted she could have—

> EDMUND
> *Sharply.*

Why don't you deal, if we're going to play.

> TYRONE

Eh? I am.

> *Dealing with very uncertain judgment of distance.*

And the idea she might have become a nun. That's the worst. Your mother was one of the most beautiful girls you could ever see. She knew it, too. She was a bit of a rogue and a coquette, God bless her, behind all her shyness and blushes. She was never made to renounce the world. She was bursting with health and high spirits and the love of loving.

> EDMUND

For God's sake, Papa! Why don't you pick up your hand?

> TYRONE
> *Picks it up—dully.*

Yes, let's see what I have here.

> *They both stare at their cards unseeingly. Then they both start. Tyrone whispers.*

Listen!

EDMUND

She's coming downstairs.

TYRONE

Hurriedly.

We'll play our game. Pretend not to notice and she'll soon go up
again.

EDMUND

Staring through the front parlor—with relief.

I don't see her. She must have started down and then turned back.

TYRONE

Thank God.

EDMUND

Yes. It's pretty horrible to see her the way she must be now.

With bitter misery.

The hardest thing to take is the blank wall she builds around her.
Or it's more like a bank of fog in which she hides and loses herself.
Deliberately, that's the hell of it! You know something in her does
it deliberately—to get beyond our reach, to be rid of us, to forget
we're alive! It's as if, in spite of loving us, she hated us!

TYRONE

Remonstrates gently.

Now, now, lad. It's not her. It's the damned poison.

EDMUND

Bitterly.

She takes it to get that effect. At least, I know she did this time!

Abruptly.

My play, isn't it? Here.

He plays a card.

TYRONE

Plays mechanically—gently reproachful.

She's been terriby frightened about your illness, for all her pretending. Don't be too hard on her, lad. Remember she's not responsible.
Once that cursed poison gets a hold on anyone—

EDMUND

His face grows hard and he stares at his father with bitter accusation.

It never should have gotten a hold on her! I know damned well she's not to blame! And I know who is! You are! Your damned stinginess! If you'd spent money for a decent doctor when she was so sick after I was born, she'd never have known morphine existed! Instead you put her in the hands of a hotel quack who wouldn't admit his ignorance and took the easiest way out, not giving a damn what happened to her afterwards! All because his fee was cheap! Another one of your bargains!

TYRONE

Stung—angrily.

Be quiet! How dare you talk of something you know nothing about!

Trying to control his temper.

You must try to see my side of it, too, lad. How was I to know he was that kind of a doctor? He had a good reputation—

EDMUND

Among the souses in the hotel bar, I suppose!

TYRONE

That's a lie! I asked the hotel proprietor to recommend the best—

EDMUND

Yes! At the same time crying poorhouse and making it plain you wanted a cheap one! I know your system! By God, I ought to after this afternoon!

TYRONE

Guiltily defensive.

What about this afternoon?

EDMUND

Never mind now. We're talking about Mama! I'm saying no matter how you excuse yourself you know damned well your stinginess is to blame—

TYRONE

And I say you're a liar! Shut your mouth right now, or—

EDMUND

Ignoring this.

After you found out she'd been made a morphine addict, why didn't
you send her to a cure then, at the start, while she still had a chance?
No, that would have meant spending some money! I'll bet you told
her all she had to do was use a little will power! That's what you still
believe in your heart, in spite of what doctors, who really know
something about it, have told you!

TYRONE

You lie again! I know better than that now! But how was I to know
then? What did I know of morphine? It was years before I discovered
what was wrong. I thought she'd never got over her sickness, that's
all. Why didn't I send her to a cure, you say?

Bitterly.

Haven't I? I've spent thousands upon thousands in cures! A waste.
What good have they done her? She always started again.

EDMUND

Because you've never given her anything that would help her want
to stay off it! No home except this summer dump in a place she hates
and you've refused even to spend money to make this look decent,
while you keep buying more property, and playing sucker for every
con man with a gold mine, or a silver mine, or any kind of get-rich-
quick swindle! You've dragged her around on the road, season after
season, on one-night stands, with no one she could talk to, waiting
night after night in dirty hotel rooms for you to come back with a
bun on after the bars closed! Christ, is it any wonder she didn't
want to be cured. Jesus, when I think of it I hate your guts!

TYRONE

Strickenly.

Edmund!

Then in a rage.

How dare you talk to your father like that, you insolent young cub!
After all I've done for you.

EDMUND

We'll come to that, what you're doing for me!

TYRONE
Looking guilty again—ignores this.

Will you stop repeating your mother's crazy accusations, which she never makes unless it's the poison talking? I never dragged her on the road against her will. Naturally, I wanted her with me. I loved her. And she came because she loved me and wanted to be with me. That's the truth, no matter what she says when she's not herself. And she needn't have been lonely. There was always the members of my company to talk to, if she'd wanted. She had her children, too, and I insisted, in spite of the expense, on having a nurse to travel with her.

EDMUND
Bitterly.

Yes, your one generosity, and that because you were jealous of her paying too much attention to us, and wanted us out of your way! It was another mistake, too! If she'd had to take care of me all by herself, and had that to occupy her mind, maybe she'd have been able—

TYRONE
Goaded into vindictiveness.

Or for that matter, if you insist on judging things by what she says when she's not in her right mind, if you hadn't been born she'd never—

He stops ashamed.

EDMUND
Suddenly spent and miserable.

Sure. I know that's what she feels, Papa.

TYRONE
Protests penitently.

She doesn't! She loves you as dearly as ever mother loved a son! I only said that because you put me in such a God-damned rage, raking up the past, and saying you hate me—

EDMUND
Dully.

I didn't mean it, Papa.

He suddenly smiles—kidding a bit drunkenly.

I'm like Mama, I can't help liking you, in spite of everything.

142

TYRONE

Grins a bit drunkenly in return.

I might say the same of you. You're no great shakes as a son. It's a case of "A poor thing but mine own."

> *They both chuckle with real, if alcoholic, affection. Tyrone changes the subject.*

What's happened to our game? Whose play is it?

EDMUND

Yours, I guess.

> *Tyrone plays a card which Edmund takes and the game gets forgotten again.*

TYRONE

You mustn't let yourself be too downhearted, lad, by the bad news you had today. Both the doctors promised me, if you obey orders at this place you're going, you'll be cured in six months, or a year at most.

EDMUND

His face hard again.

Don't kid me. You don't believe that.

TYRONE

Too vehemently.

Of course I believe it! Why shouldn't I believe it when both Hardy and the specialist— ?

EDMUND

You think I'm going to die.

TYRONE

That's a lie! You're crazy!

EDMUND

More bitterly.

So why waste money? That's why you're sending me to a state farm—

TYRONE

In guilty confusion.

What state farm? It's the Hilltown Sanatorium, that's all I know, and both doctors said it was the best place for you.

EDMUND

Scathingly.

For the money! That is, for nothing, or practically nothing. Don't lie, Papa! You know damned well Hilltown Sanatorium is a state institution! Jamie suspected you'd cry poorhouse to Hardy and he wormed the truth out of him.

TYRONE

Furiously.

That drunken loafer! I'll kick him out in the gutter! He's poisoned your mind against me ever since you were old enough to listen!

EDMUND

You can't deny it's the truth about the state farm, can you?

TYRONE

It's not true the way you look at it! What if it is run by the state? That's nothing against it. The state has the money to make a better place than any private sanatorium. And why shouldn't I take advantage of it? It's my right—and yours. We're residents. I'm a property owner. I help to support it. I'm taxed to death—

EDMUND

With bitter irony.

Yes, on property valued at a quarter of a million.

TYRONE

Lies! It's all mortgaged!

EDMUND

Hardy and the specialist know what you're worth. I wonder what they thought of you when they heard you moaning poorhouse and showing you wanted to wish me on charity!

TYRONE

It's a lie! All I told them was I couldn't afford any millionaire's sanatorium because I was land poor. That's the truth!

EDMUND

And then you went to the Club to meet McGuire and let him stick you with another bum piece of property!

As Tyrone starts to deny.

Don't lie about it! We met McGuire in the hotel bar after he left you. Jamie kidded him about hooking you, and he winked and laughed!

TYRONE
Lying feebly.
He's a liar if he said—

EDMUND
Don't lie about it!
With gathering intensity.
God, Papa, ever since I went to sea and was on my own, and found out what hard work for little pay was, and what it felt like to be broke, and starve, and camp on park benches because I had no place to sleep, I've tried to be fair to you because I knew what you'd been up against as a kid. I've tried to make allowances. Christ, you have to make allowances in this damned family or go nuts! I have tried to make allowances for myself when I remember all the rotten stuff I've pulled! I've tried to feel like Mama that you can't help being what you are where money is concerned. But God Almighty, this last stunt of yours is too much! It makes me want to puke! Not because of the rotten way you're treating me. To hell with that! I've treated you rottenly, in my way, more than once. But to think when it's a question of your son having consumption, you can show yourself up before the whole town as such a stinking old tightwad! Don't you know Hardy will talk and the whole damned town will know! Jesus, Papa, haven't you any pride or shame?

Bursting with rage.
And don't think I'll let you get away with it! I won't go to any damned state farm just to save you a few lousy dollars to buy more bum property with! You stinking old miser— !
He chokes huskily, his voice trembling with rage, and then is shaken by a fit of coughing.

TYRONE
Has shrunk back in his chair under this attack, his guilty contrition greater than his anger. He stammers.
Be quiet! Don't say that to me! You're drunk! I won't mind you. Stop coughing, lad. You've got yourself worked up over nothing.

Who said you had to go to this Hilltown place? You can go anywhere you like. I don't give a damn what it costs. All I care about is to have you get well. Don't call me a stinking miser, just because I don't want doctors to think I'm a millionaire they can swindle.

> *Edmund has stopped coughing. He looks sick and weak. His father stares at him frightenedly.*

You look weak, lad. You'd better take a bracer.

> EDMUND
> *Grabs the bottle and pours his glass brimfull—weakly.*

Thanks.

> *He gulps down the whiskey.*

> TYRONE
> *Pours himself a big drink, which empties the bottle, and drinks it. His head bows and he stares dully at the cards on the table—vaguely.*

Whose play is it?

> *He goes on dully, without resentment.*

A stinking old miser. Well, maybe you're right. Maybe I can't help being, although all my life since I had anything I've thrown money over the bar to buy drinks for everyone in the house, or loaned money to sponges I knew would never pay it back—

> *With a loose-mouthed sneer of self-contempt.*

But, of course, that was in barrooms, when I was full of whiskey. I can't feel that way about it when I'm sober in my home. It was at home I first learned the value of a dollar and the fear of the poorhouse. I've never been able to believe in my luck since. I've always feared it would change and everything I had would be taken away. But still, the more property you own, the safer you think you are. That may not be logical, but it's the way I have to feel. Banks fail, and your money's gone, but you think you can keep land beneath your feet.

> *Abruptly his tone becomes scornfully superior.*

You said you realized what I'd been up against as a boy. The hell you do! How could you? You've had everything—nurses, schools, college, though you didn't stay there. You've had food, clothing. Oh, I know you had a fling of hard work with your back and hands, a bit of being homeless and penniless in a foreign land, and I respect

146

you for it. But it was a game of romance and adventure to you. It was play.

EDMUND

Dully sarcastic.

Yes, particularly the time I tried to commit suicide at Jimmie the Priest's, and almost did.

TYRONE

You weren't in your right mind. No son of mine would ever— You were drunk.

EDMUND

I was stone cold sober. That was the trouble. I'd stopped to think too long.

TYRONE

With drunken peevishness.

Don't start your damned atheist morbidness again! I don't care to listen. I was trying to make plain to you—

Scornfully.

What do you know of the value of a dollar? When I was ten my father deserted my mother and went back to Ireland to die. Which he did soon enough, and deserved to, and I hope he's roasting in hell. He mistook rat poison for flour, or sugar, or something. There was gossip it wasn't by mistake but that's a lie. No one in my family ever—

EDMUND

My bet is, it wasn't by mistake.

TYRONE

More morbidness! Your brother put that in your head. The worst he can suspect is the only truth for him. But never mind. My mother was left, a stranger in a strange land, with four small children, me and a sister a little older and two younger than me. My two older brothers had moved to other parts. They couldn't help. They were hard put to it to keep themselves alive. There was no damned romance in our poverty. Twice we were evicted from the miserable hovel we called home, with my mother's few sticks of furniture thrown out in the street, and my mother and sisters crying. I cried, too, though I tried hard not to, because I was the man of the family. At ten years old! There was no more school for me. I worked twelve hours a day in a machine shop, learning to make files. A dirty barn of a place where rain dripped through the roof, where you roasted in summer, and there was no stove in winter, and your hands got numb with cold, where the only light came through two small filthy windows, so on grey days I'd have to sit bent over with my eyes almost touching the files in order to see! You talk of work! And what do you think I got for it? Fifty cents a week! It's the truth! Fifty cents a week! And my poor mother washed and scrubbed for the Yanks by the day, and my older sister sewed, and my two younger stayed at home to keep the house. We never had clothes enough to wear, nor enough food to eat. Well I remember one Thanksgiving, or maybe it was Christmas, when some Yank in whose house mother had been scrubbing gave her a dollar extra for a present, and on the way home she spent it all on food. I can remember her hugging and kissing us and saying with tears of joy running down her tired face: "Glory be to God, for once in our lives we'll have enough for each of us!"

He wipes tears from his eyes.
A fine, brave, sweet woman. There never was a braver or finer.

EDMUND
Moved.
Yes, she must have been.

TYRONE
Her one fear was she'd get old and sick and have to die in the poorhouse.

He pauses—then adds with grim humor.
It was in those days I learned to be a miser. A dollar was worth so much then. And once you've learned a lesson, it's hard to unlearn it. You have to look for bargains. If I took this state farm sanatorium for a good bargain, you'll have to forgive me. The doctors did tell me it's a good place. You must believe that, Edmund. And I swear I never meant you to go there if you didn't want to.

Vehemently.
You can choose any place you like! Never mind what it costs! Any place I can afford. Any place you like—within reason.

148

At this qualification, a grin twitches Edmund's lips. His resentment has gone. His father goes on with an elaborately offhand, casual air.

There was another sanatorium the specialist recommended. He said it had a record as good as any place in the country. It's endowed by a group of millionaire factory owners, for the benefit of their workers principally, but you're eligible to go there because you're a resident. There's such a pile of money behind it, they don't have to charge much. It's only seven dollars a week but you get ten times that value.

Hastily.

I don't want to persuade you to anything, understand. I'm simply repeating what I was told.

EDMUND

Concealing his smile—casually.

Oh, I know that. It sounds like a good bargain to me. I'd like to go there. So that settles that.

Abruptly he is miserably desperate again—dully.

It doesn't matter a damn now, anyway. Let's forget it!

Changing the subject.

How about our game? Whose play is it?

TYRONE

Mechanically.

I don't know. Mine, I guess. No, it's yours.

Edmund plays a card. His father takes it. Then about to play from his hand, he again forgets the game.

Yes, maybe life overdid the lesson for me, and made a dollar worth too much, and the time came when that mistake ruined my career as a fine actor.

Sadly.

I've never admitted this to anyone before, lad, but tonight I'm so heartsick I feel at the end of everything, and what's the use of fake pride and pretense. That God-damned play I bought for a song and made such a great success in—a great money success—it ruined me with its promise of an easy fortune. I didn't want to do anything else, and by the time I woke up to the fact I'd become a slave to the damned thing and did try other plays, it was too late. They had identified me with that one part, and didn't want me in anything else. They were right, too. I'd lost the great talent I once had through years of easy repetition, never learning a new part, never really working hard. Thirty-five to forty thousand dollars net profit a season like snapping your fingers! It was too great a temptation. Yet before I bought the damned thing I was considered one of the three or four young actors with the greatest artistic promise in America. I'd worked like hell. I'd left a good job as a machinist to take supers' parts because I loved the theater. I was wild with ambition. I read all the plays ever written. I studied Shakespeare as you'd study the Bible. I educated myself. I got rid of an Irish brogue you could cut with a knife. I loved Shakespeare. I would have acted in any of his plays for nothing, for the joy of being alive in his great poetry. And I acted well in him. I felt inspired by him. I could have been a great Shakespearean actor, if I'd kept on. I know that! In 1874 when Edwin Booth came to the theater in Chicago where I was leading man, I played Cassius to his Brutus one night, Brutus to his Cassius the next, Othello to his Iago, and so on. The first night I played Othello, he said to our manager, "That young man is playing Othello better than I ever did!"

Proudly.

That from Booth, the greatest actor of his day or any other! And it was true! And I was only twenty-seven years old! As I look back on it now, that night was the high spot in my career. I had life where I wanted it! And for a time after that I kept on upward with ambition high. Married your mother. Ask her what I was like in those days. Her love was an added incentive to ambition. But a few years later my good bad luck made me find the big money-maker. It wasn't that in my eyes at first. It was a great romantic part I knew I could play better than anyone. But it was a great box office success from the start—and then life had me where it wanted me—at from thirty-five to forty thousand net profit a season! A fortune in those days—or even in these.

Bitterly.

What the hell was it I wanted to buy, I wonder, that was worth—Well, no matter. It's a late day for regrets.

He glances vaguely at his cards.

My play, isn't it?

EDMUND

Moved, stares at his father with understanding—slowly.

I'm glad you've told me this, Papa. I know you a lot better now.

TYRONE

With a loose, twisted smile.

Maybe I shouldn't have told you. Maybe you'll only feel more contempt for me. And it's a poor way to convince you of the value of a dollar.

Then as if this phrase automatically aroused an habitual association in his mind, he glances up at the chandelier disapprovingly.

The glare from those extra lights hurts my eyes. You don't mind if I turn them out, do you? We don't need them, and there's no use making the Electric Company rich.

EDMUND

Controlling a wild impulse to laugh—agreeably.

No, sure not. Turn them out.

TYRONE

Gets heavily and a bit waveringly to his feet and gropes uncertainly for the lights—his mind going back to its line of thought.

No, I don't know what the hell it was I wanted to buy.

He clicks out one bulb.

On my solemn oath, Edmund, I'd gladly face not having an acre of land to call my own, nor a penny in the bank—

He clicks out another bulb.

I'd be willing to have no home but the poorhouse in my old age if I could look back now on having been the fine artist I might have been.

He turns out the third bulb, so only the reading lamp is on, and sits down again heavily. Edmund suddenly cannot hold back a burst of strained, ironical laughter. Tyrone is hurt.

What the devil are you laughing at?

EDMUND

Not at you, Papa. At life. It's so damned crazy.

TYRONE

Growls.

More of your morbidness! There's nothing wrong with life. It's we who—

> *He quotes.*

"The fault, dear Brutus, is not in our stars, but in ourselves that we are underlings."

> *He pauses—then sadly.*

The praise Edwin Booth gave my Othello. I made the manager put down his exact words in writing. I kept it in my wallet for years. I used to read it every once in a while until finally it made me feel so bad I didn't want to face it any more. Where is it now, I wonder? Somewhere in this house. I remember I put it away carefully—

> EDMUND
>
> *With a wry ironical sadness.*

It might be in an old trunk in the attic, along with Mama's wedding dress.

> *Then as his father stares at him, he adds quickly.*

For Pete's sake, if we're going to play cards, let's play.

> *He takes the card his father had played and leads. For a moment, they play the game, like mechanical chess players. Then Tyrone stops, listening to a sound upstairs.*

> TYRONE

She's still moving around. God knows when she'll go to sleep.

> EDMUND
>
> *Pleads tensely.*

For Christ's sake, Papa, forget it!

> *He reaches out and pours a drink. Tyrone starts to protest, then gives it up. Edmund drinks. He puts down the glass. His expression changes. When he speaks it is as if he were deliberately giving way to drunkenness and seeking to hide behind a maudlin manner.*

Yes, she moves above and beyond us, a ghost haunting the past, and here we sit pretending to forget, but straining our ears listening for the slightest sound, hearing the fog drip from the eaves like the uneven tick of a rundown, crazy clock—or like the dreary tears of a trollop spattering in a puddle of stale beer on a honky-tonk table top!

> *He laughs with maudlin appreciation.*

Not so bad, that last, eh? Original, not Baudelaire. Give me credit!

Then with alcoholic talkativeness.

You've just told me some high spots in your memories. Want to hear mine? They're all connected with the sea. Here's one. When I was on the Squarehead square rigger, bound for Buenos Aires. Full moon in the Trades. The old hooker driving fourteen knots. I lay on the bowsprit, facing astern, with the water foaming into spume under me, the masts with every sail white in the moonlight, towering high above me. I became drunk with the beauty and singing rhythm of it, and for a moment I lost myself—actually lost my life. I was set free! I dissolved in the sea, became white sails and flying spray, became beauty and rhythm, became moonlight and the ship and the high dim-starred sky! I belonged, without past or future, within peace and unity and a wild joy, within something greater than my own life, or the life of Man, to Life itself! To God, if you want to put it that way. Then another time, on the American Line, when I was lookout on the crow's nest in the dawn watch. A calm sea, that time. Only a lazy ground swell and a slow drowsy roll of the ship. The passengers asleep and none of the crew in sight. No sound of man. Black smoke pouring from the funnels behind and beneath me. Dreaming, not keeping lookout, feeling alone, and above, and apart, watching the dawn creep like a painted dream over the sky and sea which slept together. Then the moment of ecstatic freedom came. The peace, the end of the quest, the last harbor, the joy of belonging to a fulfillment beyond men's lousy, pitiful, greedy fears and hopes and dreams! And several other times in my life, when I was swimming far out, or lying alone on a beach, I have had the same experience. Became the sun, the hot sand, green seaweed anchored to a rock, swaying in the tide. Like a saint's vision of beatitude. Like the veil of things as they seem drawn back by an unseen hand. For a second you see—and seeing the secret, are the secret. For a second there is meaning! Then the hand lets the veil fall and you are alone, lost in the fog again, and you stumble on toward nowhere, for no good reason!

He grins wryly.

It was a great mistake, my being born a man, I would have been much more successful as a sea gull or a fish. As it is, I will always be a stranger who never feels at home, who does not really want and is not really wanted, who can never belong, who must always be a little in love with death!

TYRONE

Stares at him—impressed.

Yes, there's the makings of a poet in you all right.

Then protesting uneasily.

But that's morbid craziness about not being wanted and loving death.

EDMUND

Sardonically.

The *makings* of a poet. No, I'm afraid I'm like the guy who is always panhandling for a smoke. He hasn't even got the makings. He's got only the habit. I couldn't touch what I tried to tell you just now. I just stammered. That's the best I'll ever do. I mean, if I live. Well, it will be faithful realism, at least. Stammering is the native eloquence of us fog people.

A pause. Then they both jump startledly as there is a noise from outside the house, as if someone had stumbled and fallen on the front steps. Edmund grins.

Well, that sounds like the absent brother. He must have a peach of a bun on.

TYRONE

Scowling.

That loafer! He caught the last car, bad luck to it.

He gets to his feet.

Get him to bed, Edmund. I'll go out on the porch. He has a tongue like an adder when he's drunk. I'd only lose my temper.

He goes out the door to the side porch as the front door in the hall bangs shut behind Jamie. Edmund watches with amusement Jamie's wavering progress through the front parlor. Jamie comes in. He is very drunk and woozy on his legs. His eyes are glassy, his face bloated, his speech blurred, his mouth slack like his father's, a leer on his lips.

JAMIE

Swaying and blinking in the doorway—in a loud voice.

What ho! What ho!

EDMUND
Sharply.
Nix on the loud noise!

JAMIE
Blinks at him.
Oh, hello, Kid.
With great seriousness.
I'm as drunk as a fiddler's bitch.

EDMUND
Dryly.
Thanks for telling me your great secret.

JAMIE
Grins foolishly.
Yes. Unneshesary information Number One, eh?
He bends and slaps at the knees of his trousers.
Had serious accident. The front steps tried to trample on me. Took
advantage of fog to waylay me. Ought to be a lighthouse out there.
Dark in here, too.
Scowling.
What the hell is this, the morgue? Lesh have some light on subject.
He sways forward to the table, reciting Kipling.
"Ford, ford, ford o' Kabul river,
 Ford o' Kabul river in the dark!
 Keep the crossing-stakes beside you, an' they will surely guide you
 'Cross the ford o' Kabul river in the dark."
*He fumbles at the chandelier and manages to turn on the
 three bulbs.*
Thash more like it. To hell with old Gaspard. Where is the old
tightwad?

EDMUND
Out on the porch.

JAMIE
Can't expect us to live in the Black Hole of Calcutta.
His eyes fix on the full bottle of whiskey.
Say! Have I got the d.t.'s?
He reaches out fumblingly and grabs it.

By God, it's real. What's matter with the Old Man tonight? Must be ossified to forget he left this out. Grab opportunity by the forelock. Key to my success.

He slops a big drink into a glass.

EDMUND

You're stinking now. That will knock you stiff.

JAMIE

Wisdom from the mouth of babes. Can the wise stuff, Kid. You're still wet behind the ears.

He lowers himself into a chair, holding the drink carefully aloft.

EDMUND

All right. Pass out if you want to.

JAMIE

Can't, that's trouble. Had enough to sink a ship, but can't sink. Well, here's hoping.

He drinks.

EDMUND

Shove over the bottle. I'll have one, too.

JAMIE

With sudden, big-brotherly solicitude, grabbing the bottle. No, you don't. Not while I'm around. Remember doctor's orders. Maybe no one else gives a damn if you die, but I do. My kid brother. I love your guts, Kid. Everything else is gone. You're all I've got left.

Pulling bottle closer to him.

So no booze for you, if I can help it.

Beneath his drunken sentimentality there is a genuine sincerity.

EDMUND

Irritably.

Oh, lay off it.

JAMIE

Is hurt and his face hardens.

156

You don't believe I care, eh? Just drunken bull.

He shoves the bottle over.

All right. Go ahead and kill yourself.

EDMUND

Seeing he is hurt—affectionately.

Sure I know you care, Jamie, and I'm going on the wagon. But tonight doesn't count. Too many damned things have happened today.

He pours a drink.

Here's how.

He drinks.

JAMIE

Sobers up momentarily and with a pitying look.

I know, Kid. It's been a lousy day for you.

Then with sneering cynicism.

I'll bet old Gaspard hasn't tried to keep you off booze. Probably give you a case to take with you to the state farm for pauper patients. The sooner you kick the bucket, the less expense.

With contemptuous hatred.

What a bastard to have for a father! Christ, if you put him in a book, no one would believe it!

EDMUND

Defensively.

Oh, Papa's all right, if you try to understand him—and keep your sense of humor.

JAMIE

Cynically.

He's been putting on the old sob act for you, eh? He can always kid you. But not me. Never again.

Then slowly.

Although, in a way, I do feel sorry for him about one thing. But he has even that coming to him. He's to blame.

Hurriedly.

But to hell with that.

He grabs the bottle and pours another drink, appearing very drunk again.

That lash drink's getting me. This one ought to put the lights out.
Did you tell Gaspard I got it out of Doc Hardy this sanatorium is a
charity dump?

> EDMUND
> *Reluctantly.*

Yes. I told him I wouldn't go there. It's all settled now. He said I can
go anywhere I want.

> *He adds, smiling without resentment.*

Within reason, of course.

> JAMIE
> *Drunkenly imitating his father.*

Of course, lad. Anything within reason.

> *Sneering.*

That means another cheap dump. Old Gaspard, the miser in "The
Bells," that's a part he can play without make-up.

> EDMUND
> *Irritably.*

Oh, shut up, will you. I've heard that Gaspard stuff a million times.

> JAMIE
> *Shrugs his shoulders—thickly.*

Aw right, if you're shatisfied—let him get away with it. It's your
funeral—I mean, I hope it won't be.

> EDMUND
> *Changing the subject.*

What did you do uptown tonight? Go to Mamie Burns?

> JAMIE
> *Very drunk, his head nodding.*

Sure thing. Where else could I find suitable feminine companionship?
And love. Don't forget love. What is a man without a good woman's
love? A God-damned hollow shell.

> EDMUND
> *Chuckles tipsily, letting himself go now and be drunk.*

You're a nut.

JAMIE

Quotes with gusto from Oscar Wilde's "The Harlot's House."

"Then, turning to my love, I said,
 'The dead are dancing with the dead,
 The dust is whirling with the dust.'

But she—she heard the violin,
And left my side and entered in:
Love passed into the house of lust.

Then suddenly the tune went false,
The dancers wearied of the waltz . . ."

He breaks off, thickly.

Not strictly accurate. If my love was with me, I didn't notice it. She must have been a ghost.

He pauses.

Guess which one of Mamie's charmers I picked to bless me with her woman's love. It'll hand you a laugh, Kid. I picked Fat Violet.

EDMUND

Laughs drunkenly.

No, honest? Some pick! God, she weighs a ton. What the hell for, a joke?

JAMIE

No joke. Very serious. By the time I hit Mamie's dump I felt very sad about myself and all the other poor bums in the world. Ready for a weep on any old womanly bosom. You know how you get when John Barleycorn turns on the soft music inside you. Then, soon as I got in the door, Mamie began telling me all her troubles. Beefed how rotten business was, and she was going to give Fat Violet the gate. Customers didn't fall for Vi. Only reason she'd kept her was she could play the piano. Lately Vi's gone on drunks and been too boiled to play, and was eating her out of house and home, and although Vi was a goodhearted dumbbell, and she felt sorry for her because she didn't know how the hell she'd make a living, still business was business, and she couldn't afford to run a home for fat tarts. Well, that made me feel sorry for Fat Violet, so I squandered two bucks of your dough to escort her upstairs. With no dishonorable intentions whatever. I like them fat, but not that fat. All I wanted was a little heart-to-heart talk concerning the infinite sorrow of life.

> EDMUND
> *Chuckles drunkenly.*

Poor Vi! I'll bet you recited Kipling and Swinburne and Dowson and gave her "I have been faithful to thee, Cynara, in my fashion."

> JAMIE
> *Grins loosely.*

Sure—with the Old Master, John Barleycorn, playing soft music. She stood it for a while. Then she got good and sore. Got the idea I took her upstairs for a joke. Gave me a grand bawling out. Said she was better than a drunken bum who recited poetry. Then she began to cry. So I had to say I loved her because she was fat, and she wanted to believe that, and I stayed with her to prove it, and that cheered her up, and she kissed me when I left, and said she'd fallen hard for me, and we both cried a little more in the hallway, and everything was fine, except Mamie Burns thought I'd gone bughouse.

> EDMUND
> *Quotes derisively.*

> "Harlots and
> Hunted have pleasures of their own to give,
> The vulgar herd can never understand."

> JAMIE
> *Nods his head drunkenly.*

Egzactly! Hell of a good time, at that. You should have stuck around with me, Kid. Mamie Burns inquired after you. Sorry to hear you were sick. She meant it, too.

> *He pauses—then with maudlin humor, in a ham-actor tone.*

This night has opened my eyes to a great career in store for me, my boy! I shall give the art of acting back to the performing seals, which are its most perfect expression. By applying my natural God-given talents in their proper sphere, I shall attain the pinnacle of success! I'll be the lover of the fat woman in Barnum and Bailey's circus!

> *Edmund laughs. Jamie's mood changes to arrogant disdain.*

Pah! Imagine me sunk to the fat girl in a hick town hooker shop!

160

Me! Who have made some of the best-lookers on Broadway sit up and beg!

> *He quotes from Kipling's "Sestina of the Tramp-Royal."*
> "Speakin' in general, I 'ave tried 'em all,
> The 'appy roads that take you o'er the world."
> *With sodden melancholy.*

Not so apt. Happy roads is bunk. Weary roads is right. Get you nowhere fast. That's where I've got—nowhere. Where everyone lands in the end, even if most of the suckers won't admit it.

EDMUND
Derisively.

Can it! You'll be crying in a minute.

JAMIE
Starts and stares at his brother for a second with bitter hostility—thickly.

Don't get—too damned fresh.
> *Then abruptly.*

But you're right. To hell with repining! Fat Violet's a good kid. Glad I stayed with her. Christian act. Cured her blues. Hell of a good time. You should have stuck with me, Kid. Taken your mind off your troubles. What's the use coming home to get the blues over what can't be helped. All over—finished now—not a hope!

> *He stops, his head nodding drunkenly, his eyes closing—then suddenly he looks up, his face hard, and quotes jeeringly.*
> "If I were hanged on the highest hill,
> Mother o' mine, O mother o' mine!
> I know whose love would follow me still . . ."

EDMUND
Violently.

Shut up!

JAMIE
In a cruel, sneering tone with hatred in it.

Where's the hophead? Gone to sleep?
> *Edmund jerks as if he'd been struck. There is a tense silence.*

Edmund's face looks stricken and sick. Then in a burst of rage he springs from his chair.

EDMUND

You dirty bastard!

He punches his brother in the face, a blow that glances off the cheekbone. For a second Jamie reacts pugnaciously and half rises from his chair to do battle, but suddenly he seems to sober up to a shocked realization of what he has said and he sinks back limply.

JAMIE
Miserably.

Thanks, Kid. I certainly had that coming. Don't know what made me—booze talking— You know me, Kid.

EDMUND
His anger ebbing.

I know you'd never say that unless— But God, Jamie, no matter how drunk you are, it's no excuse!
He pauses—miserably.
I'm sorry I hit you. You and I never scrap—that bad.
He sinks back on his chair.

JAMIE
Huskily.

It's all right. Glad you did. My dirty tongue. Like to cut it out.
He hides his face in his hands—dully.
I suppose it's because I feel so damned sunk. Because this time Mama had me fooled. I really believed she had it licked. She thinks I always believe the worst, but this time I believed the best.
His voice flutters.
I suppose I can't forgive her—yet. It meant so much. I'd begun to hope, if she'd beaten the game, I could, too.
He begins to sob, and the horrible part of his weeping is that it appears sober, not the maudlin tears of drunkenness.

EDMUND
Blinking back tears himself.

God, don't I know how you feel! Stop it, Jamie!

162

JAMIE

Trying to control his sobs.

I've known about Mama so much longer than you. Never forget the first time I got wise. Caught her in the act with a hypo. Christ, I'd never dreamed before that any women but whores took dope!

He pauses.

And then this stuff of you getting consumption. It's got me licked. We've been more than brothers. You're the only pal I've ever had. I love your guts. I'd do anything for you.

EDMUND

Reaches out and pats his arm.

I know that, Jamie.

JAMIE

His crying over—drops his hands from his face—with a strange bitterness.

Yet I'll bet you've heard Mama and old Gaspard spill so much bunk about my hoping for the worst, you suspect right now I'm thinking to myself that Papa is old and can't last much longer, and if you were to die, Mama and I would get all he's got, and so I'm probably hoping—

EDMUND

Indignantly.

Shut up, you damned fool! What the hell put that in your nut?

He stares at his brother accusingly.

Yes, that's what I'd like to know. What put that in your mind?

JAMIE

Confusedly—appearing drunk again.

Don't be a dumbbell! What I said! Always suspected of hoping for the worst. I've got so I can't help—

Then drunkenly resentful.

What are you trying to do, accuse me? Don't play the wise guy with me! I've learned more of life than you'll ever know! Just because you've read a lot of highbrow junk, don't think you can fool me! You're only an overgrown kid! Mama's baby and Papa's pet! The family White Hope! You've been getting a swelled head lately. About nothing! About a few poems in a hick town newspaper!

163

Hell, I used to write better stuff for the Lit magazine in college! You better wake up! You're setting no rivers on fire! You let hick town boobs flatter you with bunk about your future—

Abruptly his tone changes to disgusted contrition. Edmund has looked away from him, trying to ignore this tirade.

Hell, Kid, forget it. That goes for Sweeny. You know I don't mean it. No one hopes more than I do you'll knock 'em all dead. No one is prouder you've started to make good.

Drunkenly assertive.

Why shouldn't I be proud? Hell, it's purely selfish. You reflect credit on me. I've had more to do with bringing you up than anyone. I wised you up about women, so you'd never be a fall guy, or make any mistakes you didn't want to make! And who steered you on to reading poetry first? Swinburne, for example? I did! And because I once wanted to write, I planted it in your mind that someday you'd write! Hell, you're more than my brother. I made you! You're my Frankenstein!

He has risen to a note of drunken arrogance. Edmund is grinning with amusement now.

EDMUND

All right, I'm your Frankenstein. So let's have a drink.

He laughs.

You crazy nut!

JAMIE

Thickly.

I'll have a drink. Not you. Got to take care of you.

He reaches out with a foolish grin of doting affection and grabs his brother's hand.

Don't be scared of this sanatorium business. Hell, you can beat that standing on your head. Six months and you'll be in the pink. Probably haven't got consumption at all. Doctors lot of fakers. Told me years ago to cut out booze or I'd soon be dead—and here I am. They're all con men. Anything to grab your dough. I'll bet this state farm stuff is political graft game. Doctors get a cut for every patient they send.

EDMUND

Disgustedly amused.

You're the limit! At the Last Judgment, you'll be around telling everyone it's in the bag.

JAMIE

And I'll be right. Slip a piece of change to the Judge and be saved, but if you're broke you can go to hell!

He grins at this blasphemy and Edmund has to laugh. Jamie goes on.

"Therefore put money in thy purse." That's the only dope.

Mockingly.

The secret of my success! Look what it's got me!

He lets Edmund's hand go to pour a big drink, and gulps it down. He stares at his brother with bleary affection—takes his hand again and begins to talk thickly but with a strange, convincing sincerity.

Listen, Kid, you'll be going away. May not get another chance to talk. Or might not be drunk enough to tell you truth. So got to tell you now. Something I ought to have told you long ago—for your own good.

He pauses—struggling with himself. Edmund stares, impressed and uneasy. Jamie blurts out.

Not drunken bull, but "in vino veritas" stuff. You better take it seriously. Want to warn you—against me. Mama and Papa are right. I've been rotten bad influence. And worst of it is, I did it on purpose.

EDMUND

Uneasily.

Shut up! I don't want to hear—

JAMIE

Nix, Kid! You listen! Did it on purpose to make a bum of you. Or part of me did. A big part. That part that's been dead so long. That hates life. My putting you wise so you'd learn from my mistakes. Believed that myself at times, but it's a fake. Made my mistakes look good. Made getting drunk romantic. Made whores fascinating vampires instead of poor, stupid, diseased slobs they really are. Made fun of work as sucker's game. Never wanted you succeed and make me look even worse by comparison. Wanted you to fail. Always jealous of you. Mama's baby, Papa's pet!

He stares at Edmund with increasing enmity.

And it was your being born that started Mama on dope. I know that's not your fault, but all the same, God damn you, I can't help hating your guts— !

EDMUND

Almost frightenedly.

Jamie! Cut it out! You're crazy!

JAMIE

But don't get wrong idea, Kid. I love you more than I hate you. My saying what I'm telling you now proves it. I run the risk you'll hate me—and you're all I've got left. But I didn't mean to tell you that last stuff—go that far back. Don't know what made me. What I wanted to say is, I'd like to see you become the greatest success in the world. But you'd better be on your guard. Because I'll do my damnedest to make you fail. Can't help it. I hate myself. Got to take revenge. On everyone else. Especially you. Oscar Wilde's "Reading Gaol" has the dope twisted. The man was dead and so he had to kill the thing he loved. That's what it ought to be. The dead part of me hopes you won't get well. Maybe he's even glad the game has got Mama again! He wants company, he doesn't want to be the only corpse around the house!

He gives a hard, tortured laugh.

EDMUND

Jesus, Jamie! You really have gone crazy!

JAMIE

Think it over and you'll see I'm right. Think it over when you're away from me in the sanatorium. Make up your mind you've got to tie a can to me—get me out of your life—think of me as dead—tell people, "I had a brother, but he's dead." And when you come back, look out for me. I'll be waiting to welcome you with that "my old pal" stuff, and give you the glad hand, and at the first good chance I get stab you in the back.

EDMUND

Shut up! I'll be God-damned if I'll listen to you any more—

JAMIE

As if he hadn't heard.

166

Only don't forget me. Remember I warned you—for your sake. Give me credit. Greater love hath no man than this, that he saveth his brother from himself/

Very drunkenly, his head bobbing.

That's all. Feel better now. Gone to confession. Know you absolve me, don't you, Kid? You understand. You're a damned fine kid. Ought to be. I made you. So go and get well. Don't die on me. You're all I've got left. God bless you, Kid.

His eyes close. He mumbles.

That last drink—the old K. O.

He falls into a drunken doze, not completely asleep. Edmund buries his face in his hands miserably. Tyrone comes in quietly through the screen door from the porch, his dressing gown wet with fog, the collar turned up around his throat. His face is stern and disgusted but at the same time pitying. Edmund does not notice his entrance.

TYRONE
In a low voice.

Thank God he's asleep.

Edmund looks up with a start.

I thought he'd never stop talking.

He turns down the collar of his dressing gown.

We'd better let him stay where he is and sleep it off.

Edmund remains silent. Tyrone regards him—then goes on.

I heard the last part of his talk. It's what I've warned you. I hope you'll heed the warning, now it comes from his own mouth.

Edmund gives no sign of having heard.

Tyrone adds pityingly.

But don't take it too much to heart, lad. He loves to exaggerate the worst of himself when he's drunk. He's devoted to you. It's the one good thing left in him.

He looks down on Jamie with a bitter sadness.

A sweet spectacle for me! My first-born, who I hoped would bear my name in honor and dignity, who showed such brilliant promise!

EDMUND
Miserably.

Keep quiet, can't you, Papa?

TYRONE
Pours a drink.

A waste! A wreck, a drunken hulk, done with and finished!

He drinks. Jamie has become restless, sensing his father's presence, struggling up from his stupor. Now he gets his eyes open to blink up at Tyrone. The latter moves back a step defensively, his face growing hard.

JAMIE
Suddenly points a finger at him and recites with dramatic emphasis.

Clarence is come, false, fleeting, perjured Clarence,
That stabbed me in the field by Tewksbury.
Seize on him, Furies, take him into torment."
Then resentfully.

What the hell are you staring at?
He recites sardonically from Rossetti.
"Look in my face. My name is Might-Have-Been;
I am also called No More, Too Late, Farewell."

TYRONE
I'm well aware of that, and God knows I don't want to look at it.

EDMUND
Papa! Quit it!

JAMIE
Derisively.

Got a great idea for you, Papa. Put on revival of "The Bells" this season. Great part in it you can play without make-up. Old Gaspard, the miser!

Tyrone turns away, trying to control his temper.

EDMUND
Shut up, Jamie!

JAMIE
Jeeringly.

I claim Edwin Booth never saw the day when he could give as good a performance as a trained seal. Seals are intelligent and honest. They don't put up any bluffs about the Art of Acting. They admit they're just hams earning their daily fish.

TYRONE
Stung, turns on him in a rage.

You loafer!

EDMUND

Papa! Do you want to start a row that will bring Mama down? Jamie, go back to sleep! You've shot off your mouth too much already.

Tyrone turns away.

JAMIE
Thickly.

All right, Kid. Not looking for argument. Too damned sleepy.

He closes his eyes, his head nodding. Tyrone comes to the table and sits down, turning his chair so he won't look at Jamie. At once he becomes sleepy, too.

TYRONE
Heavily.

I wish to God she'd go to bed so that I could, too.

Drowsily.

I'm dog tired. I can't stay up all night like I used to. Getting old— old and finished.

With a bone-cracking yawn.

Can't keep my eyes open. I think I'll catch a few winks. Why don't you do the same, Edmund? It'll pass the time until she—

His voice trails off. His eyes close, his chin sags, and he begins to breathe heavily through his mouth. Edmund sits tensely. He hears something and jerks nervously forward in his chair, staring through the front parlor into the hall. He jumps up with a hunted, distracted expression. It seems for a second he is going to hide in the back parlor. Then he sits down again and waits, his eyes averted, his hands gripping the arms of his chair. Suddenly all five bulbs of the chandelier in the front parlor are turned on from a wall switch, and a moment later someone starts playing the piano in there— the opening of one of Chopin's simpler waltzes, done with a forgetful, stiff-fingered groping, as if an awkward school-girl were practicing it for the first time. Tyrone starts to wide-awakeness and sober dread, and Jamie's head jerks back and his eyes open. For a moment they listen frozenly. The playing stops as abruptly as it began, and Mary appears in the doorway. She wears a sky-blue dressing gown over her nightdress, dainty slippers with pompons on her bare feet. Her face is paler than ever. Her eyes look enormous. They glisten like polished black jewels. The uncanny thing is that her face now appears so youthful. Experience seems ironed out of it. It is a marble mask of girlish inno-cence, the mouth caught in a shy smile. Her white hair is braided in two pigtails which hang over her breast. Over one arm, carried neglectfully, trailing on the floor, as if she had forgotten she held it, is an old-fashioned white satin wedding gown, trimmed with duchesse lace. She hesitates in the door-way, glancing round the room, her forehead puckered puzzledly, like someone who has come to a room to get something but has become absent-minded on the way and forgotten what it was. They stare at her. She seems aware of them merely as she is aware of other objects in the room, the furniture, the windows, familiar things she accepts auto-matically as naturally belonging there but which she is too preoccupied to notice.

JAMIE
*Breaks the cracking silence—bitterly,
self-defensively sardonic.*

The Mad Scene. Enter Ophelia!
His father and brother both turn on him fiercely. Edmund is quicker. He slaps Jamie across the mouth with the back of his hand.

TYRONE
His voice trembling with suppressed fury.

Good boy, Edmund. The dirty blackguard! His own mother!

JAMIE
Mumbles guiltily, without resentment.

170

All right, Kid. Had it coming. But I told you how much I'd hoped—
He puts his hands over his face and begins to sob.

TYRONE

I'll kick you out in the gutter tomorrow, so help me God.
But Jamie's sobbing breaks his anger, and he turns and shakes his shoulder, pleading.
Jamie, for the love of God, stop it!
Then Mary speaks, and they freeze into silence again, staring at her. She has paid no attention whatever to the incident. It is simply a part of the familiar atmosphere of the room, a background which does not touch her preoccupation; and she speaks aloud to herself, not to them.

MARY

I play so badly now. I'm all out of practice. Sister Theresa will give me a dreadful scolding. She'll tell me it isn't fair to my father when he spends so much money for extra lessons. She's quite right, it isn't fair, when he's so good and generous, and so proud of me. I'll practice every day from now on. But something horrible has happened to my hands. The fingers have gotten so stiff—
She lifts her hands to examine them with a frightened puzzlement.
The knuckles are all swollen. They're so ugly. I'll have to go to the Infirmary and show Sister Martha.
With a sweet smile of affectionate trust.
She's old and a little cranky, but I love her just the same, and she has things in her medicine chest that'll cure anything. She'll give me something to rub on my hands, and tell me to pray to the Blessed Virgin, and they'll be well again in no time.
She forgets her hands and comes into the room, the wedding gown trailing on the floor. She glances around vaguely, her forehead puckered again.
Let me see. What did I come here to find? It's terrible, how absent-minded I've become. I'm always dreaming and forgetting.

TYRONE

In a stifled voice.
What's that she's carrying, Edmund?

EDMUND
Dully.
Her wedding gown, I suppose.

TYRONE
Christ!

He gets to his feet and stands directly in her path—in anguish.
Mary! Isn't it bad enough— ?
Controlling himself—gently persuasive.
Here, let me take it, dear. You'll only step on it and tear it and get it dirty dragging it on the floor. Then you'd be sorry afterwards.
She lets him take it, regarding him from somewhere far away within herself, without recognition, without either affection or animosity.

MARY
With the shy politeness of a well-bred young girl toward an elderly gentleman who relieves her of a bundle.
Thank you. You are very kind.
She regards the wedding gown with a puzzled interest.
It's a wedding gown. It's very lovely, isn't it?
A shadow crosses her face and she looks vaguely uneasy.
I remember now. I found it in the attic hidden in a trunk. But I don't know what I wanted it for. I'm going to be a nun—that is, if I can only find—
She looks around the room, her forehead puckered again.
What is it I'm looking for? I know it's something I lost.
She moves back from Tyrone, aware of him now only as some obstacle in her path.

TYRONE
In hopeless appeal.
Mary!

But it cannot penetrate her preoccupation. She doesn't seem to hear him. He gives up helplessly, shrinking into himself, even his defensive drunkenness taken from him, leaving him sick and sober. He sinks back on his chair, holding the wedding gown in his arms with an unconscious clumsy, protective gentleness.

172

JAMIE

Drops his hand from his face, his eyes on the table top. He has suddenly sobered up, too—dully.

It's no good, Papa.

He recites from Swinburne's "A Leave-taking" and does it well, simply but with a bitter sadness.

"Let us rise up and part; she will not know.
Let us go seaward as the great winds go,
Full of blown sand and foam; what help is here?
There is no help, for all these things are so,
And all the world is bitter as a tear.
And how these things are, though ye strove to show,
She would not know."

MARY

Looking around her.

Something I miss terribly. It can't be altogether lost.

She starts to move around in back of Jamie's chair.

JAMIE

Turns to look up into her face—and cannot help appealing pleadingly in his turn.

Mama!

She does not seem to hear. He looks away hopelessly.

Hell! What's the use? It's no good.

He recites from "A Leave-taking" again with increased bitterness.

"Let us go hence, my songs; she will not hear.
Let us go hence together without fear;
Keep silence now, for singing-time is over,
And over all old things and all things dear.
She loves not you nor me as all we love her.
Yea, though we sang as angels in her ear,
She would not hear."

MARY

Looking around her.

Something I need terribly. I remember when I had it I was never lonely nor afraid. I can't have lost it forever, I would die if I thought that. Because then there would be no hope.

173

She moves like a sleepwalker, around the back of Jamie's chair, then forward toward left front, passing behind Edmund.

EDMUND
Turns impulsively and grabs her arm. As he pleads he has the quality of a bewilderedly hurt little boy.
Mama! It isn't a summer cold! I've got consumption!

MARY
For a second he seems to have broken through to her. She trembles and her expression becomes terrified. She calls distractedly, as if giving a command to herself.
No!

And instantly she is far away again. She murmurs gently but impersonally.
You must not try to touch me. You must not try to hold me. It isn't right, when I am hoping to be a nun.
He lets his hand drop from her arm. She moves left to the front end of the sofa beneath the windows and sits down, facing front, her hands folded in her lap, in a demure schoolgirlish pose.

JAMIE
Gives Edmund a strange look of mingled pity and jealous gloating.
You damned fool. It's no good.
He recites again from the Swinburne poem.
"Let us go hence, go hence; she will not see.
 Sing all once more together; surely she,
 She too, remembering days and words that were,
 Will turn a little toward us, sighing; but we,
 We are hence, we are gone, as though we had not been there.
 Nay, and though all men seeing had pity on me,
 She would not see."

TYRONE
Trying to shake off his hopeless stupor.
Oh, we're fools to pay any attention. It's the damned poison. But I've never known her to drown herself in it as deep as this.

Gruffly.

Pass me that bottle, Jamie. And stop reciting that damned morbid poetry. I won't have it in my house!

> *Jamie pushes the bottle toward him. He pours a drink without disarranging the wedding gown he holds carefully over his other arm and on his lap, and shoves the bottle back. Jamie pours his and passes the bottle to Edmund, who, in turn, pours one. Tyrone lifts his glass and his sons follow suit mechanically, but before they can drink Mary speaks and they slowly lower their drinks to the table, forgetting them.*

> MARY
>
> *Staring dreamily before her. Her face looks extraordinarily youthful and innocent. The shyly eager, trusting smile is on her lips as she talks aloud to herself.*

I had a talk with Mother Elizabeth. She is so sweet and good. A saint on earth. I love her dearly. It may be sinful of me but I love her better than my own mother. Because she always understands, even before you say a word. Her kind blue eyes look right into your heart. You can't keep any secrets from her. You couldn't deceive her, even if you were mean enough to want to.

> *She gives a little rebellious toss of her head*
> *—with girlish pique.*

All the same, I don't think she was so understanding this time. I told her I wanted to be a nun. I explained how sure I was of my vocation, that I had prayed to the Blessed Virgin to make me sure, and to find me worthy. I told Mother I had had a true vision when I was praying in the shrine of Our Lady of Lourdes, on the little island in the lake. I said I knew, as surely as I knew I was kneeling there, that the Blessed Virgin had smiled and blessed me with her consent. But Mother Elizabeth told me I must be more sure than that, even, that I must prove it wasn't simply my imagination. She said, if I was so sure, then I wouldn't mind putting myself to a test by going home after I graduated, and living as other girls lived, going out to parties and dances and enjoying myself; and then if after a year or two I still felt sure, I could come back to see her and we would talk it over again.

She tosses her head—indignantly.

I never dreamed Holy Mother would give me such advice! I was really shocked. I said, of course, I would do anything she suggested, but I knew it was simply a waste of time. After I left her, I felt all mixed up, so I went to the shrine and prayed to the Blessed Virgin and found peace again because I knew she heard my prayer and would always love me and see no harm ever came to me so long as I never lost my faith in her.

> *She pauses and a look of growing uneasiness comes over her face. She passes a hand over her forehead as if brushing cobwebs from her brain—vaguely.*

That was in the winter of senior year. Then in the spring something happened to me. Yes, I remember. I fell in love with James Tyrone and was so happy for a time.

> *She stares before her in a sad dream. Tyrone stirs in his chair. Edmund and Jamie remain motionless.*

CURTAIN

Tao House
September 20, 1940

NEARER
NATURE

Tree swallows house hunting

NEARER
NATURE

JIM ARNOSKY

LOTHROP, LEE & SHEPARD BOOKS

NEW YORK

Copyright © 1996 by Jim Arnosky

All rights reserved. No part of this book may be reproduced or utilized in any form or by any means,
electronic or mechanical, including photocopying and recording, or by any information storage and retrieval system,
without permission in writing from the Publisher. Inquiries should be addressed to Lothrop, Lee & Shepard Books,
a division of William Morrow & Company, Inc., 1350 Avenue of the Americas, New York, New York 10019.

Printed in the United States of America

First Edition   1 2 3 4 5 6 7 8 9 10

Library of Congress Cataloging in Publication Data

Arnosky, Jim. Nearer nature / by Jim Arnosky.

p.   cm.

Summary: The noted naturalist and artist presents sketches and
observations from his walks around the Vermont farm where he lives.

ISBN 0-688-12213-2

1. Natural history—Vermont—Juvenile literature. 2. Vermont—Descriptions and travel—Juvenile literature.
3. Arnosky, Jim—Juvenile literature. [1. Natural history—Vermont. 2. Farm life—Vermont.
3. Vermont—Description and travel. 4. Arnosky, Jim.] I. Title. QH105.V7A76 1996 508.743—dc20 95-43954

CIP AC

Trout

Contents

contents

Part Two ❧ Pickerel Cove

FOR DEANNA

Introduction

One sunny spring afternoon, a light blue pickup stopped in front of the house and from it a young woman shouted, "You really have a beautiful place!" Then she drove away. My wife, Deanna, who was busy weeding a flower bed, looked up and replied too late, "Thanks." I stood mute. We were both a bit dumbfounded. We have thought our place beautiful, but we've never had anyone driving by shout it out to us. The pickup had out-of-state plates, and I wondered if the woman was one of those whom the real-estate people tell us are making the move back to the country.

In the late sixties and early seventies, a lot of people moved from the suburbs and cities "back to the land," "back to nature." This was when Deanna and I bought a wood-frame one-room-with-a-loft cabin in the hills of southeastern Pennsylvania, a mile downhill from Hawk Mountain Wildlife Sanctuary. We fully intended to live there the rest of our lives.

While we lived in the cabin, Deanna and I learned to identify birds and recognize wildflowers growing in the woods. There we decided to grow most of our food—an impractical idea in a rocky woodland setting, but one we made happen by felling trees, pulling stumps, clearing boulders, and plowing up a plot of ground.

The cabin was heated by a small wood-and-coal stove. I cut all our firewood from the woods around the cabin. We burned it during the day and banked a coal fire at night. We had no plumbing—we had an outhouse. To cook and wash, we carried water—twenty-six gallons a day, every day, for three years. Using a plastic butter container, Deanna scooped the water from a tiny trickle of a brook and poured her scoops into five-gallon jugs.

By the time Deanna became pregnant with our second daughter, I was selling enough artwork to *Golden, Ranger Rick,* and *Cricket* magazines to afford to have a well dug and a hand pump installed. It wasn't exactly the latest in modern conveniences, but at the time it seemed a luxury.

Life was good, but rugged. We lived in the cabin twice as long as Thoreau had lived at Walden. By our fifth year, we had grown weary of the rigors of cabin life, and our daughters, Michelle and Amber, were outgrowing their small loft bedroom. We decided to make a move, and a series of turns led us to Vermont, where we soon settled in its green hills.

For the past twenty years, we have lived simply but comfortably in a 160-year-old farmhouse. We have a woodshed, a barn, three acres of open land, and forty-eight acres of woods. Our farm is tucked back against the mountains, away from the traffic of the main road and far from the sounds of the village. Here we have a rich and quiet life. We grow vegetables, herbs, and flowers for our own use and enjoyment, and for many years we kept a small flock of sheep. Only recently have we retired from sheep raising.

The farm, which we call Ramtails, is featured in all of my books in some way or other. It is the center of my universe. In this old house, I organize my thoughts and record them in my journals. The essays in this book are based on journal entries made during a seven-month period, as winter turned to spring and spring became summer. They speak more extensively about our farm, our sheep-raising days, the garden, and our home than anything I've written to date. But this is more than a book about our lifestyle. It amplifies the theme I have woven into all my books: that once you take the time to look, and realize that there is a world—animal, vegetable, and mineral—in nearly every footprint, you begin to step more carefully. It is the moments you spend looking, watching, and wondering about what you are seeing that bring you nearer nature.

Jim Arnosky
Ramtails 1996

Ramtails in summer after two days of rain

Part One

Farm & Field

One
A Summit View

I have always chosen to live inside scenery rather than look at it. Being part of the scene, I am most aware of my immediate surroundings. Like a raccoon ambling down a streambed, my focus is on the close-up details—the crystal clear water, the smooth and colorful pebbles, the tiny fish darting, the root-tangled banks, the smells and subtle sounds, the feel of every step. I sense these near things more acutely for being where I am. Once in a while, however, everyone needs to climb to a height and view the world to gain a perspective of the land and of his or her place in it.

One exceptionally warm winter afternoon, I decided to climb the wooded hill behind our farm and find myself a summit view. Dressed lightly (no thermals) for the trek, I headed up the hill on snowshoes. The snow, about three feet deep, was settling from the recent thaw and full of the moisture from its own melting. Wet snow is great molding snow, ideal for sculpture or perfect snowballs. It also has a long memory. Animal tracks print clearly. Claw marks or toe- and heel-pad indentations remain clear for a number of days before they begin to deteriorate.

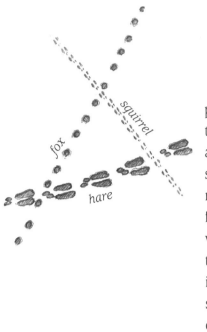

At the base of the hill, where mostly aspens grow, I saw the perfectly printed footprints of snowshoe hare everywhere. Hare tracks went this way and that, running between the aspens and around the small spruces. Some tracks showed short hops. Some showed broad jumps of five feet and more. Tracks of a red fox mingled with those of hare, and at one point, while following the fox's tracks, I came across one of my favorite sights in the snowy woods—a track triangle. This is where three sets of tracks intersect to form a triangle in the snow. A track triangle in which each side is composed of a different animal's footprints, I consider very special. One side of this one was formed by the dainty footprints of the fox. Another was the short hopping tracks of a snowshoe hare, and the third was a staccato line of red squirrel paw prints. The triangle was almost perfect, which made the finding even more splendid.

Since the fox tracks were heading uphill in the direction I was going, I followed them, stepping over a porcupine's gully trail that meandered through the woods. I followed the fox tracks to where the hill began a steep incline. There the tracks turned around and headed back downhill. I left them and continued uphill, following the rutted route of an old logging road up the rugged hillside. A raven called *"kruuk, kruuk,"* and I saw the big black bird through the treetops, flying high overhead. From the opposite direction, I heard the higher-pitched calling of crows, but they were well away and out of sight.

I snowshoed further up the hill and deeper into the woods, walking under some tall hemlocks and stepping over another porcupine gully trail. Beneath the hemlocks, I found another three-animal track triangle. This one wasn't as large and was made by smaller animals: a rather small snowshoe hare, the walking trail of a ruffed grouse, and the tiny stitchlike tracks of a white-footed mouse. The mouse track showed only hind footprints and a tail drag—it had been hopping along on its hind legs like a kangaroo, using its tail for balance.

I emerged from the hemlocks into a mixed stand of hardwood trees. Under a tall yellow birch with a twisted trunk, I sat on a boulder and rested. Just then I heard the sound of wings beating. At first I thought they belonged to a grouse, but the wing beats were spaced too far apart. A grouse flaps its wings in short, rapid beats. These wing beats also had a unique wafting sound that I finally recognized as a raven's. I looked up and searched the sky between the treetops. The large black raven was flying low and against the wind. It circled deliberately right above where I was sitting, then flapped, still audibly, back over the hill. I had been put on notice: I was now on raven property.

Up, up I snowshoed, following the winding trail. Soon I was on the back side of the hill in a wilderness of sorts, where few people go and every sound is muffled, trapped in the dips and hollows of the rocky terrain. In this remote place, four town lines meet at a single point, which is marked simply with two boulders, one the size of a hay bale, the other a much smaller cantaloupe-shaped stone sitting on top. The boulders were placed here many years ago when the trail was a busy road carrying settlers and supplies from farm to village to farm, and over which quarrymen, blasting and digging into the granite hill, brought down heavy granite blocks in horse-drawn wagons. Now the trail's only travelers are wild creatures, to whom the significantly stacked boulders mean nothing.

As I drew nearer the top of the hill, I had to pick my way between young hemlock and birch trees growing in the trail. Between the small trees were the mingled footprints of foxes and hare. On a few birch saplings, neat strips of bark had been eaten away, evidence of white-footed mice that had climbed up the slender tree stems and nibbled their way back down. The barkless

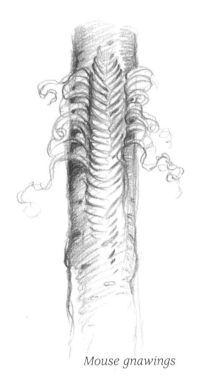

Mouse gnawings

strips were etched with chew marks, showing just how thoroughly each tree's cambium—the thin layer of cells just beneath the bark, from which new wood grows—had been consumed. The mice worked systematically, first peeling away small strips of bark, leaving each strip hanging in a curlicue from the slender tree stems, then gnawing the cambium in the green wood beneath in neat herringbone patterns.

On the summit, the tallest trees swayed wildly in the wind. Suddenly the wind died, and all around the woods were hushed and silent except for the soft swooshing of my snowshoes as I mushed along over the deep snow. I paused and checked my pedometer to see how far uphill I had hiked: one mile exactly.

I was high enough now to see for miles, but my view was somewhat obscured by trees. Squinting and peering between tree trunks and crisscrossing branches, I could make out the far horizon and the dim ice-blue outline of snow-covered mountains. As my eyes adjusted to focusing beyond the foreground, I began to recognize broad features in the landscape—the dark brown swatches of winter hardwoods, the black blotches of evergreens, and the gleaming white of snow-covered fields. Immediately below me, I located the saltbox shape of our red barn and the weathered brown woodshed beside it, but the white house was lost to me against the white snow. I heard Yoko bark once. Then from the barn the sheep began to baa, and I knew Deanna had gone out to take them grain or hay.

It was worth the hike a mile uphill to view from afar things near and dear. The sight of my world without me in it made me see where I belonged—back down below, working on the farm, exploring the surrounding woods, focusing on close-up things, appreciating detail.

Since that winter day, I hike up to the summit at least once every fall and once every winter. I've cleared the trail to the hilltop and cut away the trees whose branches most severely blocked the view. Though the view is now more thrilling, its effect on me remains the same: the spectacle of hills and trees, fields and farms, makes me eager to get back down and take part in the scene.

Blueberry's twins, just born

Two 🌰🍂
Lambing Time

Our flock of sheep consists of a breeding stock of eight ewes and one ram and the lambs produced each spring. We've had to keep the flock small as our pasture grass can support no more than fifteen grazing sheep. To prevent sporadic breeding, we keep the ewes and ram apart most of the year. When autumn comes, we send off to the butcher the few lambs we have earmarked for the freezer. The rest stay.

Our reasons for raising sheep are twofold. First, to keep the pasture grass grazed short, especially around the barn. This eliminates the danger of tall, dry grass being set on fire, either by some careless act or by lightning. Second, because we are not vegetarians, to supply ourselves with lean meat from animals raised as humanely and naturally as possible. But no matter how free we allow our sheep to be, or how carefully we tend them when they are sick or injured, each year there is the matter of the few that must be killed. Every year it becomes harder to decide which sheep go to the butcher, and it is difficult to watch them being herded onto the truck. But a worse sight is a farm overrun by "pets"—too many sheep, all raised as darling lambs, pathetically competing for every square inch of grass; a concentration camp of animals packed into pens and corners, suffering from the cruelty of good intentions. Our choice has been a judicious one. With a little over one and a half acres of pastureland, we can raise sheep as a crop or not raise sheep at all. Since we believe the sheep enrich our lives in many ways, including diet, we choose animal husbandry and accept its inherent difficulties as necessary threads in the fabric of farm life.

Our sheep spend the first half of winter outdoors in a corral. There they have sunlight to warm them and snow to quench their thirst whenever the water bucket is empty. On windy or bitterly cold days, the sheep walk into the snowless, windless barn basement. During gentle snowfalls, they stand outside in the corral. I think they like the cool feeling of snowflakes landing on their faces and accumulating on their wooly backs.

As the snow becomes deeper, the sheep stomp paths from the barn, across the corral to the water bucket, and to the place where they are fed grain and hay. The more snow we have, the deeper the path gets, much like the trails through the deer "yards" in the winter woods.

In February we herd our sheep out of their comfortable snow rut in the corral and lead them up the plank steps to the second floor of the barn. Inside, there is clean hay on the wooden floors, where the expectant mothers can lie down, and heavy latched doors to keep our husky, Yoko, and the local coyotes from the newborn lambs.

Usually it is Soybean, our oldest and most even-tempered ewe, that gives birth first. This year, however, Blueberry, a highly temperamental ewe and our only brown sheep, began the lambing season, giving birth to completely white twins. It happened just after supper, right before nightfall. After the second lamb had emerged, Deanna went out to the barn hourly to check that both lambs were suckling. The cold night could be lethal for a little lamb going without milk. Once Deanna saw that the twins were both nursing, she noticed Soybean pawing at the floor, an early sign of labor. Deanna rushed into the house to tell Amber and me that more lambs were on the way.

As we entered the barn, Soybean's water broke. She was surely going to lamb right away, we thought. But she did not. We waited and watched in the cold barn for nearly half an hour. Then Amber returned to the house to finish her homework. Shortly afterward, I left the barn too, but Deanna stayed with Soybean. She felt she might need help. Soybean is almost thirteen years of age, quite old for a sheep. But though her labor takes a greater toll on her than it did when she was younger, Soybean is the best of mothers. Except for her very first lamb, she has always had twins. Deanna suspected she would have twins again, and this time she was concerned about the aging sheep's ability to deliver them on her own.

By alternating watches, Deanna and I kept vigil all evening and late into the night. Soybean's contractions were prolonged and obviously painful, and a few times we thought a lamb was coming. But no lamb showed. Eventually, both very tired, Deanna and I left the barn and went to bed. Sometime in the early morning hours, Soybean had her twins—two lively little rams—apparently without any major difficulty. We named them Belker and Briar.

The next lambs born were also twin rams. Since their mother's name was Strawberry, we named them Jam and Jelly. Jelly was no problem. He found his mother's udder right away, and within an hour of his birth he was exploring his new world. Jam was a weakling. He was also not very alert. He couldn't find his mother, let alone her teats, no matter how she tried to call and help him.

Every once in a while, we get a lamb like this. The procedure is the same for each. We bottle-feed it milk replacer to keep it

Twins 3 1/2 hours old, one still groggy

23

fortified until we hope it can find its mother's udder and nurse. But all too often the lamb gets only our feedings, and since they are nothing compared to rich ewe's milk, the lamb dies in a few days.

Nevertheless, we go through the moves, hoping this one will be an exception. We once tried bringing a weak lamb into the house, the way some other sheep farmers do, but the warmth seemed to be as harmful to the lamb as the cold barn. It developed pneumonia and died. With Jam we made no attempt to bring him indoors. We just tried to keep him fed. Deanna stayed with him all evening. I brought some warm water mixed with molasses for Strawberry and another bottle of warm milk replacer for her weak lamb. The little guy had trouble drinking. He coughed and choked milk up into his nasal passages. We had to hold him upside down a few times to let the milk drain from his nostrils.

That night the moon was only half full but nearly as bright as if it were full. Around midnight, after Deanna and Amber had gone to bed, I went out with another bottle of warm milk. Stars twinkled in the clear sky. It was getting cold, and it was colder still for a little lamb with hardly any food in his belly. Yoko followed me in the moonlight but left me to go alone into the barn. As always at this time of the year, the room smelled like wool and manure and ewe's milk. The lamb was crying softly in the dark room. I turned on a light and fed him. When I left, he was asleep beside his warm mother, and I felt he just might make it after all.

Deanna fed the lamb at five a.m. and again at eight a.m. He seemed to be getting stronger, and we wondered if he might be nursing between our feedings. His mother stood and called softly, encouraging him to come to her. Things were looking good.

The day had turned warm when we left the lamb to his own resources, hoping he would nurse along with his brother. But when I went out to the barn at noon, Jam was lying motionless on his side. I was certain he had died. I wondered: if we had milked

Strawberry and bottle-fed her milk to the lamb, would he have gotten stronger? But catching a ewe for every feeding, holding her still for milking, then transferring the milk into a bottle, hoping it would stay warm enough, would have been too difficult.

The other lambs were running and hopping about the sunlit room. The ewes were crowding around the feed trough, waiting for their grain. Amid all this commotion, the little ram lay still until I nudged him with my boot. Then, amazingly, he struggled to his hooves, hobbled pathetically over to me, and poked his tiny muzzle against my pant leg. I knew then that we had a bottle baby for sure.

In the kitchen, I stirred up a concoction that our sheep book says will substitute for colostrum—the first and richest flow of mother's milk. Into a bowl I poured a mixture, half of regular milk and half of evaporated milk (the book calls for half water). I added some sugar, a little vegetable oil, and a beaten egg yolk. This nutritious blend, I hoped, would make up for the missed feedings that had so weakened the helpless lamb. While Deanna fed the rest of the sheep, I bottle-fed little Jam. He was so starved, he had to have another bottle. As he suckled, he whimpered all the while like a baby. It made me uncomfortable to see how dependent on us he had become. I knew it would be better all around for him to need his mother most.

At five the next morning, despite all our care, Deanna found Jam dead. He had lived less than three days. We felt a deep sense of failure. I recounted the hours, trying to understand how much so short a life could have experienced. The lamb had felt the pressures of being born and of struggling from the placental sac. He had known the relief of breathing his first breath of air and had felt the muscles in his long legs as he stood and took his first wobbly steps. He had lived long enough to feel the pang of hunger, to search for food and find none, to learn that someone would help, to have his hunger satisfied. Jam had seen the sunlight and felt its warmth. For two nights, he had lain in darkness surrounded by the rhythmic sounds of older sheep chewing their cuds. The little lamb had not known about death. He had known only life.

After we lost Jam, the lambing ceased for almost three weeks. Then, in the midst of a subzero cold spell, Charcoal, a dark black sheep whose slim appearance had made us think she was the only ewe that was not pregnant, gave birth to an enormous lamb—another ram. It was five A.M. and minus twelve degrees in the barn when Deanna noticed Charcoal's hind end had a nose and two small hooves protruding from it. This was a very difficult birth and one of our bloodiest. Charcoal is small as well as slim. Halfway out, the big lamb tore her skin and she began to bleed profusely. There was little we could do but watch. In her pain Charcoal, still standing, pressed against the wall, smearing blood all over the whitewash. The blood froze in minutes on the cold wall, turning a bright, fluorescent red.

The sun was up when Charcoal's lamb finally slid completely out, its body covered with Charcoal's blood. The red lamb was actually white and nearly as big as Soybean's growing twins. For a newborn he was exceptionally strong. He popped up onto all fours to get his first drink of Charcoal's milk. The lamb's warm body kept his coat of blood from freezing, and it remained deep red in color, in contrast to the bright red of the frozen blood smeared on the wall. As he nursed, a pinkish steam issued from his back. By noontime Charcoal had cleaned most of the blood off her lamb and he turned fawn colored. We named him Buffy.

Lights, a ewe almost as old as Soybean, also surprised us, by giving birth to her first set of twins—a ram and ewe. But since she had always had only one lamb, Lights favored the ram and pushed the little ewe away. We tried to trick her into accepting the second lamb by rubbing the little castaway all over with a towel smeared with her brother's scent. But Lights could tell the difference and she kicked the ewe away. The ewe lamb was not a weakling. She tried her best to nurse, only to be butted by her mother and shoved across the floor. It was painfully obvious that we had another bottle baby.

We took turns bottle-feeding the little ewe, which Amber named Cauliflower. It was a good name. The lamb was exceptionally white and her wool was long and curling and knotted like whorls on ripened cauliflower. Deanna and I complemented Amber's lamb name by naming Cauliflower's twin brother Broccoli.

Cauliflower, 8 hrs. old

When it was my turn to feed Cauliflower, she came readily to the black rubber nipple and she sucked strongly. Her little tail wagged as she drank. I was feeling pretty good about her health, until I saw Broccoli nursing vigorously at his mother's teats.

One of Soybean's lambs ambled boldly up to me and began nibbling the top of my rubber boot. When I jerked my knee, the lamb scrambled away. There is nothing more healthy-looking than a lively, active youngster, and nothing more pathetic than one that is sickly and weak. I finished feeding Cauliflower and left the barn, hoping she wouldn't end up weak and dying, as Jam had.

Cauliflower made it through her first, most crucial week. She grew stronger with each feeding and even gained some weight. Then came a week of thaw, and the warm weather furthered Cauliflower's progress. Soon she was hopping around and exploring nooks and crannies in the room.

Cauliflower became my favorite lamb, and I looked forward to my turn to feed her. As soon as I entered the barn room, she came running. Whenever she drank all the milk in the bottle and seemed hungry for more, I went back to the house to heat a few

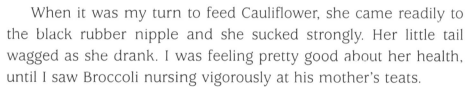

more ounces. Once, while I was waiting for an overheated second helping of milk to cool, I held Cauliflower and stroked her bushy forehead. She fell asleep in my arms. It was then that I realized how lonely she must have been. Her mother paid no attention to her and wouldn't even let her near. Cauliflower was all alone among the other sheep whenever we weren't there, which was most of the time. I checked the milk again. It was just the right temperature, and Cauliflower woke to drink it down. As she drank, I petted her head and brushed her back, all the while speaking softly to her. She needed the affection as much as she needed the milk.

Cauliflower thrived on bottled milk and our affection. In time she was able to hold her own and play with her twin brother and the other, older lambs. We weaned her off the bottle. She began to eat grain right along with the rest of the sheep. But because of her unique bond with us, she always stayed nearer to the barn door than the other lambs did, as if she were waiting for one of us to come. When we did, she was up and hopping, wiggling her tail, baaing, wanting to be talked to and petted and held. She rubbed her tiny white face against our legs and followed our every step around the room.

Lambing time was over. The barn was a sweet and happy place, filled with the smells and sounds of mother sheep and lambs. In the barn it seemed like springtime. Outside it was still winter, with deep snow all around.

Three

More Tracks and Trails

$\mathcal{I}$ am a compulsive tracker. Whenever I find one footprint, I simply have to search the ground for more, then follow to see where they go. All winter long I read stories from the animal tracks in the snow. This winter there was one week of prolonged overcast. A light snow fell constantly, keeping a quarter-inch layer of dry crystals on the old snow crust. In this powdery layer, every creature that had been out left a perfect, clearly printed record of its doings. But the page had to be read quickly. In no time at all a new snowfall covered the information over.

One morning the snow on the snowmobile trail that runs beside our river was imprinted with literally thousands of footprints of minks, foxes, otters, squirrels, white-footed mice, snowshoe hare, and domestic cats, all freshly made within a few hours. The hodgepodge of footprints made it look as if all the animals had traveled at once, passing one another, stopping to make way, tailing each other, piling up at busy intersections. Of course this wasn't so. The snow travelers had all gone their separate ways, and except for mates traveling together, most probably did not meet one another.

Mink tracks

The next morning there were patches of blue in the gray sky. The clouds were beginning to move on, pushed by a stiff breeze. From the top branch of a riverside maple, a red-winged blackbird called. The branch on which it was perched whirled around in the wind, and the bird was given quite a ride. But with its black toes gripped around the branch, the blackbird rode out the gust, keeping perfect balance by raising and lowering its long tail feathers.

The only tracks in the fresh snow were those of minks—a male and female—hunting close together. All five toes of each mink foot were recorded in the snow. A male mink is one-third larger than a female, and so are its tracks. This male was above average in size, and his trail showed how he had lightly scraped his claws in the snow as he loped along. The smaller, female trail was much neater. The tracks showed where both minks had dug down under the snow into leaf litter, hunting for tunneling voles and hibernating salamanders or insects.

At the frozen river, the minks had plunged one after the other through small holes in the ice and come up with their catch. On the ice beside one hole were bits of crayfish shell and, near another hole, spots of bright red blood and a tiny minnow tail. On the bank, the minks had inspected a deep hole, perhaps looking for a future den. They hadn't stayed inside it for long, but hopped back out to continue their morning hunt. Nearby was a larger woodchuck hole in which, by the look of her tight-circling tracks, the female mink had taken quite an interest. I wondered if she had smelled the hibernating woodchuck below. While the female had lingered around the woodchuck burrow, the male had been busy poking his pointed snout here and there into the snow, sniffing through the crystals for a scent of vole.

Side by side, the minks had made their way from the river, over the snow-covered dam of a beaver pond, to the man-made trout pond behind our farm. The trout pond was frozen over everywhere except for a large open hole near the granite dam. Both minks had slid into the hole, but I saw no signs of anything they'd caught, and I presumed they had come up empty.

From the trout pond, the minks had backtracked to the beaver pond. But instead of recrossing it, they had run along the frozen shoreline, then together turned abruptly away from the pond and cut across a snowy meadow. Around midmeadow, the female's trail turned off at a right angle to the male's, made a wide two- or three-acre loop, and finally rejoined her mate's at the end of a long stone wall in which they had a den.

On another cold morning, when a full moon still shone brightly in the predawn sky, I followed the male mink's tracks when it left its den to hunt alone. It headed straight for the beavers' pond. A little way out on the very thin ice, it dove into the water through a beaver's plunge hole. I didn't have to walk out on the thin ice to see where the mink had emerged and relieved itself. I reached out with a long stick and poked the feces. The stools were still soft enough to separate. Inside were crunched up crayfish shells.

From the beaver pond, the mink climbed up a brushy bank and made its way through the tangle to the open snowfield that in summer is our sheep pasture. The energetic mink's trail followed the edge of the pasture, weaving through prickly berry bush stems. It followed the line of our wire fencing, sometimes hopping through the openings to run inside on the pasture snow. The tracks formed S's and figure eights, circling here, looping around the base of a tree there, headed in no particular direction. Then, abruptly, they cut out on a long, straight run toward our barn.

The mink trail crossed over the farm lane and went through the open barn doorway into the barn's basement. The dirt on the basement floor, which is always dry and stays soft even in winter, was imprinted all over with the mink's footprints. It had sniffed nearly every square inch of the earthen floor. Then, having found nothing to kill and eat, it had left the place the way it had entered and headed back down over the pasture.

It left the pasture with a short hop through the wire fencing, veered away from the beaver pond, and made a beeline over the snowy meadow to its den in the stone wall.

*B*esides the mink pair, we had a pair of red foxes hunting in the area. On my way home from the minks' den, I noticed the fox tracks—two dotted lines of paw prints interwoven as the foxes hunted together. Sometimes they spread apart and hunted separately, but they always stayed just a bark away from each other. One of the foxes had smaller paws and made a daintier trail. Since, as with minks, female foxes are smaller than males, I assumed the smaller tracks were the vixen's. I set out to follow her trail, knowing that in the long run I would be following them both. Predators of different species often share hunting ranges. On the meadow, the vixen's tracks paralleled the mink's. At one point near the beaver pond, they crossed an otter's sliding tracks.

I followed the fox prints to the river, where they led me along the riverbank, then into an open farm field. In summer and early autumn, when the field is full of corn, it is a productive hunting ground for predators that feed on birds, mice, rats, squirrels, insects, toads, and snakes that live in the jungle of tall stalks. But in winter, with the corn cut and the field under deep snow, the place is little more than an open thoroughfare from one hunting ground to another.

The fox crossed the cornfield at a steady trot, stopping only once to dig in the snow to a stump of corn stubble, which she pawed and shredded with her sharp teeth.

She rejoined her mate in the next field, a snow-covered cow pasture and a much more promising place to hunt. Beneath the snow, the pasture was a thick mat of dry grasses riddled with vole tunnels. By now the snow was deep enough to have vole tunnels as well. The two foxes ranged all over the pasture, sniffing for tunneling voles. In some places a fox had only poked its nose down into the snow to sniff a tunnel underneath. But in one spot, the larger fox had jammed its snout deep, pushing with its hind legs, and shoved its entire head forward under the snow. In the process it had made an impression of its head, neck, breast, belly, and haunches. I pulled out my tape measure. From the tip of its nose to its hind feet, the fox was thirty-six inches long, excluding its tail, which it must have been holding in the air, for there were no tail marks in the snow.

Between the two of them, the foxes had poked dozens of nose impressions in the snow to sniff out voles and had dug thirty holes. Some of the holes had uncovered vole nests. Others had uncovered tunneling voles. I found a fresh spot of vole urine in one hole and fresh vole droppings in others, but I found no signs of the fresh, frantically made tunnels or tiny tracks that would suggest a vole had escaped. I believe the foxes had caught and eaten all the voles they uncovered. In the still, moonlit night and perhaps on into the morning, the pristine snow-covered pasture had become a killing field.

At the very end of the pasture, I did come across two tiny sets of vole tracks emerging from the snow, just three feet apart. Both made a beeline across the pasture, headed for the protection of something solid. One vole had tunneled back down into the snow at the base of a sturdy fencepost, the other near the crooked stem of an alder tree. There were no fox prints around either hiding place. As far as I could tell, those two voles had survived.

Red fox tracks and full body print

*I*t occurred to me that I hadn't seen a deer track all winter. The deer that live in the woods and fields around our farm migrate sometime in December to "yard up" in thick stands of evergreen trees that grow on hillsides or in hollows with a southern exposure. Tall evergreens provide shelter from the wind and from heavy snow. Small evergreens and low-hanging boughs provide soft needles, twigs, and buds the deer can eat. The browsing deer stomp paths in the snow, eventually creating a maze of passageways that are sometimes deeply walled. Within the maze, deer can outrun and outmaneuver most marauding predators. But outside of it, they can get bogged down in deep, soft snow and become easy prey.

One splendid afternoon, as the sky brightened to cobalt blue and the temperature climbed into the midthirties, I visited a deer yard a few miles from our home. In the sheltering evergreen forest, I stripped a sapling and poked it through the snow. It measured two and a half feet deep.

The deer themselves kept out of sight, but they had left signs everywhere. Under the thickly matted evergreen boughs, hoofprints showed where deer had browsed. Hemlock, fir, and cedar trees had all been browsed to heights of up to six feet. The terminal buds of small birch and maple saplings had all been nipped off. Many maple saplings that had been mercilessly pruned by browsing deer over the past few winters now looked more like Japanese bonsai trees than wild American hardwoods.

By following the browsing trail, I came across six deer beds. A deer's body heat melts the snow on which it lays, forming an impression the same shape and size as the deer's torso. In one bed, I could make out the impression of the animal's tail, its folded hindquarters, its breastbone, and two deep hoofprints, made when the deer pushed with its front legs to stand up. I also found

Deer hoofprint

34

what appeared to be communal beds made by six or seven deer lying close together. All around the beds and along the browsing trails, deer droppings littered the snow. The pellets were a dark brownish-green from the evergreen needles and woody in texture from the twigs and bark the deer had eaten.

The deer tracks intermingled and overlapped in both directions along the trail. Only by singling out one set of tracks at a time and steadfastly keeping to them could I follow the movements of individuals. One of them had stepped down a gully to the deeply snow-covered frozen spring, stood on the ice, and stretched its long neck to drink. I could hear the water running under the small opening in the ice through which the deer had sipped.

The freshest tracks led uphill beyond the softwoods and into the hardwoods growing along the crest of a ridge. The snow was deep, and the bounding and slipping tracks showed that the deer had expended a lot of energy to get up the hill. Suddenly I realized that it was I who had sent the deer bounding out of their yard. We were close indeed. I wanted to see them, but not at the expense of their comfort and well-being. So rather than pursue the tracks up the hill, I followed another deer trail that was not as fresh.

The trail led downhill to an abrupt drop-off. Below flowed a good-sized brook. I stood at the edge of the cliff and stared down at the rushing stream. The deer had not paused at the top of the cliff but had simply taken the drop in their stride, moving fluidly down the snowy, bouldery slope to the brook. There they drank, then walked through the stream to the opposite bank and on into more softwoods—a continuation of their winter yard.

I dared myself to follow, but the slope was too steep. Carefully holding only healthy stems and branches that would not break, I edged closer to the brink. With my binoculars, I focused on the sparkling stream and thought I saw the dark black shape of a trout swimming. It was only a slender stone.

Porcupine hair and quills

Four 🌰

A Confrontation under the Stars

Where we live, winter's worst usually comes a month or so before winter ends. In late January or February, when a bright full moon or starlit sky means there are no clouds to blanket the land, the temperature can plummet to twenty, thirty, even forty below.

On one such night, with the Milky Way spilling its billions of stars across the blue-black sky, a large porcupine left its den in the woods at the foot of the old quarry, waddled on its big oval feet along a worn trail that led downhill through granite boulders and a thick patch of young Douglas firs, and emerged on a snow covered road in the woods. The porcupine crossed the road and picked up the trail on the other side, heading toward the stream.

At the same time, a fisher (a member of the weasel family) crossed the stream, moving in undulating hops up the sloping land toward the woods road and the quarry. It was following the scent of porcupine and made very few stops along the way. As it closed the space between itself and the oncoming porcupine, the fisher moved more briskly, sliding under one deadfall, leaping over another. At a stand of hemlock trees where the snow was firmly packed and had a sprinkling of finer snow on top, the fisher's feet made perfect prints.

The porcupine had moved past a stand of aspens and into the hemlock area when it suddenly came face to face with the fisher. The fisher stood awhile, then lunged at the porcupine. Fishers are the only animals that regularly eat porcupines, but this attack was not successful. The fisher got a pawful of quills.

The porcupine stood its ground and the fisher circled, preparing to lunge again. The porcupine watched, keeping its back to its adversary, every quill up. Whether from nerves or fear or just the long time it was being kept from its normal routine, the porcupine urinated heavily on the snow where it stood. Its urine was dark green from the tannic acid in the hemlock bark and inner wood it had been eating. The porcupine also dropped one pellet. The fisher, being smaller than average and facing an especially large porcupine, seemed also unnerved. It too urinated, the liquid pale yellow on the snow.

The fisher wheeled around and lunged another time, again to no avail. After some more circling, it suddenly gave up and ran off. When it was about fifty feet from the porcupine, it took to the trees, traveling limb to limb, leaving no more prints in the snow.

The porcupine turned around and headed back the way it had come. Where its trail crossed the road, it stopped and combed its coat where the fisher had clawed it. Some broken quills and a tuft of long black hairs fell out. It shed a few more broken quills as it continued on its way across the road and back to the old quarry.

Three times it stopped to eat along the way: once from a white pine, once from a cinnamon birch, and last from the base of a spruce. Each feeding was halfhearted—only a tiny square inch or two of bark was chewed. With the odor of fisher still on its fur, the porcupine climbed the trail up the steep incline, between the huge granite boulders, and returned to the depths of its den.

This drama was told by the tracks. The fisher in the story was a small one, probably a female, since fisher females are considerably smaller than males. The porcupine, on the other hand, was very large. Its footprints were huge, and the entrance to its den was large, brushed all around the sides by the porcupine's quills and hair as it entered and left. Because of the porcupine's formidable size, I believe the confrontation with the fisher lasted a long time, with the porcupine slowly pivoting and turning in place while the fisher circled. Leonard Lee Rue III says in his book *Furbearing Animals of North America* that when a fisher attacks a porcupine, it tries to keep to the front of the animal in order to avoid its quill-filled tail. A fisher will try to flip a porcupine over in order to tear into its soft quill-less belly. The small fisher in our story may have been attempting to get hold of the porcupine to flip it over when the porcupine lashed out and smacked the fisher with its tail. I know the fisher was hit hard. The broken quills that the porcupine later combed out show that it made solid contact with the fisher, and the tuft of long black porcupine guard hairs that combed out with the quills suggests that the fisher got quilled in the front foot while clawing at the porcupine.

I brought home the tuft of porcupine hairs and a few broken quills. Each hair was over two inches long and very fine. The quills were hollow and very light in weight. In most reference books, porcupine quills are described as being barbed; that is what makes them stay stuck in whatever they stick into. In looking at the broken quills under my microscope, I was surprised to see that the barbs were more like ridges or ripples in the quill, all pointing away from the quill point. Each broken quill had many minuscule barbs around its terminal end. It was easy to imagine how, together, so many small barbs could hold the quill fast into flesh and, over time, work the quill in deeper.

The next day, I was curious to see if anything more had happened between the porcupine and the fisher. As always in winter, the tracks in the snow told the tale. The porcupine had gone out again that night, but instead of heading downhill toward the stream, it had climbed uphill into the high-ground woods.

About two hundred yards from its den, the porcupine had stopped to eat bark from the lower part of a yellow birch trunk. The highest chew marks were twenty inches off the ground, which meant the porcupine was at least twenty inches tall sitting on its haunches.

In *The World of the Porcupine,* David Costello states that a day's meal for a large porcupine consists of a patch of bark (and the cambium beneath the bark) about the size of a piece of typing paper. The porcupine I was following had eaten that much off the yellow birch. Then it had waddled on to a hemlock tree and spent considerable time nipping off small branches, but not a needle had been eaten from them. Perhaps the porcupine was removing them so it could get its teeth into the large limbs on which they grew? I searched the tree for any light patches where bark may have been freshly removed, but saw none.

The porcupine had climbed down the hemlock, stepped on the boughs it had just chewed off and dropped, and continued on its way. Its trail was so fresh, I couldn't resist following it farther, even when it took me up a rocky slope where the hemlocks were so thick that their snowladen boughs made the going hard. I stooped and walked in a squat until the prickly hemlocks gave way to softer Douglas fir. I followed the big oval footprints upward, between massive boulders and over fallen tree trunks to a spot where the porcupine had paused to taste the bark of a small spruce tree.

Beyond the spruce, the trail veered downhill and meandered through piles of logging slash (leftover treetops and branches)—dangerous stuff to walk on if you are not a porcupine. I stood and stretched to relieve the tension in my back. I was standing on a ridge just above the rock pile surrounding the porcupine's den.

Then I turned, squatted again, and headed back.

*F*ishers are difficult to track because they often take to trees. If the trees are growing close enough together, fishers can travel half a mile by leaping from tree to tree like squirrels do. A fisher's hunting circuit can be anywhere from ten miles around for females to thirty miles around for males. Since the small quarry was the next logical place in this one's path, I concentrated my search for fresh tracks there, where there are not enough trees for the fisher to take an arboreal route.

I searched for about half an hour and found many snowshoe hare prints and pellets but no tracks of the fisher. It was beginning to snow, and what fisher tracks there were from the night before would, within the hour, be covered.

I had just about given up when I spotted a darkly smudged patch of snow around an aspen tree. The smudge had been made by my fisher. Something had soiled its front paws, and their impressions were printed in black on the white snow. What luck! The new snow was beginning to cover the prints, but when I knelt and blew gently, the clear black footprints were revealed.

The fisher's front paw measured only two inches across. An average-sized fisher's front paw would be at least two and a half inches across, so the tracks confirmed my suspicion that the small fisher had been intimidated by the much larger porcupine. The fisher had been in the porcupine's neighborhood, less than two hundred yards from the feeding porcupine and less than fifty yards from the porcupine's den. Yet it had not once ventured in the porcupine's direction. Instead it had climbed the aspens and fed meagerly on the black fungus that grows on the branches. The fungus was what had blackened the fisher's feet.

From its tracks and its claw marks in the aspen bark, I saw that the fisher had climbed the tree, scraped off a bit of fungus with its

41

front paws, then returned to the ground to claw the clump apart and eat it up. As the fisher's front feet became more soiled, they printed more darkly in the snow; but because its hind feet became only slightly soiled, they printed more gray than black.

The fisher ran from one aspen tree to another, eating the black fungus. Sometime between feedings, it dug three holes in the snow, one-two-three in a row. The last was the deepest. I couldn't tell what the fisher was digging for. Maybe it was just cleaning off its feet. Beneath one aspen was a large piece of fungus still lying on the snow. I poked at the black wad with a twig. It was soft and gooey and adhered to the wood. Apparently the fungus doesn't freeze. It may be this quality of remaining soft and chewy even in the cold that makes the fungus a poor but palatable substitute for the fisher's preferred foods, which are small birds and animals, especially porcupines.

The fisher made a wide loop around the aspens, back to where I had noticed the first black smudge, then picked its way through a thick growth of small balsam trees to the pile of granite boulders on the other side. There I lost its tracks amid the giant stones.

The confrontation under the stars had been traumatic for both the fisher and the porcupine. All the next day, though well within each other's drifting scents, they patently avoided each other. That a porcupine would avoid its only mortal enemy besides man was not a great surprise. It was surprising, though, to learn that a fisher could have its confidence so shaken that it would spend an entire day eating gooey fungus rather than hunt for another, smaller porcupine in the area, especially when the old quarry is home to dozens of porcupines.

My two-day study yielded another surprise: the black fungus on the aspen trees is food for wildlife. Like sap, wood, bark, stems, leaves, buds, blossoms, and fruits, the fungus is, in its parasitical way, another nutritious gift from trees to ever-hungry animals.

Five

Boiling Sap

Our maple-sugaring season begins in March and runs through the end of winter and into spring. In our dooryard is a century-old sugar maple, four feet in diameter. All around it are tapholes from previous years. I used to drill five tapholes into the tree and hang five sap buckets. The tree kept all five full of sap. Now, though, the tree is slowly dying of old age, and it just doesn't seem right to take so much sap from it, though I've no doubt it would still give generously.

This March I put only two taps in the maple, one on its north side, the other on its south side. When I drilled the north hole, the wood that curled out along the drill bit was as dry as sawdust. The south hole yielded soggy, wet wood, and the sap began dripping even before I could tap the spigot in. On the south side of the tree, it felt like spring; on the north, it was still winter.

About forty gallons of sap boils down to one gallon of maple syrup. Since we have only the one tree, the most syrup we've ever produced in one sugaring season was a gallon and a half. This year, with only two taps in the tree, we were lucky to make half a gallon.

When the sap is rising in our maple, I know it is rising in thousands of other trees as well, and my expectations rise with it—winter is coming to an end. When the dripping sap slows down or stops, so has the advance of spring.

Generally the sap runs most in daylight hours, especially on sunny days following freezing nights. But this year the trees defied convention and ran all one day and into the night as well. That evening, every sugarhouse had its rig fired up, trying to keep up with the flow of sap. After supper I drove to a friend's sugarhouse to visit while he boiled sap.

Guy's sugarhouse is tiny, eight feet by twelve feet, and picturesquely situated on a woodsy knoll. Steps dug out of the earth lead up to the tiny sugarhouse door. In the moonlight, the little building looks straight out of a fairy tale. It always amuses me that much of the essential maple-sugaring equipment is manufactured by a company named Grimm. In fact, the whole maple syrup industry seems elfin to me, especially the small one-person operations. Go into a sugar woods in early March and you'll hear the rhythmic sound of a light hammer tapping spouts into the trees. You'll often not see the tapper, though, hidden by the woods, moving quietly from tree to tree. Later, after all the spouts have been inserted and the buckets hung or pipelines attached, the sugar woods is magical—abandoned for a time by the owner, yet filled with his tools and handiwork.

I walked up the steps and through the door into the tiny building. Guy was absorbed in his work, looking like an elf scientist as he dipped a long thermometer down into the boil, lifted it out, and held it high to read. He ladled some steaming sap from the pan, inspecting it closely as he poured it back. The last half ounce from the ladle is the most crucial clue. If the liquid sheets together and hangs apronlike from the ladle's rim, the sap is almost syrup.

I found a place out of Guy's way to stand and watch. The little room was crowded, with the rectangular sap-boiling rig in its center and the other tools of the trade all around the walls. Guy opened the red-hot door of the rig and fed more wood into the fire. The heat required to boil cold tree sap and keep it boiling as fresh cold sap enters the pan is tremendous. The little rig was fired up hot, its draft wide open. Guy poked the coals, then shut the door and sat to visit.

The sap in the pan bubbled into a rolling boil. The room was filled with maple-scented steam, rising in a column to the rafters, where it escaped through a vent in the roof. Guy and I chatted about a dinner we had attended the night before, about the sap run, and how odd it was for the sap to be running after dark. We talked of TV shows and the Olympics and politics. As the sap boiled down and thickened in the pan, our conversation boiled down and thickened too, our subjects turning to living well, old age, our wanting to stay forever, enjoying this place, this earth, watching its creatures, hearing its sounds, smelling its smells.

The room began to smell like a candy factory: the sap in the pan was sweetening. Guy turned a nozzle and let more fresh sap in, then stoked the fire. The coals were becoming embers. He didn't add new wood.

Around eleven o'clock, the sap was still coming, but the flow was petering out. Guy had made half a gallon of maple syrup in the last three hours and a few gallons more during the day. He was tired. It was time to call it a night.

As I left, Guy joked that we'd solved most of the world's problems inside his little sugarhouse that night. In truth, most of what we'd said had risen with the steam and escaped through the roof into the cold night air.

Six
Losing a Limb

After sugar season, we had some very windy weather. One morning, the wind was roaring all around the house, buffeting the clapboards, threatening to burst the windowpanes. We stopped feeding the woodstove for fear the draft would become so great it might whip the fire into an uncontrollable frenzy. The oil furnace kept the house warm, but not toasty the way the woodstove does. All the time the wind roared, Deanna's long silver porch chimes sang, and the three tall Norway spruce trees in the front yard swayed to the music.

In the woods, the wind blew rotting branches off the trees. A falling limb, even a small one, is a dangerous thing. It can crack a skull or break a neck. Our maple tree's largest limb had become diseased and weak. It was ripe to fall, and we were lucky not to lose it to the wind. For the past few years, we've avoided walking beneath it. This year, when the wind subsided, I decided to have the limb removed.

The tree surgeon (he would call himself a woodcutter, but it was nothing less than surgery that he performed) sawed the limb off close to where it grew from the maple's trunk. Then he cut the felled limb into firewood logs.

The limb had reached farther across the yard than any other. In health, its leafy branches had shaded the lawn and supported the swing our daughters shared. Without it, our maple tree seemed to be standing off-center, incomplete.

The logs, piled high on the ground, ranged from six inches to over a foot and a half in diameter—almost half that of the tree itself. I couldn't accurately determine the limb's age by looking at the cross sections of the logs because many of the growth rings had been obliterated by decay. Still, it was clear that the limb was not very old compared to the tree. A limb can grow fast, reaching out to expose itself to more and more sunlight. The tree's trunk, on the other hand, stands in the shadow of its own branches, so it grows more slowly.

Some of the logs had smaller branches attached, and on these, buds were beginning to sprout into tiny maple leaves. The sprouting maple buds had a red tint. I looked across the field to a hill covered with maples. Their buds combined to create a red cast over the entire hillside.

Most of our maple's amputated limb showed wood that was dead and rotten, and the rotten areas in the logs created wondrous patterns. Each cross section looked like a work of art—free-form shapes, carefully inlaid, each a different shade of sepia, beige, or olive-tinted tan. One log had a cross-section design that looked like something the painter Georgia O'Keeffe might have created had she worked in inlaid wood.

One gnarled log was splitting from the deep rot inside it. I pulled it apart. Inside, the wood had been transformed into humus: deep, black, moist, with the texture of used coffee grounds and the aroma of maple sap. Also inside the log was a cache of milkweed seeds, their down dyed pale green from the wood. Each seed case had been opened, and the seeds were missing. A couple dozen brown maple leaves were stuffed inside the log as well. Protected from the rain and snow, they were soft, leathery, and remarkably resilient. I crumpled some in my hand; they slowly uncrumpled and regained their shapes. There must have been a hole somewhere in the limb for all these things to have gotten inside.

The huge limb yielded nearly a third of a cord of sixteen-inch firewood logs. A whole cord is a stack of logs four by four by eight feet. Considering the size of the limb, I estimated that the entire maple tree, if felled, would yield over four cords. That's enough firewood to heat a small home for one Vermont winter.

But our dooryard maple won't be cut down for firewood—not yet. It could live on for many more years. When it finally does die, there are a number of young maples, offspring, growing wild around the yard, any one of which could grow to be as big, as grand, and as old as its parent.

When I'd finished moving the logs from the dooryard to the woodshed, Deanna suggested that I plant one of those small maples in the sunny spot created by the missing limb. I dug out a three-foot-tall sapling and transplanted it beside the old tree, then covered the ground around it with the dark, rich humus from the rotted log. As I spread the maple-scented humus around the young tree, I noticed the fuzzy green fiddlehead of a fern just beginning to unfurl from the ball of earth I had taken up with the sapling's roots.

Beaver from behind

Seven 🌿
Watching Beavers

One chilly April evening, I walked to the hollow just beyond the trout pond. Last fall, beavers had dammed a brook that flows into the pond to create a second pond, and I was curious to see it now, in the spring.

There was still a lot of snow in the shaded hollow and the beavers' tiny pond was still mostly frozen over, but there were narrow pockets of open water on both sides of the dam—one on the trout-pond side and another on the beaver-pond side. On the beaver-pond side, I noticed the ripples made by a beaver swimming toward the dam. I watched from only fifty feet away as it climbed out of the water and onto the snowy ground near the dam.

It was a large beaver, dark brown in color. As it lumbered over to a clump of alder stems, its tail dragged on the snow. I expected it to begin chewing one of the stems, but it was intent on something else. Partially hidden from my view was another beaver, equal in size to the first. There was a brief scuffle. The first beaver, a male, attempted to mount the second, which I presumed was a female. There was another scuffle, after which both animals entered the water on the trout-pond side of their dam.

51

There was only about ten feet of open water in the trout pond. The male swam to the edge of the ice and pawed at it. Then he turned and pursued the female, chasing her around the small pool. Twice he mounted the swimming female in the water. Each time, her head went under. She was not a willing partner. A fight ensued. The beavers scrapped in the water near the dam, rolling and tumbling, kicking up a lot of mud and splashing muddy water onto the snow.

Then the female made her escape. She swam to the edge of the ice and crawled out. She appeared to be nursing a spot on the inside of her hind leg: the male may have bitten her or she may only have been grooming. When the male swam up to the ice near the female, she leaned forward and arched her back defensively like a hissing cat. The male swam a few feet away, then crawled onto the ice as well.

It's interesting to watch heavy beavers on thin ice. The male tried twice to climb out onto the ice before he was successful. Both times the ice crumbled under his weight, sending him plunging back into the water.

The female stood on her haunches while she groomed her fur. Once, when she plopped onto all fours, her front feet broke through the ice and she fell forward, clunking her chin.

It was getting dark in the woods. As my vision dimmed, my hearing became more acute. I heard the slight swooshing made by the beavers' feet and tails moving across the ice. When the male began to chew on an alder stem, the sound of his teeth against the wood was clear and sharp. I must have made a sound myself, because suddenly both beavers looked in my direction, stood up tall on their hind legs, and sniffed the air, trying to catch a scent. In the near darkness, I could hear the faint sound of them inhaling.

Eight 🌿
The Fox

Around dusk on another April evening, I came upon a red fox hunting in a field. In the waning daylight, the fox looked gold, like the dry grasses in the field. I'm convinced that it became aware of me by sight alone as I was downwind in a strong breeze that would have kept my scent from reaching it and drowned out any sound I may have made. When it saw me the fox took off, running across the field, which is long and wide. It had to run a long way to the woods, and through my binoculars, I admired it all the way.

As it bounded over the grass, the fox held its pointed ears high. The backs of its ears were long and convex and covered with short, luxurious fur. Its tail looked as thick as its body, brown with a distinct black band around it before the pure white tip. The running fox held its tail stiff and parallel to the ground, but the white tip bobbed up and down like a baseball bouncing over the field. By the time the fox reached the woods, all I could see was the bouncing white tip of its tail.

The next evening, at precisely the same time I had seen the fox the day before, I revisited the field. This time, though, I approached the field more cautiously. Again the wind was blowing

Fox eating vole

strongly in my favor. Silently I made my way from the woods into the open field, then up a knoll at the field's edge. I slowly crawled to peek over the grassy knoll and look across the broad field. There was the fox! It was close—fewer than sixty feet away. If I hadn't been downwind in such a strong wind, it surely would have sensed me coming.

The fox was hunting in the dry grass. From so close a vantage point, I could now see that its hind end was russet brown with blond highlights, very much indeed like the dry field grasses. Its long and furry tail was also russet colored, but tinged throughout with black. The animal was brighter at its front, a reddish orange on the shoulders, neck, and face. In sharp contrast, its ears were velvety black, fringed exquisitely in white. Its front legs were also velvety black. Its hind legs were dark brown. This fox was absolutely gorgeous. Its fur was prime, and every hair in place. Because of its dapper look, I concluded that it was a male. In spring, female foxes look quite disheveled from their fur being pawed and pulled at by nursing pups.

I was really close—too close, I thought. I was sure the fox would soon discover me, but it seemed intent on something in the grass and moved ever so slowly, lifting each foot carefully and placing each step lightly. Then it froze in its tracks, staring at the grass ahead. A few minutes passed. I was beginning to tremble slightly from trying to be as still as the stalking fox. It remained frozen in place for a minute or so longer. Then its entire body flinched with tension. It crouched, getting ready to pounce. Its long tail arched stiffly high, with the white tip curving down, indicating the fox's intense anticipation. *Pounce!*

The fox leaped into the tall grass and came up with a vole. The rodent wriggled in the fox's mouth, and the fox shook its prey all around. I was surprised to see how big the vole was and how very

dark brown its fur was. The animal was a mouthful. The fox didn't drop it onto the ground to eat it as a dog often does with something it has caught and killed. As the fox chewed, parts of the vole stuck out, first from one side of the fox's mouth, then from the other side. It munched the vole, breaking the tiny bones, then swallowed bones and all in one piece.

The fox resumed hunting, keeping downwind from each spot it approached. It was hunting by sight, its eyes fixed on the ground before it. It was also hunting by smell: after every few steps, it paused to sniff the air—ahead, to the left, to the right. But mainly the fox hunted by sound. After each move, it froze and listened for the sound of a vole rustling in the grass. At one point in the middle of the field, the fox sat back on its haunches. Its body leaned forward. It cocked its ears, catching a sound ahead and pinpointing its exact location. The fox flinched once, slowly stood, then crouched, digging in with its hind feet. *Pounce!* Then POUNCE! It missed a vole twice.

The fox was getting farther and farther away from me. I wanted to be closer, so when the hunter walked, I moved too. After moving a few dozen feet more across the field, the fox again became intent on one place in the grass and began stalking toward the spot. Suddenly it leaped six feet forward—POUNCE! Another miss. Comically the fox looked all around to see where in the world this vole had gone.

The fox was nearly at the other end of the field when it turned and began hunting its way back. This time it followed a long ridge in the land, stopping every few steps to listen. It was hunting upwind now and having to locate its prey by sound and sight alone.

The fox kept coming toward me. I grew concerned that it would detect me. I lay down on the field, trying to be invisible. The fox kept coming. With my binoculars, I could see its face up close: mostly orange, it was delicately fringed with white fur. Its forehead was yellow, and a brown patch surrounded each of its amber eyes.

The fox froze in midstep, its right forefoot held off the ground, and stayed that way, on point, looking and listening. Then it pounced! Another vole escaped. This one ran overland and dove into a clump of matted grass. The fox dug at the clump, poked its nose inside, and became highly excited by the hidden vole's scent. Its back was arched; its tail stood straight up.

Then, abruptly, the wind shifted. The fox got a whiff of my scent and stared in my direction. I didn't move. I tried not to breathe. But the fox burst into motion and sprinted away. At the other side of the field, it slowed to a trot, then a walk. The wind had shifted back; I could feel it blowing in my face again. The fox casually walked into the bordering woodland. Under the trees it became totally relaxed. It sat and looked out at the field. It yawned, then scratched its side. Then it stood, turned, and romped into the darkening woods.

Nine
Shearing Time

*E*ach spring, when the pasture begins to "green up," as the old Vermonters say, we make arrangements for our sheep to be sheared before we let them out of the barn to graze. This year we were dismayed to find that the fellow who had sheared our sheep for the past ten years had given up the practice. For the comfort of the animals and the cleanliness of their wool, sheep should be shorn once a year, and many of the people who raise sheep, Deanna and I included, have never shorn one. It is an art that takes practice and skill, along with a great deal of strength in the lower back. A friend gave Deanna the phone number of an apprentice of our regular shearer who was now working on her own. We called, and on the appointed day the new shearer arrived. She set up her station quickly and was ready to begin. Deanna and I had to catch the sheep one at a time and force the unwilling customers to the shearer's mat.

There are a number of ways to catch a sheep. You can corner it and pounce, grabbing its wool and holding on as the sheep jumps and spins to get free. You can surround it, one person attracting its attention from the front while the other sneaks up from behind and jumps onto the sheep, straddling its back as it bucks and kicks. Or you can reach out and grab an animal that is running by you, taking hold of whatever wool you happen to get your hands on. Deanna usually grabs a running sheep and lets it drag her along until she can get it to go where she wants it. I am not as cavalier. I plan my attack carefully, corner the sheep I've targeted, and pounce, going always for the long wool on the sheep's back.

The shearer followed the same procedure for each sheep. Using one hand to hold the sheep by the ruff of its back and the other to firmly grab one of its front legs, she flipped the animal over carefully in one quick motion. Then, with the sheep upside down in an awkward humanlike sitting position that seemed to immobilize it, she began shearing wool. First she sheared the sheep's forehead, then around the eyes, cheeks, ears, neck, throat, and chin. As the woman sheared, she rolled the shorn fleece down in one piece. Wool fibers have microscopic loops that cause shorn wool strands to cling together. The shearer sheared the sheep's breast, then each front leg. She was good at her trade, always cutting close to the skin, but keeping the blades just above the thin layer of lanolin that sheeps' skin exudes. There is so much lanolin within the skin that accidental nicks or scrapes, or even deep cuts, do not bleed badly. The blood thickens and coagulates in the oil.

The woman sheared the sheep's rump and then its underparts, carefully manipulating the electric shears around the sheep's udder (or in the case of the ram, its scrotum) and anus. She sheared the hind legs last, then gently rolled the sheep over on the mat and off of its completely detached fleece.

Deanna systematically rolled each fleece and stuffed it into an empty grain bag. One fleece usually fills one bag. Deanna can often tell which animal's fleece is in each bag by examining the tint, texture, and length of the wool.

Next the shearer trimmed the hooves. If they are not trimmed at least once a year, sheep hooves grow long and eventually curl under, making the animal less sure-footed and more susceptible to parasites and other infections that harbor within the curl. In size and shape, a sheep's hoof is very much like a deer's. Yet deer hooves never grow too long; they are kept trimmed naturally by the abrasive stones and sand that deer walk on. Hoof trimming is a delicate operation. A sheep's kick can seriously injure a person. And a hoof that has just been clipped is razor sharp. The shearer has to hold the foot she is trimming with one hand and keep the sheep's three other feet still with her legs and knees. There is little or no lanolin in a sheep's hooves, and a hoof trimmed too closely bleeds profusely. Our shearer trimmed all the sheep's hooves flawlessly. After each sheep was shorn and trimmed, it was given a worming pill and then released to return to the flock.

The shorn animals looked odd. The white-wooled sheep were now pink. The brown-wooled sheep, because of their very black skin, looked strangely dark. And the lambs, none of which had been sheared, suddenly appeared nearly as big as their mothers.

The sheep remained in the barn a week or so longer while I spent the days working in the pasture, mending the fencing that had been damaged by winter snow. One morning, as I was working on the pasture fence, a mole tunneled close to the surface of the ground. I squatted beside it and watched as it dug upward, pushing up small clods of earth that tumbled down the sides of the mound the mole was creating. The mole stayed underground, out of sight. The earth seemed to pulsate as the mole moved under it, like a small heart beating in the ground.

I continued working, replacing the old fence post and hammering the wire fence onto the sturdy new post. Then I followed the fence around, checking for and repairing damage as I went.

By noon the fences were all secure and Deanna and I ceremoniously opened the barn door to let the sheep out. Old Soybean headed the stampede through the open door, down the wooden ramp, and out to the sweet green grass. The lambs were another story. They were all frightened of what was, to them, the never-before-opened door. They kept well away from it, staying inside the barn room after their mothers had all gone. Deanna was for rounding them up, catching lambs one by one, and carrying them outside to the pasture. I suggested we simply leave the door open, go out ourselves, and hope the lambs would eventually lose their fear and venture out on their own. "Uh-huh," Deanna said in mock agreement. I suggest this every spring, and every spring we end up having to round up the lambs, catch them, and carry them one by one to the pasture.

Consider for a moment: the lambs' world had been only the barn. They knew nothing of the outside, save the fresh air flowing through the broken panes in the barn windows. They had never even gone through a doorway to someplace else. Now, suddenly without their mothers, the frightened lambs stood huddled in the room they were born in. They looked lost and confused.

Out in the pasture, the mothers were enjoying the time they had to themselves, away from their offspring. Only when the lambs in the barn began baaing did any of the ewes look toward the barn.

Cauliflower was the first lamb to step through the open door. All alone she hopped down the steep wooden ramp and ran out into the sunlight. She did not go to her mother in the pasture. She came to me and began to follow me around. I started shoveling a load of manure, the first of the season for the garden, from the barn basement. Cauliflower walked back and forth beside me—to the manure on the floor, then to the cart. She was never underfoot, however, and the work seemed more pleasant because of her company.

Above us, in the barn room, the other lambs were still huddling together, their tiny hooves shuffling on the floorboards. I stopped shoveling, fetched a can of grain, and took it upstairs, passing the lambs so they could smell it. I sprinkled grain on the floor, to the open doorway, and down the steep ramp. The lambs began inching en masse toward the door. I left without looking back at them so I wouldn't spook them. Little by little, the lambs came out and down the steep ramp. I noticed one or two peeking over the rail board at me, but I pretended not to see them and continued my shoveling.

When the ewes had had enough time to themselves, they became anxious about their missing lambs. A few mothers walked over and called into the barn, but by this time the lambs had lost their fear. They could see their mothers outside, but they did not answer the calls. The lambs were enthralled with the new world of the barn basement. They wandered around sniffing the earth floor, tasting the concrete foundation, sills, posts, and wallboards. The ewes gathered at the entrance of the barn and called for their lambs. Soybean baaed loudest. Surely, I thought, her twins could hear the concern in her voice; yet they paid no attention. The lambs were all being disobedient. Finally I walked over, waved my arms and stomped my feet, and chased the bad lambs out of the barn to their mothers. All except Cauliflower. She stayed around me the whole time it took for me to load up the manure cart. When I started the small tractor to pull the cart to the garden, the noise of the engine startled Cauliflower and sent her running out of the barn and into the pasture, where she rejoined the flock.

Ten

The Shape of Our Garden

Sheep manure is a wonderful fertilizer. Each manure pellet is a capsule, dry to the touch, filled with nutrients that are slowly released into the garden soil as the pellet disintegrates. Sheep manure is nearly odorless, except when you shovel it up off the ground or barn floor. Then, mixed with strands of hay and bits of chaff, it smells like seaweed.

I used the small tractor to pull a cart full of manure to the edge of the unplanted, untilled garden. Nearby a chickadee sang a sweet little song, one I had not heard before. There was a light, shifting wind. Watching the weather vane on the house roof so I could stay upwind of my shovel and avoid inhaling dust the wind might blow up, I began unloading the manure. I distributed the stuff carefully, spreading each shovelful down on the garden, not hurling it into the air. Spaced evenly apart, the shovel-sized piles of manure and hay looked like tiny muskrat houses. If they were left standing in the air, the mounds would dry out and lose some of their strength and goodness. So as soon as I had covered the garden with manure mounds, I started up the tiny yellow rototiller and began tilling the manure under to mix it with the soil.

Writer and countryman Hal Borland once said that he was

fortunate to have "escaped early success" and enjoyed independence in his later life. I can say that I too am fortunate to have escaped early success. It wasn't until I was thirty-five that I finally began to see fruit from my labors. I did, however, achieve independence at an early age. Not through any financial success; Deanna and I never had more than minimum income for the first ten years of our marriage. We achieved independence through the way we chose to live—outside conventional measures of comfort and standards of living. Early on, we decided to plant a garden in order to grow our own food. Our garden is small, less than a sixth of an acre. But in it we grow a full year's supply of vegetables. Being able to feed ourselves no matter what the economy was up to has given us a great measure of independence. Our garden has given us the freedom to be ourselves. That is no small thing.

As I walked slowly behind the rototiller, guiding it along a straight line, I kept my eyes on the ground. I watched the tiller tines bite into, chew up, and spit out the remains of last year's garden. It was surprising to see how many edibles we had either missed or chosen not to harvest.

The tiller's turning blades unearthed potatoes, their thick skins black and shriveled and filled with rotting potato goo.

I tilled up dried beanstalks with hard beans rattling inside dry pods. The tiller pulled the beanstalks out by the roots, then plowed stalks, roots, and bean pods back into the sandy soil.

All that was left of last year's tomato plants were withered stalks and about half a dozen empty yellow tomato skins. The skins were lying flat and round on the soil like tiny collapsed paper lanterns.

I tilled a whole row of leftover cabbage heads that insects had destroyed in the fall before we could harvest them. The chopping tiller released their rotting odor into the air, then mixed the heads and much of their smell back into the soil.

There were a few small squash lying on the garden ground. Their skins were brittle, and inside each were dried and preserved squash seeds. The tiller tines broke open the squash and sowed the seeds.

I tilled up chalky white bones Yoko had buried in the garden and forgotten. The tiller broke the bones and reburied the pieces.

As the tiller churned the earth, I looked for earthworms. None showed up. The subterranean worms had not yet migrated up into the topsoil.

Hundreds of small spiders were living in the soil. The tiller shook them up out of their burrows, where they scattered before the blades like the crowds of frightened people running from monsters in old horror films.

North, then south, north, then south, I tilled the length of the garden. As I tilled in one direction, my footprints in the row I had just tilled went by me in the other.

Our garden is shaped something like the state of Pennsylvania, from which Deanna and I both hail, with a little rectangular annex on the Ohio side, where we grow tomatoes. The shape evolved unintentionally, though perhaps subconsciously, over the planting seasons.

Every summer the wild meadow on what would be the New York border reclaims some of the garden soil. Each spring I till the dry weeds back into the ground, redrawing the line between wild and domestic. The weeds take good care of the soil they steal. Their roots keep the ground moist, and their tall leafy stems shade the ground, preventing nutrients from being leached out by the hot sun. Wherever the weeds have been growing, the soil is a moist, rich, dark brown. Whatever vegetables we plant in the disputed border soil grow lush and green.

In order for us to take care of the garden soil as well as the encroaching weeds do, we must add mulch and fertilizer every season and produce our food organically. This means strict avoidance of most commercial herbicides and pesticides. Instead of dusting or spraying our crops, we keep the garden weed-free by pulling the weeds by hand and rototilling the soil between the vegetable rows. We depend on birds and toads to help control the harmful insects. Many insect-eating birds nest around the farm. In the outbuildings, barn swallows construct their mud-cup nests against the beams and on the rafters. Phoebes nest in the garage. We encourage tree swallows and bluebirds by providing nesting boxes for them. All day long, the birds snatch insects from the air and nip them off of the vegetable leaves. At night, toads patrol the garden, eating many insects that are hidden from the birds.

It would be nice if you could catch toads and transplant them into your garden, but you can't. I've tried. A transplanted toad seems to have little else on its mind than finding its way back home. So the only way for a garden to be blessed with toads is if they move in on their own. To lure toads to our garden, I provide them with housing by placing clay flowerpots upside down here and there around the garden. Each pot has a small entry hole chipped into it so a toad can come and go. Inside the pot, the shaded earth floor keeps the air damp and cool, just the way a toad likes it.

Once I had rototilled the entire garden, I tilled once more around the borders to make sure the edges were neatly squared—except for the side where Pennsylvania is bordered by the great Delaware River. That border I tilled in a long curving line.

My tilling was now complete. I stopped the engine and walked around on the earth I had just manured and tilled, enjoying every deep and soundless step in the soft, rich soil.

Toad house

Eleven

A Walk on the Morning Frost

In rural places, the burning of fallow fields, those left unplanted, ungrazed, and unmowed, is a rite of spring. Landowners burn their fields to rid them of dead grasses that will inhibit new growth and to prevent the dry fields from being accidentally set afire. I don't agree with the practice. Burning encourages the takeover of a field by coarse weeds, shrubs, and trees, the roots of which are deep and less apt to be burned out than grass and clover roots. And the fire burns more than weeds and grass. Many small animals are consumed by the flames, especially slow ones such as salamanders, snakes, and insects, which cannot quickly burrow underground or get deep enough to escape the tremendous heat. These animals die horribly, burned and blackened to a crisp. The burning of even a small field takes its toll on wildlife and creates a great amount of heavy smoke that pollutes our clean country air. People and wild animals would all be better off if we controlled the occasional brushfire rather than purposely setting more. Perhaps someday the practice of burning fallow fields will be recognized as counterproductive. But for now the burning persists as a rite of spring.

One April evening, firemen arrived to help burn the large field adjacent to our property. I went outside to watch and to be on hand to help in case the fire spread too near our barn. But firemen are experts on fires, not only at putting them out but also at controlling them. The firemen kept the fire restricted to only the areas the landowner wanted to burn by creating a fire line and controlling the burning with water from heavy packs strapped to their backs. The fire burned in the directions the firemen made it go, away from the neighbor's house and a safe distance from our barn.

Whenever the wind picked up, the crackling blaze whipped high, to five feet and more above the ground. When the wind died, the fire calmed. The firemen stayed upwind of the burning grass. Downwind, thick gray smoke peeled off the field and rolled in the air.

As the flames spread evenly across the field, I thought of the miles of vole tunnels that would be destroyed. The firemen worked steadily until the entire field had been burned. Then, as soon as one rite of spring was over, another began. Across the blackened field, down near the river, spring peepers started peeping for the first time this season. Had the warm air created by the fire spurred the frogs? I wondered. The peeping began softly and sporadically, then grew stronger, building to a crescendo of sonorous peeps—hundreds, perhaps thousands, of tiny tree frogs singing in the smoke-scented air.

The air smelled of smoke through the rest of the night. We could smell it in the house, and the odor kept me from sleeping soundly. I awoke in the early hours. Outside, the moon was bright. Its blue light shone through the windows. Yoko was sprawled on the lawn. She had abandoned her wicker chair on the porch to sleep out in the open on the frosty grass.

After seven I went out to walk on the frost before the rising sun burned it away. Frost covered every place the sun's rays had not yet touched. Where the sun was shining, the ground was damp and the grass wet.

I walked to the beaver pond. The beavers had been working in the moonlit night. The dam had fresh pilings on it, including a long, fully-needled white pine bough that the beavers had cut from a larger fallen limb. Something rippled the water near the bank, and I crept closer, fully expecting to see a beaver putting in a little overtime. Instead it was a pair of hooded mergansers swimming close together. As I approached, the pair swam away toward the center of the pond. The male was wary and kept one eye looking back toward me all the time. The female murmured her misgivings.

I followed the pasture fencing away from the pond. Evidently the fence wire had also been coated with frost. It was dripping moisture as after a shower. The pasture, which was exposed to the earliest morning sunlight, was frost free. Only in the great rectangular shadow of the barn was the ground still frosty white.

The adjacent meadow, whose longer grasses are shaded by dips and rolls in the land, was heavily frosted. Individual leaves, grass blades, pebbles and stones, sticks and fragments of bark were exquisitely decorated with tiny ice crystals. And though the field's general coloring was hoary white, pastel shades showed through the coating of ice.

In the burned meadow, a dark brown woodchuck was feeding on some bright green grass shoots the fire had not scorched. When it saw me, the woodchuck ran over the meadow to its hole—a woodchuck is never far from its hole.

I walked over the burned field to the old railroad bed, passing under the low branches of a hawthorn. The hawthorn's sharp spikes looked like long, ghostly fingernails. Each was covered with frost.

The railroad bed led me to the fox field where, in a border tree, a single crow was harassing a red-tailed hawk. When the hawk left its perch and glided, the crow followed, diving and screaming. The hawk seemed unconcerned. Rather than head for the cover of the evergreen woods, it alighted on a branch in the wide-open crown of a leafless poplar. The crow perched in the poplar too, hunching its back and lowering its head, giving the hawk the evil eye. The hawk ignored it until the crow flew off and circled just above the hawk's head, its feet hanging down as if to reach out and claw the hated hawk. Then the hawk swiveled its head this way and that to watch the circling crow. Finally the crow returned to its perch and resumed its silent, evil-eye treatment.

The sun was well up and shining on the hawk's cream-colored breast when the black crow flew again, diving repeatedly at the hawk. But though it called out its alarm each time it attacked, no other crows appeared. The crow, alone with its enemy, perched again and stared.

I left the two antagonists in the tree to continue their frosty relationship and headed home. On the ground, the frost was disappearing fast.

Twelve

Scared Lifeless

From the day we turned the sheep out to pasture, Cauliflower had enjoyed a carefree and relatively limitless existence, hopping through the wire from one side of the fence to the other, joining the flock when she wished and leaving them to wander the lane or walk along with us as we did our chores. As long as we were present, Yoko never bothered the lamb, and Cauliflower showed little fear of Yoko.

Then one morning Deanna and I went into town to buy seeds. When we returned, Yoko was outside the pasture fence, standing over a dead-looking Cauliflower. The lamb was not dead. She had been scared lifeless. Her eyes were glazed, her breathing shallow. Apparently Cauliflower had wandered out of the pasture and up the lane to the house. And Yoko, with no one around to inhibit her, had begun to run the lamb—to play with her. The chase must have frightened and exhausted Cauliflower. It did the opposite for Yoko. The dog had become so excited, she'd begun to pull bits of wool from Cauliflower's neck. We've seen Yoko do this with kittens. She never means to hurt. In her excited state, however, she'd bitten into Cauliflower's shoulder and tasted blood.

We came home in time to prevent Yoko from reverting to instinct and killing Cauliflower. The sight of Deanna and me snapped her out of it, and she instantly realized she had done something wrong. She cowered away as we inspected Cauliflower's condition. Then she came back and stood near us, watching, as if she'd had no part in the matter.

Cauliflower appeared to be in shock. As I carried her to the pasture, her neck was limp and her head hung down. I thought she might die in my arms. I laid Cauliflower on the green grass. She did not move. When it began to rain and the other sheep took shelter, she lay on the grass getting wet. I moved her to the dry sheep shed and covered her with a towel.

For hours Cauliflower did not move under the cloth, though her breathing did get stronger. Finally, slowly, she raised her head. Her eyes lost their glaze. She could see, but she would look only at the floorboards directly before her. Even when we took turns going to soothe her with touch and soft talk, Cauliflower would not look up.

Around suppertime the rain stopped. Deanna saw Cauliflower walking very slowly toward the rest of the flock, her head still held low, her eyes looking only at the ground. The flock met her approach with skittishness and alarm. The ewes stomped their hooves and snorted. The other lambs would not go near her. Cauliflower stopped a dozen feet away and remained still, keeping her head down, looking pathetic. We couldn't understand the flock's behavior toward Cauliflower. She had always been accepted by the other sheep. Then I realized that she probably smelled of Yoko. The sheep were reacting just as they would if Yoko were stalking toward them.

I took a can of Lysol out to Cauliflower and sprayed her all over. It was then that I discovered the extent of her wound. Yoko's bite had gouged Cauliflower just above the shoulder. There was an inch and a quarter cut in the skin and blood had congealed in the lanolin around it. I sprayed the wound with Bactine and covered it with a thick glob of petroleum jelly to serve as a bandage. The Lysol spray solved the flock's problem with Cauliflower. They approached and accepted her. Some of the lambs even lay down beside her.

Later on we tried to feed Cauliflower milk, but she wasn't hungry. She grew listless again and would not get up after the flock moved on. At night, when I went out to check on her, she was in the same spot, all alone in the dark pasture. The other sheep were under shelter in the basement of the barn.

Cauliflower was lying on the ground, sprawled out as if she had been hit by a truck. All around her, night crawlers were moving across the rain-soaked ground. The slimy worms shone in my flashlight beam. It was an eerie sight: all those worms crawling around, with Cauliflower lying motionless among them. Some of the night crawlers were feeding on the ground surface. Others were mating. I walked up and down the width of the pasture, amazed at the number of them. There were worms in the way of every step I took. On each square foot of ground, close to a dozen long worms were oozing out of the soil! They flinched when they sensed the light. As I walked, the vibrations of my steps reached the worms just before I did, and they quickly contracted, pulling their bodies out of my way.

I picked Cauliflower up off the ground and carried her into the barn, upstairs to the room she had been born in, and laid her on the fragrant hay. I left expecting her to die overnight.

The next morning Cauliflower was standing up and baaing and wiggling her tail. She still kept her head down, but it looked as though the life that Yoko had frightened out of her had been restored. I took her back out to the pasture and she rejoined the flock. But her ordeal had transformed her from carefree to fearful. She walked around the pasture slowly, timidly, as if at any moment the dog would again be at her throat. I spent some time with her, and once, as I was petting her chin, she rested her head in my hand. I held her head a long while. It was all I could do to comfort her.

Fear, not death, is the enemy of life. It robs the body of rest and tortures the mind even during sleep. We all have latent fears, wild dogs lurking somewhere at the edge of our sense of well-being. That night I awoke suddenly in a cold sweat. The Cauliflower experience had struck me deeply and awakened a wild dog of my own. My fear was real, but its cause was imagined. Cauliflower's fear, on the other hand, was based on real and recent experience. What courage she must have had to muster to venture back out into the open, with Yoko in full view patrolling the pasture fence.

Eventually Cauliflower's timid and fearful state passed. Day by day, she learned to enjoy life again—uninhibited by and regardless of the ever-present dog.

Thirteen

Spring Wildflowers

A gentle-as-can-only-be-in-May sporadic two-day rainfall sprinkled the lawns and gardens, fields, and woods. In the lulls between rains, the peepers rose in song, insects swarmed, and swallows snatched them on the wing.

Some insects continue flying during the rain, maneuvering between the falling raindrops. Think of it! A raindrop hitting so small an airborne body would surely knock it down.

In the wild meadow adjacent to the pasture, a kingbird perched on a sprig and watched for insects flying in the rain. Though the bird was mostly gray, in the rain it looked colorful, and when it flew, the white tips of its tail feathers flashed brilliantly against the meadow greens. Colors reflect more vividly through rainwashed air. Reds and yellows are especially vibrant, violets and blues are penetrating, and greens are overwhelming. In the rain, the pasture looked yellow-green; the meadow, emerald. The lawn was a true or Kelly green, and the woods were a soft blur of every green from nearly yellow to quite blue.

The rain rejuvenated all of Deanna's transplanted plants, which had been looking limp, suffering from the shock of being dug from one place and moved to another. In the rain, the transplants began to actually look comfortable in their new surroundings.

The tiny maple I had planted near the old tree spread its small wrinkled new leaves and held each out to the falling rain like tiny umbrellas. The heaven-sent water coddled the old maple, washing its branches, limbs, and trunk and running along its exposed roots. Wet with rain, the ancient tree looked whole, even young again.

I walked around the farm, listening to the rain fall, smelling the freshly scrubbed air, soaking in the loveliness. Every twig and leaf was bejeweled with clinging water drops. Millions of drops, and every one a lens forming an upside-down image of a scene. In the raindrops clinging to a willow branch, I saw the upside-down figure of one of our sheep grazing. In another drop, topsy-turvy spruce trees. I saw the pasture, barn, woodshed, house, and garden turned upside down, all squeezed inside a single drop dripping from the needle of a white pine tree.

Bloodroot

Bloodroot

After the rain, I found new wildflowers in bloom on every walk I took. Down by the river, bloodroot was blooming all along the banks. Bloodroot has a sleight-of-hand manner of secretly sprouting, then suddenly appearing fully bloomed. Its single leaf, which reminds me of a catcher's mitt, closes glovelike around the plant's stem and developing bud, keeping the whole growth process hidden. Then one day the leaf opens, and presto! A lovely flower! Even after first blooming, the bloodroot's leaf occasionally closes around the stem and flower, hiding its beauty, then opening to show it off again.

I examined one bloodroot flower closely. It had nine white petals arranged around a bright orange central clump of stamen and pistils. Bloodroot flowers close and open again and again, the way crocuses do, according to the weather. Warm and sunny, open; cold and rainy, closed. Although the petals form a tight white ball in closed bud, when opened they are long and narrow.

If you broke a bloodroot stem it would ooze a red-orange "blood" that would stain your skin and clothing. I suppose the root is its "bloodiest" part, but I've never dug one up to see because I hate uprooting wildflowers.

There were large congregations of bloodroot blooming on the riverbank, thriving in the wet sandy soil, and smaller numbers clustered here and there under the tangle of vines and brushy stems above the bank. More grew amid the tall stalks of primitive horsetail in the near woods.

Colonies of bloodroot become established along a spreading root system. Under the arch of a fallen branch, I spotted a solitary plant, its blossom semiclosed, cupped in the open palm of its leaf. It was the first colonist of many that will someday bloom in that secluded place.

Trout Lilies

One afternoon Deanna came back from a walk along the brook and mentioned that she'd seen red trilliums up and nearing bloom. The next day, late in the afternoon, I went to the brook to find Deanna's trilliums. I found them, and they were indeed near blooming, but I also found some trout lilies in full bloom.

The trout lily is a favorite wildflower of mine, partially, I think, because of its name. I love anything "trout"—trout streams, trout ponds, trout rods, trout fishermen, and of course, trout themselves. The trout lily's long narrow trout-shaped leaves are olive green, mottled with purple markings that resemble the dark wormlike patterns on a brook trout's back. The center vein in its leaf is nothing more than a slight crease and can easily go unnoticed, like the lateral line down the side of a trout's body. Trout lily leaves are shiny and always look wet: so wet that every

Trout lily

spring, when I rediscover them, I catch myself touching the leaves to feel if they are wet or dry. A group of trout lily leaves looks like a mess of just-caught trout flip-flopping on the ground.

There are always more sprouted trout lily leaves than flowering plants. I found only one cluster that was all in bloom. It filled a sunlit patch of ground, and the yellow lilies further brightened the spot. But to see the trout lily's real beauty, you have to get down on your knees and elbows. Like most lilies, the trout lily does not face upward toward the sun, but hangs its lovely head humbly toward the earth.

Painted Trilliums

In the woods, the boulder-strewn paths were lined with painted trilliums. The painted trillium is a hardy flower that resembles its cousin the red trillium, except that the painted trillium grows taller and straighter. Its snow-white petals are wrinkled around the edges. At the flower's center is a burst of crimson that veins upward and outward on each petal. On exceptionally dewy mornings or just after a rain, the painted trillium's furled leaves cup little pools of water that reflect the forest canopy. Its white flowers become beaded with water drops—tiny liquid lenses that magnify the petal's crimson veining.

Spring Beauties

On a woodland walk, Deanna and I saw thousands, maybe millions, of spring beauties. Spring beauties are small: rarely over six inches high, eight inches if you count the length of their stems that is covered by the debris from the woods' floor. The spring beauty plant has a single stalk, whitish below the leaf litter, turning to pink and then light brown as it ascends into the light. It has two elliptical leaves, green and soft, without much visible veining. Above them the stalk branches into a cluster of slender flower

Painted trillium

Spring beauties

78

stems. Spring beauty flowers take turns opening and closing, depending on how the light reaches them. Sometimes only one or two flowers in a cluster will open, while the rest remain tightly closed. Closed, the spring beauty flower resembles a long white tooth protruding from the mouth of a green bud case. Opened, the flower forms a dainty star of five white petals, each with delicate red veins. Some spring beauty flowers are so heavily veined that from a distance they appear pink.

Dutchman's-breeches

Growing here and there among the spring beauties were the taller stalks and carrotlike green tops of Dutchman's-breeches. Amid each cluster of the Dutchman's-breeches' leafy stalks, one stalk grows taller than the rest. On it the flowers are formed four to eight, all in a row. Each small flower looks like a white-legged, yellow-belted, baggy pair of pants hanging legs-up from a clothesline. In fact, the Dutchman's-breeches flower looks so much like the thing it is named for, it robs your imagination. Though I always take notice of this wildflower, I never spend much time thinking about it. I'd rather sit among the spring beauties and admire their delicate individuality, imagining the many millions of them in bloom throughout the woods, tiny earthly stars shining all day long and winking out at night.

Moccasin Flower

I took Deanna and Amber to a place deep in the forest where, exploring on my own a few days earlier, I'd found moccasin flowers. They bloomed in the place where, while I was working on a book of autumn sketches last fall, I saw my first lynx. Deanna, Amber, and I searched for the flowers in sunny patches and dark shaded places, amid crowds of hardwood seedlings and under sprays of tall ferns. All together we found a couple dozen. All were

Dutchman's-breeches

pink, from a slight blush to a deep rose. One was so light, it was nearly white.

Just as we were about to leave, I spotted a pure white moccasin flower growing near a deadfall. In the dark spot, the flower seemed to glow. I've never seen a completely white moccasin flower before. The wildflower guide books say these members of the orchid family range from deep rose to white in more northern climates; what they don't mention is that you can search for years, as I have, and perhaps never find a pure white specimen.

Moccasin flower

The white moccasin flower was growing right beside another that was deep pink, and so less conspicuous. Amber, Deanna, and I knelt beside the blooms. It was a sight to behold—the two extremes of moccasin-flower color side by side. I was tempted to run home for my camera, but the three of us decided we'd rather preserve the image in our minds.

*R*ed Trillium

On another wildflower safari, this time on my own, I walked toward the brook to see if the red trilliums had bloomed yet. A small garter snake that had been basking in the morning sunlight slithered under a mat of dry grasses as I passed. Nearer the brook, the sunlight was dappling down through the treetops. The ground was moist and the grasses green and damp.

The little brook winds its way in and around large moss-covered boulders and tumbles over steps of a granite ledge, forming swirling pockets and deep, still pools. I paused at one small pool to watch a brook-trout fry, not much longer than an inch. It was holding its own against the current, feeding on microscopic particles that were apparently drifting downstream. I bent near to the water to see the tiny fish up close, and a water strider skating on the stream surface passed right under my nose. The baby brookie's head seemed to be nothing but enormous eyes and a small pouting mouth. The little fish's sides already showed typical trout markings. I counted seven dark "parr" spots on the fry's side.

I got up and made my way upstream, stepping on wet stones and moss-covered boulders, careful not to tear the moss with the rough soles of my boots. A stream boulder, with moss and other small plants and fungi growing on it, is a world unto itself—a miniature planet Earth with a rock core, a soft crust, water, vegetation, and even animal life.

On the bouldery stream bank, I saw a few trilliums not yet in bloom and, farther upstream on a boulder-free bank, a few more, these nearer to bloom. Their elongated green buds were slightly opened, each showing a little of the red flower packed inside.

Close by the trilliums, in a sun-dappled spot, three slender ferns were unfurling upward amid a crowd of low green plants. Each slender fern stalk was speckled with black bits, either some growth of its own or residue of the dark soil from which the plants had emerged. Up the sloping bank there were more ferns—one cluster, two, three, four, and more. All backlit by the morning sun, they glowed a light translucent green. Suddenly I began noticing ferns unfurling all along the stream bank. They looked as if they'd heard someone was coming and were stretching tall to see who it might be. I walked very slowly, placing each step in a fern-free spot.

Farther up the stream, I sat on a large dry boulder to rest and listen to the running brook. As I sat, my boot loosened a small stone, disrupting the streambed and releasing a brown cloud of sediment into the flow. I watched the water until it cleared again. It took some time, even from such a small disturbance.

Across the water were the trout lilies I'd discovered the other day. On my side of the stream, I spotted three red trilliums in full bloom. Like the trout lilies, the red trillium flowers each faced downward, though they were not as bowed as the lilies. The red trilliums looked more shy than pious. With a fingertip, I turned a trillium blossom toward me and admired its soft, pretty face: three deep red petals delicately veined with maroon. In the flower's center stood seven pale yellow stamens, each marked with maroon. In the center of them, the pistil. I released the flower and it slowly turned on its stem to face away and downward once again.

While I know this flower as red trillium, it has a few other, more imaginative names. The naturalist John Burroughs called it wake-robin. He loved this wildflower and named his first book after it—the first outdoor book I ever read, *Wake-Robin*. Another name for red trillium is birthroot, which to me is most apropos, for it was while reading *Wake-Robin* that the naturalist in me was born.

Red trillium

Part Two

Pickerel Cove

Pickerelweed

One
The Cove

When we came to Vermont, one of the first places Bernard (the farmer who sold us our place) showed us was Pickerel Cove. He pointed around, directing our attention to various nooks and crannies, as if he had made them himself. He didn't own the cove, but it was obviously a place he loved dearly.

An old gentleman named Ray was fishing from the bank. Bernard and I chatted with him. He'd caught nothing that day, but there had been other days when he'd caught many trout in the cold water. I asked Ray if he'd ever caught any pickerel. He said there never were any pickerel in Pickerel Cove; the place took its name from the pickerelweed growing in it.

Ray and Bernard are both gone now, but the cove remains. It is a wetland that was once a large bend in the river. Years ago when the railroad laid track along the river, it altered the watercourse, straightening the river so the track could run straight. That cut off the cove from the main flow. Most of the water of the cove comes from seepage of the river under the porous railroad bed and from a brook that spills down from above, overflow from a trout pond in the woods. The rest comes from rain.

Our farm is on a great knoll of grassy land just above the cove. When there is enough water in the cove, its surface reflects the upside-down image of our red barn and the sheep on the green knoll. Our barn cats hunt along the cove's banks. The swallows that nest in the boxes around our yard hunt insects in the air over the cove. In early spring, the first peepers we hear are all singing from the cove.

We've seen deer, foxes, otters, minks, muskrats, beavers, turtles, and all kinds of birds at the cove. Every few years moose wander through the water. Once in a while a bear moseys through.

When the weather is hot and dry, the cove's water level lowers drastically, but it never completely dries up. There is an ancient beaver dam that helps hold some water in the cove no matter how dry the weather, and each year a migrating beaver or two will stay long enough to repair the old dam, raising the water in the cove to the very top of its banks.

The wildlife observations in this part of the book were made from March, when the cove is winter frozen and covered with snow, through June, when the cove is brimming with water and alive with activity.

Two 🌰 Otter Spotter

The snow on the meadow had a hard crust and it could nearly support my weight, but every few steps, I plunged in knee-deep. It was hard going, so I went back home and put on snowshoes for my trek to the cove.

The otter tracks on the snowy cove were fresh, and I kept an eye out for an otter emerging from one of the many holes in the ice. I'm an expert otter spotter and can spot an otter's nose sticking out of an ice hole from over two hundred yards away.

I've read that river otters are rare in Vermont and seldom seen, but I don't find this true. Otters are my constant companions on winter snowshoe treks along the river, and in trout season I've had to share my favorite fishing holes with otters more often than I'd like.

It wasn't long before I spotted an otter emerging from a plunge hole. It must have broken a small opening in the new ice that had formed over its original hole: through binoculars I could see that most of the hole was frozen over, with a small black opening in one corner just big enough for an otter to slip through.

The otter was eating something, a crayfish perhaps, that it had apparently dug out of the cove's muddy bottom. When it climbed out of the hole, its feet made mud-brown prints on the white snow. The cove is deep at that spot, and the otter had to have been at the bottom to get such muddy feet.

I watched as the otter stood up on its hind legs and looked around, then gracefully curled back on itself to groom the fur under its right hind leg.

The river otters I watch in the wild are the same as the ones you see in zoos, and just as lively and comical. In the wild, though, they are wary and will dive as soon as they become aware that they are being watched.

The otter on the cove groomed for a few minutes, then casually plopped back into the water. I took advantage of its absence and ran closer to its plunge hole, keeping low and downwind. When I was about a hundred yards from the hole, the otter emerged again, but this time it wasn't eating anything. Its wet, slick fur looked very black against the bright white snow. Its tail was thick and long, and its face was broad. Its whiskers looked like a bushy, gray mustache. Its nose was rounded and constantly sniffing, it had a gray patch of fur under its tiny chin, and its eyes were two pin dots.

The otter moved away from the hole and paused to look all around. Then it began to scrape at the snow with its right front paw, preparing a spot on which to relieve itself. It walked gingerly all around the spot, its back hunched, its tail held up. Then, its hind end facing me, it pooped. As soon as the otter had finished its business, it ran back to the hole and into the water.

I took the chance to get even closer. The otter emerged again, but instead of coming out of the water, it stayed in, holding its head in the air as it ate another crayfish. A crow flapped overhead. Though the otter hadn't noticed me, the crow had and it let out a danger cry, *ca ca caw!*

I don't know if it was the crow's warning, a shift in the wind, or my own movement, but something spooked the otter and it dove under. I waited a long while for it to emerge again, but it was down for good this time.

I had been working intensely on the drawing board the past few days and feeling a bit cooped up. It was good to be out walking again, and seeing the otter was an added pleasure. Even though my best view of the day was its hind end, I was happy to have gotten it. All the way back home, I felt exhilarated by the sighting.

*A*round noontime, I caught the otter out again on the snow beside another of its plunge holes. It had just been underwater and was busy grooming itself, combing its wet fur with the sharp claws of its front feet and brushing itself with its whiskers. It scratched its rump with its teeth, then its neck with its right hind foot. How good that scratching must have felt! As the otter scratched, its chin pointed up in ecstasy. It scratched its ear. It rubbed its fur with its paws. It scrubbed its snout in the wet snow. Then it lay down flat and simply lounged.

The otter looked comfortable. I was not, having been crouched for so long in the cold, wet snow. So when the otter popped up from its catnap and returned to the water, I was determined to find a more comfortable position. I found a spot on the bank where the snow was ledged like a chair. Placing my snowshoes on the ledge and my red scarf on top of the snowshoes, I made a comfortable and dry seat.

The otter had been alternating between two plunge holes all morning. Fresh otter prints surrounded both holes. I was sitting at an equal distance from each (about fifty yards), with the wind in my favor and not even a twig blocking my view.

As soon as I sat down, the otter emerged. Its muddy feet again made dirty brown prints on the snow. It was chewing on a crayfish, which it finished off in less than a minute. Then it rolled on the snow. Through my binoculars, I could see that the otter was covered with green weeds and slime. It was rolling to clean itself.

The otter rolled onto its back and paused, paws up like a puppy, looking at the sky. "What a carefree life!" I thought. The otter lay flat on the snow and pushed its nose into it, first just a poke, then deeper, finally bulldozing the snow into a small mound. Then it stood up on all fours and glanced around: south, west, north—then east, in my direction. But I stayed very still and the otter didn't notice me.

This particular plunge hole was elongated, about six feet by two feet, and most of it was sealed over with thin ice. The otter plopped right through the ice and back into the black water. When it dived, its tail pushed up bunches of green slimy-looking reeds. It seemed to be searching for something in the reeds and stayed near the surface, its back humping up out of the water like a miniature whale's. When it submerged completely, its back bumped against the thin ice, pushing the ice up here and there but not breaking through it. Then the otter went under. I waited and waited for it to emerge again, but it didn't. I was cold from all my sitting and waiting: it was time to go home.

I was snowshoeing around the cove, looking for mouse tracks or tunnels, when I spotted the otter suddenly emerging from another plunge hole in the ice in such a fluid motion that it looked as if it had been squirted up like a line of toothpaste from a tube. Out on the snow, it immediately began to groom itself, and it groomed for a long time: at least ten minutes. When it had finished, its fur looked dry. Then it rolled over and rubbed its back on the snow, twisting its body back and forth as though scratching an itch. After much rubbing, the otter rolled over again and stretched out on its stomach to rest. It popped its head up once to look toward our barn, which is only a few hundred yards away, and then toward me, but again it didn't notice me. Satisfied that all was well, it curled up and fell asleep.

While the otter slept, I continued my search for signs of mice, being careful to remain downwind of the otter. I found none. As I headed back to where I'd been squatting when the otter fell asleep, the otter awoke, sat up, and yawned two long, neck-stretching yawns. Then it stood and dove into the water.

I quickly ran to a closer spot and waited for the otter to re-emerge. When it did, it had a mouthful of what looked like shiners—three of them, each about four inches long. It dropped all three minnows on the snow and ate them one at a time. While the otter was eating one fish, the others flipped and flopped in the dry, cold air. When it had eaten them all, the otter returned to the water.

I had run about a dozen feet closer when the otter suddenly emerged again, this time with only one fish, which it gobbled down quickly.

When the otter submerged again, it stayed down longer than I cared to wait. I began to circle the cove, heading back home. When I reached the other side, the otter emerged again. This time, however, I was upwind of it. The otter immediately picked up my scent and dove back under the ice.

A blizzard we had expected petered out before it reached us, bringing only rain, which has helped melt away more of our snow cover. Today a light snow is falling, but the air feels warm. I figured the mild temperature might trigger an emergence of winter stone flies and was searching for them (I'd spotted one in flight) when I noticed not one but two otters emerging from a plunge hole. My otter, the one I've been seeing all winter, is a large male, and now he has found a female companion. She is considerably smaller than he, and her facial features are more delicately formed. She has a darker muzzle and darker fur under her chin, and she is more active. While the male lolled about on the ice, the female ran off, following the narrow channel of open water. As she ran, she dove on the ice and slid on her belly. When she stopped, she gathered her feet under her and ran for another diving slide. When she was about twenty five feet away from the male, she turned around and headed back to him, diving and sliding all the way. She slid along until her chin hung over the edge of the hole. She peered down into the black water for a while, then crawled and slid up to the male and rolled over. The male curled himself beside her and rested his fuzzy gray chin on her slick back fur. After a few minutes, something alerted them—maybe my scent, since I was slightly upwind. One after the other, they slid into the water and out of sight.

As I walked along the cove edge looking for an airborne stone fly to follow, the female otter suddenly squirted up out of the plunge hole and onto the ice. She was eating minnows; I couldn't see how many she had. Suddenly the water in the hole began bubbling like a pot boiling. A school of minnows was frantically swimming and squirming, flipping and flopping near the surface. I thought at first that the male otter must have been chasing the minnows, setting them into a frenzy, grabbing all he could. But then I saw that he had come back out of the water at a different hole, nearly a hundred feet away.

Amid the boil of minnows, I saw the dark shapes of larger fish, their finny sides breaking the surface. As odd as it seemed—it was still only early March—the larger fish appeared to be catfish. Could the cove's catfish have roused from the mud and be actively feeding already? With my 7 X 50 binoculars, I couldn't see the shapes well enough to make a positive identification.

When the female otter dived back through the hole, the fish shapes disappeared, though the minnows continued to boil. A few minutes later, the otter popped back up with a madtom (a small species of catfish) clenched in her teeth. It was about six or seven inches long. Evidently the otter had discovered the madtoms all

94

nestled in the mud bottom and stirred them to a frenzy.

It took a while for the otter to eat the fish, and she was facing me as she ate. Her sharp canines shone white each time she opened her mouth. From that angle, she looked just like a dog chewing up its food. When she'd finished, she cleaned up all the fish pieces she'd dropped on the snow, then dove back into the water.

While the female otter was underwater, the male became alert and stared in my direction, sniffing the air, trying to get a fix on my scent. I was directly upwind from him, but the light snow that had been falling all morning had turned heavier now, and the wet snowflakes created a curtain between me and the otter and partially blocked my scent. The otter looked puzzled. Now he smelled something: his neck stretched long, his nose wrinkled; now he lost the scent and his body relaxed. After a few minutes, he gave up trying to locate me and resumed his grooming and rolling on the snow.

The female climbed out of the water, this time with a crayfish in her mouth. She crunched it up, then dove again. A minute later, she popped back up with another crayfish. In the next five minutes, the otter caught and ate five more crayfish. Her appetite was enormous. While the male always paused awhile after eating something—to look around, to groom, to lie on the snow—before  going back under to hunt for more, the female ate, dove, emerged, ate, dove, emerged, nonstop. In fifteen minutes, I watched her eat minnows, a catfish, and seven crayfish. She was no doubt carrying kits, probably in about the last week of gestation. That would explain her appetite.

The snow began to let up and the curtain between me and the otters dissipated. They caught my scent and simultaneously dove out of sight.

*U*nder a creamy inch of new snow was a layer of hard ice crust. Walking was very slippery, and I slid a little with each step I took. The otters have been in their glory! Even on the levelest of surfaces, where they normally would have to run, now they could slide. In the middle of the afternoon, I picked up the male otter's tracks near our brook. He'd been hunting in the pockets of open water in the tiny stream. What, I wondered, could he catch in that water? Caddis larvae? Crayfish? Minnows?

The brook flows into a culvert under a lane and empties into the trout pond on the other side. The otter had followed the brook to the culvert, run up to the lane, then belly flopped into a long slide across the level lane and down the short slope to the pond. It was the longest continuous otter slide I've ever seen on so level a surface, roughly twenty-four feet. What a ride!

After his slide, the otter had broken through the thin, just-formed ice that covered a small entry hole in the still-frozen trout pond, swum under the thick ice, and eventually emerged 100 to 150 feet away through a large hole near the dam. Then he slid over the snow on the dam to hunt in the short stream that connects the pond with the cove.

I finally caught up with the otter just as he emerged through an ice hole in the center of the cove. He appeared to have finished hunting for the afternoon: he spent a little while grooming his wet fur, then rolled onto his side to nap on the sunlit snow.

I haven't seen the female otter in four days. I suspect that she has given birth and is in her den beside the cove, curled around a couple of kits. I know she has been out to hunt—the snow trail leading from her den is soiled from her feet—but exactly when she comes out, how often, and how long she stays out, I can't tell. The male otter at the cove has stayed around, but doesn't go near the female's den or the trail leading to it.

The ice on the cove is melting rapidly. In some spots it's so

96

soft, you can poke a stick through to the water below. The male otter has broken a few new holes in the ice simply by bumping through from beneath or jumping from above, and he was fishing in one all afternoon. This new hole happens to be close to the shore. I had a front-row seat downwind and was able to watch the otter close-up as it caught and ate about a dozen crayfish in as many minutes.

Otters must find whole clusters of crayfish at a time to be able to dive and emerge with a fresh one at such regular intervals. It got so I could time each dive, rest my eyes from staring through my binoculars for about sixty seconds, then lift the lenses back to my eyes the second the otter came up with another crayfish.

After being underwater for a considerably longer spell, the otter emerged with a lively, pink-sided minnow in its mouth. It was exactly three o'clock. In the distant village of Groton, the church bell rang three times.

The otter disappeared and reemerged many times more, and the hole was becoming wider from his comings and goings. As usual after so many dives, he didn't even bother to climb out onto the ice to eat his catch, just held his head up out of the water and chewed his food.

I spent much of the afternoon sitting motionless on a nice dry fallen tree limb, watching the otter do things I'd seen many times before. Still, everything he did fascinated me: sliding on the ice, rolling on the snow, digging holes in the cove bank, grooming his thick, oily fur, rubbing his whiskers dry with his front feet. I even saw him use a claw to pick his teeth after he had eaten. There is a joyful thrill in being so close to a wild animal, going unnoticed while it behaves naturally. It is during these times, when I'm not thinking about much other than the creatures I'm observing, that I experience total tranquillity.

Portrait of mink by river

Three
Mink

This morning Deanna and Amber saw a mink running on the frozen river. When I reached the river on my afternoon walk, I looked for its tracks where Deanna said they'd seen the dashing mink, and I found them. The mink had been going upstream, walking on a tiny shelf of ice next to open water. At one point it had gone into the water. Just think of the exceptional coat an animal must have to keep warm in the cold, dry air and dry in icy water!

The river looked black where it flowed between white snowy banks, but in one place where the banks were bare, the water was bright and I could see through it to the stony bed. I looked for things the mink might be feeding on in the water, but saw no trout or any other likely meal.

I saw fresh mink tracks along the river, made late this afternoon, perhaps only an hour or so before I came by. The mink had come to the river across the meadow. It hadn't stopped once to sniff or dig for mice under the snow. This mink was going fishing. It had entered the river through the open crevasse along the river's edge. When it left the river to romp on the bank, its wet, warm paws made perfect impressions in the snow crust.

Where the mink had run up to the edge of a high bank and popped to a stop in that wonderful way weasels do to survey the scene, its front tracks were deep and parallel. After a good look around, it had turned right and gamboled farther downstream along the high riverbank. As its feet dried, its footprints became less clear in the snow's crust.

Under some alders, the mink had dug into the snow and relieved itself. Its warm stool had sunk an inch or so into the snow by the time I found it.

I followed the mink tracks along the river wherever I could (I was on snowshoes), but I finally lost them in a thicket of red osiers and young willow trees.

*T*he river ice is breaking and sinking. I was snowshoeing again along the river with the sun at my back when I spotted a tiny ledge of ice gleaming under the water. Catching the sunlight, it gleamed red, orange, yellow, blue, and white in the sunlight against the otherwise dull green river. But if I stepped either way, upstream or down, I lost sight of the bright image.

I could hear the ice breaking farther downstream like the discharge of a small handgun. Closer to me, the ice was making all sorts of sounds: snaps, pops, and hissing cracks; some, very subtle little smacks of thin ice flexing, other sounds loud and startling. Tiny tickings came at regular intervals, sounding like a slow clock. Some sounds I could pinpoint as coming from a ragged crack in the ice. After a particularly long *cra-a-a-ack,* I swear I saw that opening widen! A sound like a pane of glass breaking came from a deep place in the river, where the water freezes in alternate layers of thin and thick ice. Some dull thuds and bumps came from a shallow section where the ice is rippled.

*O*n another day, I found a small hole in the ice near the cove shore. Around it were mink tracks and a spot of bright red blood. The mink had probably caught a large minnow and eaten it on the snow, tearing the fish into small mouth-sized pieces. (Otters don't leave blood on the snow when they eat. They hold the whole food in their mouth while they chew it up.)

The cove ice had melted drastically since morning. By late afternoon there were as many watery places on its surface as there were snow-covered places. Across the cove, on a bright patch of snow, I spotted a dark figure, too small to be an otter. It was the mink! My heart quickened as I focused my binoculars. Mink are so shy and elusive—all winter long I had known them only by their tracks on the snow. This was my first sight of one.

Compared to the otters I've been watching on the cove, the mink looked diminutive. I couldn't tell if it was male or female; the size of an animal is difficult to judge at a distance, binoculars or not. The mink was brown, with a white patch under its chin. The shape of each mink's white chin patch is distinctly different from every other mink's, so chin patches are used by biologists to identify individuals. This one's chin patch was so round and white, it looked as if the mink were carrying a snowball in its mouth.

Mink with snowball-like chin pattern

I could tell the mink was on to me. It kept looking in my direction, nervously bobbing its neck and head up and down. Its head looked large in comparison to its slender neck. Maybe it was bristling the hair on its head in reaction to my presence? The mink stood up on its hind legs and sniffed the air. Then it dove into the snow and vanished. A few seconds later, it reappeared about ten feet away. In the next instant, it dove and disappeared again. I walked around the cove, my eyes glued to the snowy spot where the mink had disappeared, watching to see if it would show itself again. It didn't.

On the other side of the cove, I found the mink's tracks on the snow. It had been fishing in a narrow channel of open water; a channel invisible to me from the other side of the cove. Each time the mink slipped into the channel, it appeared to me to have vanished in snow.

*T*he mink that has been living much of the winter at the end of the stone wall is now keeping company with another mink. I discovered the pair's tracks today. The new one is the female; her footprints are a full third smaller than those of the male. And I believe it was this female which I saw and whose tracks I found out on the cove snow.

Mink tracks are the most expressive of all animal tracks. Following a trail, you can visualize the mink running, hopping, looping around a stem or tree trunk, shooting off at a right angle up over a hill, galloping in a straight line, slowing down to poke around some interesting area, dashing down into a gully, skidding to a halt, stalking a spot in a pile of brush, stepping along a ledge of ice at the edge of a stream, diving into the water.

Early this morning, the minks left their den. They went around the cove and into the river, where their tracks mingled on the ice with otter tracks. After traveling upstream a ways, the minks separated. The female headed into the woods. The male hunted in the open area at the edge of the cornfield. A quarter mile on, the two met up briefly, but they soon separated again. This time the male mink went into the woodland and the female traveled out in the open. By splitting up like this, the minks cover much more ground than they could by hunting either on their own or closer together. I presumed that if one made a kill, they would share the food at their next reunion.

The first time the minks' trails split, I followed the male's tracks; the second, the female's. After each mink had made a wide oval, they met near the cove, about where they'd split up the first time. Combined, they had covered at least six miles of territory.

On the way back to their den, the female veered away from the male to spend some time at a new den she has been digging out of an old woodchuck burrow. She didn't stay there today, but rejoined the male in the stone-wall den.

It was just beginning to rain. I was walking toward the cove when suddenly I heard a splash, then *splash, splash, splash!* A mink ran through the shallow water near the shoreline. It must have heard my footsteps on the slush, but it didn't know exactly where I was—instead of running away from me, it ran closer, toward a hole in the rotting old beaver dam. How close we were! Less than ten feet apart. Up close, the mink's fur is a rich chocolate brown. I was standing on higher ground than it was, so I couldn't see its white chin. Its legs were very short, and overall the animal looked small and delicate. After it had disappeared down the hole in the old dam, I went to the shoreline and found its footprints. It was the female. Her tiny prints were unmistakable.

Stooping to watch a winter stone fly

Four
Winter Stone Flies

It is March and Deanna has started tomato plants. Small green pots line the sunny windowsills. I've been leafing through seed and fishing catalogs, dividing my daydreams between the garden and the streams. Patches of brown earth have begun to appear where yesterday there was snow. On the roof eaves, dripping water has replaced the icicles. Along the roadsides, freshets drain from the melting snowfields.

But it isn't spring yet, and we're reminded of the fact every time the weather shifts. The crows that only a few days ago seemed to be pairing off—the males gurgling love notes to the females, completely enthralled with themselves—are all behaving normally again. Yesterday a sentry crow sounded an alarm as I approached the river, and the others flew in circles, complaining all the time I was there.

I was there again to search for winter stone flies. Deanna had first noticed them when one landed on the kitchen windowpane. I thought I'd seen one days before, but when I'd stooped to identify it, I'd clumsily stomped it down into the snow with the webbing of my snowshoe and didn't see it again.

Today there were hundreds of winter stone flies in the air and on the snow. The stone flies I'm most familiar with are the big, coarse-looking ones that emerge from the streams in spring, summer, and fall. These winter stone flies have the same features as their larger relatives, but they are tiny and delicate: no longer than one quarter inch and as slim as needles.

Winter stone flies emerge from rivers and streams through holes and cracks in the ice. The tiny stone fly nymph swims or drifts in the current under the ice until it finds an opening to climb through. Then it clings to the ice until its back breaks open and a winged stone fly climbs out of the nymphal skin and flies off.

I found two types. One had long wings, as long as its abdomen. The other's wings were only half the length of its abdomen. The long-winged stone fly's wings lay flat on its back when the insect was at rest, whereas the short-winged type's wings looked rolled up and useless. I didn't see any of the short-winged insects flying, only crawling on the snow. Also, the short-winged stone flies were a bit smaller than the long-winged ones. Since I believe both to be the same species, I assume the smaller fly is the male, the larger and longer-winged, the female. This is usually the case with insects: the females are larger than the males.

Since stone flies emerge from the water for the sole purpose of mating and reproducing, I arranged a meeting. Scooping a smaller fly off the snow, I placed it within an inch of a larger female that had just landed. The flies walked toward one another, but upon meeting, they jumped back and headed off in different directions. So much for matchmaking.

Watching a winter stone fly travel across a snowfield is puzzling. The stone fly moves rather quickly on the snow, clambering over and crawling under the snow granules the way a crayfish bulldozes its way through the gravel of a pond bottom. I wonder, though, where the stone fly could be going. To a spot of

Winter stone flies
(enlarged three times)

female　　　*male*

bare ground? Perhaps to some vegetation on which to cling while it waits for a mate? Why don't the stone flies stay nearer to brush and trees where they would be better protected from birds? Instead they seem to purposely move toward the open, some toward acres of open snowfield. To cross such an expanse would take a tiny stone fly more time than its life. Are the stone flies simply wandering? Do they find a mate and reproduce purely by chance?

The answers may lie in their different wing types. Most of the stone flies crawling on the snow were the smaller, short-winged types. Perhaps their short wings are used only to carry them off the ice to the land. Once there, the wings may indeed become useless. The long-winged stone flies, however, flew and landed and flew again. They picked up off the snow in an instant, like tiny helicopters.

I may be way off in this, but it makes some sense that the long-winged female flies seek out a crawling male mate. This would explain why the short-winged flies crawl out into the open: in order to be spotted by a flying female. The female flies down, the two mate, and the female flies off again to deposit her fertilized eggs in the icy stream. (Both male and female die soon after).

I must follow the next winter stone fly I see flying through the air and watch where it heads and what it does. I could probably find a book that would tell me all I want to know about the winter stone fly, but how much fun would that be? First I'll try to find the answers from the stone flies themselves.

I always read the "book of nature" first. Then I check my findings against known facts, and the research I do forms the bulk of my pleasure reading. Today I can add—after consulting some books and calling an expert, who called one or two more—that it appears that my conclusions about the behavior of the winter stone flies are correct. I've also learned that stone flies appearing in fall and winter feed as adults. This is most interesting! It means that the male stone flies I watched climbing over and under the snow granules were probably not just traveling aimlessly; they were feeding on whatever microorganisms they found growing on the snow. If you look closely at the snow at this time of year, you can see it has some greenish stuff clinging to it, perhaps a form of algae.

The behavior of small winter stone flies was known by others, even published in books, before I came across them the other day. Yet I was able to enjoy the thrill of discovering them for myself, of learning the stone flies' behavior from observation alone, and of forming conclusions about their lives based solely on what I had observed the insects doing. This is how I've always studied nature, and I believe it's why, after twenty-five years of field studies, I continue to be fascinated and challenged by the things I see around me. Sometimes my subsequent research proves my original conclusions wrong. But most of the time, the conclusions I come to on my own are very near the truth. A naturalist must believe his own eyes, trust his own logic, and be willing to be right on the mark as well as dead wrong.

Five ❧ Crows

The river's refrozen surface is silvery and speckled with silver dollar–sized white spots, each spot composed of tiny crystalline formations. I'm not sure what causes these spots. Perhaps—and this seems logical—as the ice was melting, it caused bubbles of air to rise to the surface of the water. These bubbles, caught in the water as it refroze, would appear as white dots on the newly frozen surface. Whatever, it looks lovely.

Deer mice are climbing the sumac, eating the soft red tops. I saw one sumac with three of its red flower clusters nibbled into; bits of red lay on the white snow. Some of these flower clusters are six feet above the ground. A deer mouse climbing a six-foot sumac is like a person climbing three telephone poles! And how do the mice know the flowers are up there to begin with?

Most of the milkweed pods sticking up through the snow are finally emptied of seeds. The wind has blown them all away. Every so often now, I see a downy milkweed seed rolling like a tumbleweed across the snow. When I walk through a crowd of milkweeds, the empty pods click and chatter as if applauding my passing.

I was walking through some milkweeds when I heard the call of a sentry crow. It had spotted me from its perch high in a treetop and was announcing my progress to all the crows within the sound of its voice. As far as I could tell, it was on the alert and calling a warning *ca ca ca caw*.

I remembered Ernest Thompson Seton wrote that he would point his walking stick at a sentry crow as if he were aiming a rifle, and the crow would respond with the frantic danger call: *ca ca ca caw*. I didn't have a walking stick, so I lifted my left arm and held it straight and aimed my finger at the distant crow. The crow immediately called a rapid *ca ca ca caw*. I dropped my arm, then lifted it slowly again, aiming at the crow. Again the crow called a loud *ca ca ca caw*. I did it again, and again the crow called. Then I held both arms down and stood still. The crow called out once more. Finally I stomped toward the tree the crow was perched in. The crow immediately took wing and flew behind a ridge, calling the danger call *ca ca ca caw* even more rapidly. A little while later I heard the crow again, out of sight behind the ridge, this time calling *caw caw caw*: "All's well."

I've always been fascinated by crows, but I've had some misconceptions about them. For instance, I thought they were anarchistic—that they had little organization among themselves. It turns out they are highly organized.

I began to see their wonderful organization one day five winters ago. Out on one of my snow walks, I suddenly found myself beneath a sky full of crows. Ahead of me, crows were congregating in the trees and bushes in an area where I knew a stillborn calf had recently been buried under fresh snow. The generosity of crows seems unbounded. When one strikes it rich, they all share in the good fortune. And so these crows, perched around the carcass, were calling for others to come. And others *did* come. Dozens flew in from all directions. Three passed quite low over me, but as soon as they recognized my human form, they quickly veered away over some birches. I could hear the loud flaps of their wings beating the air in the maneuver.

Then I saw one crow silently flying in a straight line in the opposite direction. I watched until it was just a black speck in the eastern sky. There it hovered, alone at first, but soon in the company of more arrivals. The guide crow continued to hover while the newcomers circled nearby. More crows appeared, and more. Then the guide crow turned and flew in a straight line back to the area of the carcass. The others followed at some distance behind their leader.

I tried to imagine the spectacular view of the guide crow—hovering high above the pattern of farm fields, watching its comrades appear one by one out of the clouds. The dimensions of such a world are enviable.

Muskrat house under snow

Six ❦ Muskrat Houses

*T*here are five muskrat houses in the cove, three of which have been visible throughout the winter as lumps in the snow. All five were constructed last year, and all five are situated in mucky, swampy, hard-to-get-at places. Only now, with the snow almost gone but the cove's swampy spots still frozen solid, have I been able to safely approach the houses on foot to look each one over closely and listen to them through my stethoscope.

The first muskrat house I walked to is the largest, three and one half feet high and six feet wide at its base. Sturdily constructed of clumps of fine, short grasses pulled out by their roots, it's built on a small elevation. The muskrats enter from the cove through a twelve-foot-long tunnel under the swampy land.

I felt around the house. The top was soft and dry; the sides, hard and full of moisture. I pushed the loose material away from the side of the house and rested my stethoscope against the mound. Distinct erratic sounds came from inside. Keeping very still and holding my stethoscope lightly so as not to pick up my own pulse, I heard what sounded to me like someone chewing celery.

I cleaned my stethoscope, then left what I'd decided to call the

The big house

Willow house

Reed house

Goldenrod house

Coarse loose grass house

big house and made my way across the cove.

The second muskrat house is only a few feet from shore. Built in the center of a thick growth of willow stems, it is loosely and sloppily constructed from grasses. There is no solid place on which to rest my stethoscope. I tried holding it against the soft side of the mound, but heard nothing. I named this one the willow house.

The third muskrat house is located in the center of the cove. I found a safe walkway on a raised strip of land running between two stretches of still-frozen water. Many thick hollow reeds grow in the center of the cove, and this mound is made mostly of these tan-colored reeds, each about a half inch in diameter. The reed house looked distinctly different from the other darker houses. I pressed the stethoscope against the mound, but all I heard was air flowing through the hollow reeds.

The fourth muskrat house is on swampland that has already begun to soften. I stepped carefully on tussocks of grass and held on to willow stems as I walked out to it. This house is constructed of long, coarse broom grass, goldenrod stems, and fine roots. It has two tunnels leading out of it—one of them short, the other about twenty-five feet long—each leading to a small pool of weedless water. I held my stethoscope against the mound, but heard no sounds coming from inside the goldenrod house.

The fifth muskrat house is in a corner of the cove surrounded by mushy land. I couldn't walk out to it, but I looked it over with binoculars. It is made of short, coarse grass that grows up out of the muck all around the house. This house will be the grass house.

Each of the muskrat houses is different in shape and made of different materials. Even though I only heard signs of life coming from the first house, all five appear to be in good condition and could very well be occupied. My approach may have vibrated the marshy ground enough to alarm the inhabitants and keep them very still inside their chambers.

Seven

Painted Turtles

The trail used all winter by snowmobilers is actually an abandoned railroad bed. It is many miles long and, typical of a rail route, much of it passes through backwoods country. Three miles north of the cove, it cuts through a large clearing surrounded by hills. On one side of the raised bed is a cow pasture; on the other side is a beaver pond.

This morning I drove north to the town of Groton, parked my truck off the road, then hiked the three quarters of a mile down the railroad bed to the clearing. It was a glorious spring morning, sunny and warm. Gentle breezes carried the smell of thawing earth. Birds were chirping and insects were flying.

On the way to the clearing, there's a place where the railroad bed cuts through ledge rock. For a hundred yards or more, rock stands on both sides of the bed. Suddenly, in this shaded alley, the air was shiveringly cold. Snow still covered the slanting earth. Thick ice encased the ledge rock and coated the surface of the bed. It was like walking through a mausoleum where winter, temporarily preserved, was lying in state. Emerging from the frigid passageway, I stepped once again into warm sunlight and the clearing.

In the clearing, the beaver pond was still very much frozen. Last year's cattails stuck up through the ice. Floating bits of wood were frozen in place. Except for a set of raccoon tracks in the nearby mud, there were no signs of beavers or any other wildlife.

On the other side of the railroad bed, between the bed and the cow pasture, there flows a brook, created in part by the water that seeps underground from the beaver pond. Some discarded auto engine parts had been thrown in the water and the brook was filled with rust. But because rust is heavy and settles, the running water remained clear. Much of the vegetation along the banks was a dull red-orange, thoroughly coated by rust churned up from the stream bottom. I was pondering this when, out of the corner of my eye, I saw something bright yellow drop off the grassy bank and plop into the water. It was the yellow plastron of a painted turtle.

I located the turtle as it slowly swam and crawled over the brook's rust-covered bottom. I've seen painted turtles many times before and have always thought they were pretty. But against the red rust color of the stream bottom, this one's colors looked more vivid and its markings were bright and clearly defined. In the tainted stream, the turtle was untainted.

The turtle's six-inch shell was a deep forest green, separated into patterns by light gray dividing lines that looked as if they'd been painted on with a delicate brush. The scalloped edging all around the shell appeared to have been carefully dipped in red-orange paint, and the turtle's black legs were dotted with the same red-orange color. Its head and neck were the same deep green as its shell, with perfectly symmetrical bold yellow markings on each side of its expressionless face. The light yellow of the undershell, which showed a bit every time it clambered over a submerged branch, was brilliant against the rusty surroundings. The turtle's very short tail suggested a female. Male turtles have much longer tails.

I found two more painted turtles, both about the same size as the first, in the rusty brook. One was a male that appeared to have recently come out of hibernation. Its shell looked dull and was still dirty with mud.

Watching the colorful painted turtles in the water and sunning themselves on the warm sunlit bank, I felt as if summer were here already. When I left, I had to walk back through the cold winter alley before returning to springtime.

The trap

Eight 🌿

The Trap

In water that only yesterday had been covered with ice, today I found a wire-mesh minnow trap lying on the cove's muddy bottom. I immediately recognized the trap as one I had lost near the cove over six years ago. I'd left it empty in the weeds on the shore overnight. When I returned the next day, it was gone. Evidently someone had found it and, instead of taking it, pitched it into the water. The old trap was rusted but still intact and, as far as I could tell, still effective. There were some crayfish caught inside it. I saw their white underparts as they crawled on the wire walls.

Figuring to let the crayfish free, I reached into the water with a long broken branch and slowly rolled the trap toward the shore. It took quite some time. As I rolled it closer, I could see that there were more than just a few crayfish inside. I picked it out of the water. It was jammed full of minnows, crayfish, tadpoles, sunfish, and newts, squirming together in a writhing ball, imprisoned in that terrible trap tossed so innocently into the water six years ago.

The trap is a simple and efficient contraption, a wire-mesh cylinder with a cone-shaped wire entrance at each end. Small animals enter the trap easily, but once inside, the cones confound them. They cannot find the hole through which they entered and are trapped. The trap is opened and closed by means of a hinge and a wire clasp. I undid the rusty clasp, opened the trap, and dumped the wad of creatures into the water. Almost a third of them were dead, massed in the center of the wad, surrounded by the living. All of the occupants were scavengers—the living had been preying on the dead.

The animals that were alive looked to be in extraordinarily good condition. The minnows were bright-eyed, brilliantly colored, and shiny. The crayfish were strong, fighting among themselves like tiny armored gladiators. The crayfish's armor was richly hued, some reddish brown with yellow lines, some olive green. The larger crayfish were two-toned, with reddish brown bodies and bright blue-green claws. The tadpoles were bullfrog tadpoles: green with black spots and about the size of large gumdrops, not including their tails. Each was plump and wriggling.

There were more newts in the gang than anything else, and they were absolutely beautiful: green on top, bright yellow below, and as healthy-looking as the tadpoles.

It seemed strange that the animals were in such good condition, apparently not ill-affected by being in the trap—except, of course, for those that had died. It occurred to me that the dead minnows, crayfish, tadpoles, and newts had also enjoyed a period of such robust health and extraordinary beauty. Initially life in the trap would have been easy. Plenty of water had flowed through the wire to provide the prisoners with oxygen, and the mesh had protected them from predators such as larger fish, otters, diving ducks, turtles, and mink. There had been plenty of food in the trap as well: those animals that had been trapped before. In order to get the food that was in the trap, an animal would become trapped itself and eventually became bait for more animals.

The trap had been in the cove for six years, and this cycle had been going on for all that time. The bodies of the weak and dying were pulled apart by their hungry predators or decomposed by water and rot, and the pieces filtered out through the trap's wire walls, making room for more animals to come in.

As the crayfish, minnows, newts, and tadpoles I had just dumped into the water swam, crawled, and wriggled away from the wad they had become tangled in, I quickly counted all I could see. There were at least one hundred fifty living animals in the trap, and between fifty and seventy-five dead ones.

How long, I wondered, had the cycle taken—from entering the trap in robust health to weakening to dying and becoming the bait that would lure more animals into the trap. A month? A few weeks? How many thousands of crayfish, newts, minnows, and tadpoles had died in that trap during the six years it had been lying in the cove?

Nine
Muskrats

It is cold and windy today, and the wind has carried all the floating grasses and weeds to the leeward shoreline of the cove. The old beaver dam is leeward, and the debris has clogged the dam's leaks, so more water is being contained. The big muskrat house is now an island. The next largest, the house of reeds, has almost been submerged: it sticks up out of the water less than twelve inches. Where yesterday there had been grassy hammocks, today there are only weedy shallows. Swimming muskrats have made clear-water channels all through the weeds.

Looking over the windy cove, I noticed one muskrat standing on a clump of submerged grass, its body half in and half out of the water, eating some greens. It looked like a tiny beaver. Muskrats are a lot like beavers in appearance and behavior. But unlike beavers, which are slow and deliberate, muskrats always seem to be in a hurry. The one feeding in the cove ate quickly, its front feet fidgeting continuously with its food. As soon as it had finished, it turned, plopped into the water, swam through a narrow channel through the weeds to deeper water, and dived. I could follow its course underwater by the air bubbles that rose to the surface every couple of feet.

Suddenly the muskrat emerged with another mouthful of green reeds. It swam hurriedly back through the channel, climbed up on the clump of grass, and immediately began to feed.

The reeds looked like horsetails to me. The muskrat dropped its load. Then, using its front feet, it pushed one reed at a time into its mouth, the way we eat celery. The muskrat's mouth was going a mile a minute and so were its front feet. But the rest of its body, including its long tail, stayed perfectly still.

I lowered my binoculars and looked at the muskrat with my naked eyes. The little animal blended into its surroundings, a small brown lump in the weedy water.

The muskrat ate the reeds it had, then, without skipping a beat, turned, swam through the channel to deeper water, and dived again. It emerged with more reeds and swam back to its feeding spot. Water dripped from its head onto its face. It shook its head, sending the water flying. I love to watch an animal shed an annoyance—the muskrat shedding the dripping water, a deer flicking its ear to swoosh away a biting fly, a fox scratching a flea. Only during those times do I know exactly how the animals are feeling.

The muskrat finished eating, then headed back out to the deep water. This time it didn't dive, but continued swimming through the wind-rippled water toward the middle of the cove, moving fast, kicking itself along with its hind feet and steering with its tail. A wake formed around the muskrat's face, cresting just below its nose. When the muskrat reached a reedy patch of water, it stopped and floated awhile and rested. Then it continued through the weeds, creating yet another channel in the weedy cove. When it was only a few feet from the reed house, the muskrat dived and disappeared.

The wind died. The water became still. I watched the reed house and the water around it but saw no sign of the muskrat, no

V-shaped wave that a swimming muskrat makes, just tiny wavelets made by the wind tickling the water's surface.

The muskrat seemed to have gone inside the house of reeds. Evidently there is still some dry room inside the drowned-looking mound.

Down by the big house, a muskrat came paddling out. I was sneaking along the shore to get a closer look when it spotted me. But instead of swimming away, it ran in splashy bursts back and forth in the shallow water, chattering and squeaking as it splashed. I took this little outburst to be a territorial show rather than an act of fear. Afterward the muskrat swam openly back to its mound and dived out of sight.

Compared to the other muskrat houses in the cove, the big house is a marvelous thing. It's made almost entirely of fine weeds, grasses, and roots packed into clumps and piled around a large dead stump that is anchored firmly to the cove's muddy bottom. Here and there around the mound, a root of the stump sticks out. The big house sticks up like a fortress three and a half feet above the water. The house has all entrances underwater.

I watched the house and the water around it for a long time, waiting for the muskrat to reemerge. The sun came out strongly, spilling yellow light through the gray clouds. Suddenly I felt too warm to sit in a heavy winter coat. No more muskrat. I left.

*I*t began to rain yesterday evening and it poured throughout the night. Around midnight I heard water dripping and, because we have some small holes in our shingled roof, I ran around placing sap buckets under each leak. Then I settled on the couch and listened to the rain on the roof, the drops in the buckets, and the music of Delius on the stereo.

The beavers in the trout pond spent the night working in the rain, adding height to their dam to keep up with the slowly rising level of the pond. They used everything they could move: poplar and alder branches, grasses, weeds, mud, whole small spruce trees, which they chewed off at the ground, even discarded wire they had found in the water.

By morning over an inch of rain had fallen, and water had begun to spill over the beavers' freshly heightened dam, which is built on top of a man-made dam. Combined with the heavy rain, the additional weight of water being retained by the beaver dam could burst the main dam. I hated to do it, but in order to relieve some of the pressure on the dam, I pulled apart a section of the beaver dam. In the next few minutes, thousands of gallons of water (at about eight pounds per gallon) poured out of the pond. The waterline dropped an inch in less than fifteen minutes. Thousands more gallons of water will empty out of the pond through the holes I created in the dam before the beavers come out again this evening to repair the damage. But tonight there will be no heavy rains to compound things.

Some of the muskrats in the cove had to evacuate their homes during the night. The high water completely submerged two of their five houses. This is the time of year for the natural dispersal of muskrats anyway: flood or no flood, many younger muskrats are leaving (or being forced out of) their birthplaces to make room for new offspring due to be born in April. The outcasts wander away, not too far if possible, and establish home ranges and families of their own. There are numerous empty bank burrows where flooded-out or cast-out muskrats can take refuge. I saw one muskrat on the opposite side of the cove from where most of the muskrats live, swimming toward the abandoned beaver lodge that was piled against the cove bank. Another one had left the cove altogether, followed the feeder brook upstream to the base of the trout-pond dam, climbed over the dam, and this morning was swimming in the still water of the trout pond. The river muskrats may not have been as lucky as the ones in the cove, who had plenty of time and still water to swim in when they were flooded out. The swollen river is flowing over its banks, flooding the surrounding land. The muskrats that live in the riverbank may have been drowned inside their burrows or may have had to swim all night in the torrent.

On the riverbank, I saw a large beaver taking a rest from swimming in the powerful stream. The beaver was on what is normally a very high bank. Today it is only a swatch of green grass surrounded by brown swirling water. Years ago I saw another beaver resting on the same spot during high water. It was so tired, or else so unconcerned about the flood, that it napped there on the spot for nearly an hour. This one didn't nap but groomed itself, beginning with the short dense fur on its belly. Using its front claws as combs, it spread the fur outward from the center of its belly. It twisted its body around to comb the right side of its back, then twisted the other way to comb its left side. The beaver had been sitting on its tail, which was folded under its hind end. I noticed this when the animal lifted the tail to clean and groom the fur around its base.

*T*he river continues to rise over its banks. There is flooding everywhere. The fields all have puddles in their low places, some of which are like small ponds. Riverside willows are standing in floodwater. Since the river beavers' bank burrows are flooded, the beavers have had to move. Happily, one has already moved into the cove, and the old rotted dam shows signs of being repaired! The big muskrat house still stands as an island, but that island has shrunk in size. The reed house is also now completely surrounded by water. The house in the clump of willow stems has a pool close enough to reflect the willows of the house. The goldenrod house is not entirely engulfed, but has water filling its underground entrance. The coarse grass house in the marshy center of the cove has a series of water-filled channels leading right up to it.

This evening four muskrats were out swimming. One small, light cinnamon muskrat was swimming in the vicinity of the goldenrod house. Another swam near the coarse grass house. The third, dark brown and quite large, climbed around the top of the reed house. And the fourth was in the water near the big house, floating as still as a stick. Through binoculars I could see how intently it was eyeballing me. Its wet gray-brown fur clung close around its face, its eyes were little black beads, its whiskers stuck out, their tips tickling the water, and its tail, floating motionless, looked like the thick tail of a huge Norway rat. The muskrat looked ratty indeed.

*T*he next evening I revisited the cove. The angle of sunlight was just right for me to watch a muskrat swimming underwater, propelling itself along with its webbed hind feet. It came to a dense bed of light green weeds and, by slowly twisting its body, corkscrewed through the tangle. Its long tail curled and waved eellike in the weedy water.

For a few feet, the submerged muskrat swam on its back, and the light tan fur of its chin, chest, and belly glowed yellow in the sunlit water. It searched among the green weeds for a particular type. When it found the ones it wanted, it pulled a bunch of stalks to its mouth and chewed them off. I had known that folds of skin in muskrat and beaver mouths can close behind the teeth, enabling a submerged animal to gnaw and dig with its sharp rodent teeth without swallowing water, but this was the first time I'd witnessed a muskrat gnawing underwater. These animals also have a separate set of transparent eyelids that close independently of their outer lids, enabling them to see underwater. A muskrat's nose and ears are valvular, and they close when the muskrat dives. And when a muskrat, beaver, or otter swims underwater, its heart and pulse rate slows to reduce the body's depletion of oxygen.

*A*ll of the cove's muskrats have become exceedingly wary and territorial. This evening I witnessed three separate fights among them. It would be easy to say that this is because by now young muskrats are being born and nursed and the mothers are safeguarding their nests. This is it, I'm sure, but the intensity of the aggression is more than what I imagined it would be. One muskrat left the big house and swam in a beeline across the cove, far beyond its own territorial boundaries. As it swam by a small spit of shore, a muskrat that lived on the bank ran into the water and attacked the swimming muskrat. The swimmer clumsily splashed away, only to be attacked again, this time in deeper water. The muskrats fought fiercely, splashing and rolling in the water until both sank. I lost sight of them for a long while. Then the first muskrat emerged and swam, again in a straight line, back to the big house. The whole thing seemed odd.

Ten Mergansers

*T*his noon I got a good look at a pair of hooded mergansers. A male and female were cruising the river when I spotted them. The current carried them downstream, and they crossed in a long diagonal line to the other side of the river. The male, fighting the drag of the current, raised his crest feathers in the way that birds do when they are uncomfortable. The bright white patch on either side of his head widened, giving him a white hood—the mark of the species.

My favorite duck of all is the wood duck, but whenever I'm asked to draw a duck, I invariably draw a male hooded merganser. Its stark white and black markings are a natural for pencil or pen.

I saw the pair again later in the afternoon, swimming in a quiet eddy. This time they spotted me first and took off together upstream, flying low over the water.

The river has been rising steadily. North of us, snow is melting in the mountains. The river ice is breaking up. All day yesterday chunks of it floated downstream, some the size of tabletops. Pieces floating near the riverbanks became snagged against overhanging branches, twisting and turning until they worked free, splashing loudly as they tumbled in the moving water. One large block made such a commotion, I thought an animal had slipped and fallen in. As the blocks drifted down the river, most of their bulk was beneath the surface of the water. Each piece was a mini-iceberg. What must it be like for the mergansers, swimming and diving amid the floating ice?

*T*he river, still high, has calmed and is running free of ice. Along the bank, red osier dogwoods have turned a lively crimson. This afternoon, through the spaces between osier and sumac stems, I spotted the bright white chest of the male hooded merganser again swimming in the river. The brown-and-gray female was also there but much harder to see through the thicket. Looking through binoculars, I followed the male as it moved upstream. When it dived, I ran to a place where the brush along the river is less dense.

The mergansers swam into an eddy and rested there away from the current. The male relaxed, flattening his crest feathers; the wide white hood on each side of his head contracted to thin white stripes. The female, though calm, seemed wary. Her gray-and-red crest was raised. When the male dived, she swam about in tight circles, never diving herself, her red-brown eyes looking this way and that way.

The male hooded merganser has yellow eyes with deep black pupils. Set in the velvety black feathers of his face, they are strikingly beautiful. When the male swam directly against the current, he leaned forward with his head and neck low. His crest flattened further. His long bill pointed straight forward. He looked streamlined rather than sharp-edged, like an entirely different duck.

Mergansers have the sharpest shapes of all the ducks. Their bills are sharply pointed. Their head crests raise to a high sharp edge.

Their wings are wedge-shaped and come to sharp swallowlike points.

The current pulled the mergansers out of the eddy, into the mainstream. Drifting, they twirled slowly along, gently out of control.

Yesterday was glorious! The sun shone, the sap flowed. I spent another day watching mergansers. Now there are two pairs. They were in the cove fishing in the open water amid the ice. When mergansers dive, they flatten their head crests, creating a sort of skullcap or diving cap. When they emerge, they raise their crests high. They may dive three, four, even five times before they come up with a fish. Unlike otters, which can remain submerged by allowing their bodies to sink, mergansers are buoyant and can stay down only by forcefully kicking their feet.

When a merganser had a fish, the catch wriggled and flopped in the duck's bill. Sometimes the struggling fish jerked the merganser's face down into the water. Mergansers, like all fishing birds, have to manipulate their food in their bills in order to swallow it head first. Otherwise they would choke on the fish's spreading fins.

The females were so busy fishing and the males so concerned with guarding their territory (one circle about eighteen inches in diameter around itself and another around its mate) that I was able to stalk very near the water's edge.

At one point the ducks split up. One pair swam down a long channel and away. The other stayed near the shore, climbed out of the water onto ice, and rested. The female laid her head on her back, her bill tucked under her feathers. The male relaxed his neck and sank his head into the soft white feathers of his breast.

I wanted to continue on my way, but I didn't want to disturb the resting mergansers. I was so close that any movement or sound would certainly alert the male, who was facing in my direction. I focused my binoculars on the male's head: his eyes closed slowly as he dozed off, then slowly opened again. I watched the merganser's eye. Each time I saw it close, I ran a dozen feet. By quietly running every time the merganser dozed, I was able to sneak by the birds.

Eleven

Close Encounters

*T*he cove is fast becoming a favorite spot for ducks. This afternoon the four mergansers were joined by a flock of ten mallards. Mallards are wonderfully vocal ducks. One female kept up a monologue of quacks, squawks, and mumbling grunts while the others in her flock rested, swam, or fed in the shallow weedy water. I thought the noisy duck had sensed me sneaking across the pasture toward the shore, but she hadn't. She was just gabbing. Neither she nor the other ducks, including the mergansers, showed any sign of tension or alarm.

Six of the mallards were on a small grassy island in the center of the cove. On the island with them, an otter lay resting. The ducks paid little attention to this predator in their midst. And when the otter rose and walked around in the grass, they showed no fear.

The otter romped across the grassy island, slid into the water, and swam amid the swimming ducks. The ducks simply went about their business. Then the otter submerged and swam nearer the ducks and under them. Twice it tried to pull a mallard under. Each time, the targeted duck suddenly squawked and splashed in the water, beating its wings to fly off the spot, then settled down again four or five feet away. After one miss, the otter swirled in the water near the surface in much the same way as a big fish does when it attacks some large prey.

Except for those two close encounters, the ducks seemed unconcerned about the otter swimming below them, and when the otter emerged and swam again in full view, they continued to act nonchalant.

The otter dived again. After a long time underwater, it finally emerged some distance from the ducks, crawled out onto another small island, and disappeared in some tall grasses. Curious to see what the otter was up to, I ran around the cove, over the trout-pond dam, through the woods, and down the back side of the cove to a place on the opposite shore—only to find that the otter was now swimming back toward the ducks. It swam purposefully right through the middle of a group of six mallards. The ducks watched it move past them, only inches away. The otter continued down a long channel that is fed from above by the trout pond's overflow. I guessed it was heading to the pond to fish there. I ran back around the cove, and just as I reached the dam, so did the otter, making its way up the overflow side of the dam, cracking twigs and shaking small brushes as it climbed.

The otter came up over the spillway, less than five feet from me. We were too close. As soon as the otter stepped into the water running over the dam, it spotted me. It made an about-face to go back down over the spillway, but it got caught in a tangle of branches. As the otter struggled to untangle itself, I crouched low, hoping to drop out of sight and lessen its anxiety. But dropping low brought me even closer to the frightened otter. It let out a loud coughing-hissing sound, then suddenly broke its way out of the tangle and slid back over the spillway, where it took refuge under a pile of sticks and brush.

I felt bad that I had shocked and frightened the otter in such close quarters. I left quickly so it could regain its composure and perhaps continue its hunting.

*T*his evening I made up for clumsily cornering the otter. In the waning daylight, as I made my rounds from home to trout pond to beaver hollow to river to cove to meadow and back home, I trod lightly and moved slowly. The beavers that lived in the hollow were out working. The female, who was near the dam, was eating the bark off a pencil-thin twig. She held it in her paws like an ear of corn, turning it as she gnawed. Then she added the barkless twig to the dam. The beaver swam up to a large piece of floating ice and crawled onto it as if it were a raft. But as soon as she boarded, the ice raft began to sink under her weight. She comically rode it down as if it were an elevator descending into the water.

I heard loud chewing noises: the male was busy working on the stem of a flooded alder.

From the beaver hollow I walked to the river. At a place where it flows very near the cove, I saw the large river beaver near the bank. The beaver had made a scent patty by piling mud on the grass, then squirting the mud with the sweet-smelling oil from its castor gland. The "beaver patty" is evidence that this beaver is living alone. It had made the patty, and perhaps others around the river, to attract a mate.

I turned my gaze from the beaver on my left to the cove on my right, and so help me, there was the otter I had frightened earlier. It was a comfortable distance away this time, though still close enough that I could see it plainly even in the dimming light. The otter was stretched out at the water's edge, its long tail laying in grass, its front feet standing in water. It was looking in my direction, and I focused my binoculars on its face. Its eyes looked sleepy. I passed by slowly, taking extra care not to alarm the otter twice in one day.

137

The ducks were out on the cove, mallards and mergansers together. A third pair of hooded mergansers had joined the others. All were still and quiet.

The rest of my way around the cove and over the meadow, I kept a sharp lookout for mink and mice, but I'd seen all I was going to see for one day.

Twelve

A June Frost

BEFORE:

This has been an unusually cool June. The month began with warnings of possible frost in the "normally colder pockets" that include most of northern Vermont. Today the forecasters are issuing frost warnings again. This frost seems imminent.

At six P.M. the temperature was in the forties, and the air was getting cooler as the sun sank nearer the horizon. At the cove, the cooling air mingled with the much warmer water and created steam. It drifted low like smoke across the still surface.

A cove muskrat swam through the mist. Its wake shone bright white on the dark green water surface, forming a V like that made by flying geese. Because the muskrat was swimming far and straight, the arms of the V lengthened. Even after it had reached the other shore, its wake was still visible as white lines breaking up into glistening white dashes.

A kingbird flew over the cove to snatch an insect, then back to its perch on a branch above the old beaver dam. I noticed that the dam had more fresh twigs and grasses on it. The river beaver was

Beaver head

swimming in the middle of the cove. I was looking through my binoculars when its head suddenly surfaced in my view. I sharpened the focus on the beaver's face, which was big and dark brown.

The beaver stayed a long time in that spot, with only its head sticking out of the water. Its nostrils were near the surface, and when the beaver exhaled, it blew the water into a fine spray. Hippolike, it swiveled its round ears, listening in different directions. I listened too.

Birds warbled in the surrounding brush. Up on the road, a car motored by. Here and there in the cove, a feeding tadpole or fish flipped up to the surface with a sharp smack. A red-winged blackbird called to its mate. Across the cove in the pasture, sheep baaed and lambs baaed back.

There was no wind and I made no sounds, but the beaver must have heard something that made it wary. It dipped underwater and swam away. It didn't surface again until it was all the way across the cove, in the cover of weeds.

Throughout the evening something continued to bother the beaver. It kept slapping its tail on the water for no apparent reason. Even after I'd left the cove and was walking home, I heard it slap its tail twice more. Perhaps, like us, the beaver was just feeling a little odd about the unusually cold weather.

After sunset the air changed from cool to downright cold. Deanna and I covered all the garden plants that a frost could kill. We covered the tenderest herbs. We covered the rock gardens. We covered the climbing rose and the red geraniums that she had just put out. Deanna brought all her porch plants into the warm kitchen. When darkness fell, the temperature outside was thirty-three degrees and still dropping.

Turtle on muskrat house

AFTER:

I was out of the house soon after sunup. Already the morning rays had melted much of the frost. In the hollows and at the bases of hills, hoarfrost still covered every stem, blade, leaf, and bloom, but away from those spots, all that remained of the frost was the moisture of its melting. Tall grasses rubbed frost water onto my pant legs, and by the time I had reached the cove, I was soaked from the knees down.

A large painted turtle crawled out of the water onto the big muskrat house and up to the top. The turtle seemed extra wary, unusually so for the ideal position it was in. It jerked its head to left and right, looked up into the sky and down into the water. As soon as I stepped out from behind the cover of a honeysuckle bush, the turtle looked at me and instantly dropped off the mound, somersaulting into the water.

Frosty air enlivens hardy plants. Their stems firm up and their leaves freshen in the cold. This morning's frost did little damage to the wild plants. It nipped only the very tops of sumac and browned some fronds of sensitive ferns. The hawthorn had blossomed overnight in the midst of the frost: clusters of snow-white, musky-smelling flowers dressed its branches. Even its long nasty thorns looked less hostile, glistening in frost moisture. Poison ivy, shut down for the cold night, had not yet awakened. Each plant's three shiny red-tinted leaves drooped in the state of suspended animation that cold and dark trigger in such plants. With its leaves drooping, the poison ivy looked as innocent as young bean plants.

The water in the cove was murky. Either the drop in temperature had caused a turnover in the water body, bringing the lower level of water to the surface and sinking the upper level, or the cove had been ready to turn over, frost or no frost. In any case, a turnover had occurred. This is the way a pond or lake breathes, preventing stagnation.

During turnover, the bottom of the cove gets slightly disturbed. Silt is loosened and set adrift, causing the cove to become murky. Where sunlight poured into the cove, I could see particles of silt. Even where the water is very shallow, I couldn't see the bottom clearly through its haze. In a few days, the silt will settle, the water will clear, and the turnover process will be complete.

The river flows as clearly as it flowed yesterday and the day before. How I love our little river! It's such a sparkling stream, full of living things.

On a pebbled shoal in its center, a pair of sandpipers were feeding on insects. Their short tails bobbed constantly as they scoured the shoal. From the way they fed, there must have been some insects on the dry tops of stones and others floating in the water-filled crevices between the stones.

I followed fresh deer tracks along the river until they faded on the hard cinders near the railroad bed. Then I headed home.

Thirteen

Hummingbird Perched

There are a few dead trees standing near the water. On one of them, three very different birds all perched at the same time. On a high top branch was a red-winged blackbird—a sentry overlooking the cove, the railroad bed, and for all I know, the whole valley. (It's hard to tell just how much area a red-winged blackbird considers its own territory.) Clinging to the tree's graying trunk, a hairy woodpecker chipped away at loose bark, searching for insects in the dead wood. And on a long slender branch that overhangs the water like a fishing pole was a tiny hummingbird, so small that I had to look again to be sure I was really seeing it. Perched, the hummingbird looked dark green, almost black. But when it flew off to a nearby honeysuckle and sipped nectar from the pink blossoms, its dark green feathers shone iridescently, its head sparkled emerald and gold, and I could see its tiny white breast and bright ruby throat.

We tend to think of hummingbirds flying, not perched. Almost every picture we see of them, whether photo or illustration, shows them in hovering flight. This is probably why we hardly ever notice perched hummingbirds.

Sleeping hummingbird

Hummingbirds perch to rest, to preen their feathers, to take shelter, to nest, and to sleep. In sleep, a hummingbird holds its long bill nearly straight up. This stabilizes the bird while it is unconscious. I once had the rare opportunity to observe a sleeping hummingbird for many hours—twenty-one to be exact! It was perched on the wire support that runs from the outside sill of our kitchen window to the tall post of a bird feeder. Each spring, ruby-throated hummingbirds migrate from Central and South America to as far north as Quebec and New Brunswick. On one leg of that trip, the tiny birds fly nonstop for five hundred miles across the Gulf of Mexico. The hummingbird outside our kitchen window looked wiped out, unkempt and disheveled, more like a stuffed specimen than a living bird. When a hard rain began to fall, the bird, sheltered by the feeder's tray, slept right through the downpour.

I went outside to look at it closely. From a foot away, I could see how tightly its tiny toes grasped the wire. From six inches away, I could see a minuscule barb on the base of the bird's bottom bill, a feature I hadn't known existed. What could the barb be for? Every few seconds the bird's tiny chest heaved in deep breathing. The sleeping hummingbird lacked the male's ruby throat; it was a female ruby-throated hummingbird. She slept all day and all the next morning. Finally in the afternoon, after at least twenty-one hours of sleep (we have no idea how long the hummingbird was there before we noticed it), the sleeper began to awaken. Her eyes still closed, she began to breathe more rapidly, and every so often she shook her bill. The muscles in her hind end pulsed, raising and lowering her tail feathers. She stretched her wings, then began rocking back and forth, lowering her bill and snapping her head this way, then that. She swallowed hard and opened her bill wide as if yawning. Then she shook her head wildly. Finally she opened her eyes and looked all around. She defecated, then flew directly down to Deanna's ground phlox to breakfast.

Fourteen 🌰

In the Wind

Strong winds today. A massive cold front is moving through. There are tiny whitecaps in the trout pond. Small cyclones of dust whirl up from the road. The tall meadow grasses move in waves. Great gusts toss the evergreen boughs and flatten the windward sides of leafy hardwood trees. Yet through it all, birds are flying, winging expertly in the wind.

The top of a bird's wing is curved; its underwing is less so. When a wing cuts through air, the air divides over and under it. Because the wing's upper surface is curved, the air traveling over it must go farther and therefore move faster in order to reach the end of the wing at the same time as the air passing under it. This produces what is known as the Bernoulli Effect, named after Daniel Bernoulli in the eighteenth century. The faster-moving air above the wing exerts less pressure on the wing surface (because it has less time in which to do so) than the slower-moving air under it. Since the air pressure is greater under the wing, the wing is pushed up. In addition, a suction is created that pulls the wing forward.

The same principle applies to airplane wings; but to me, a

Cross section of wing showing lift effect

Air flows faster

Air divides

Air rejoins

Air flows slower

plane is nothing compared to a bird in flight. Watch a swallow speeding over the grass suddenly ascend, beating its wings to climb the wind, then fold its wings against its sides, dive toward earth, and—only a few feet above the ground—spread its wings to glide again over the grass. That's flying!

Today, despite the wind, the swallows were flying to perfection. When the streamlined birds flew broadside to the wind, their sharp-edged wings clipped through the crosscurrents like scissor blades. Wings outstretched, they sailed downwind. Barely flapping, they tacked upwind. When a gust blew a bird off course, it simply incorporated its sideward movement into its flight, cutting this way and that way through the heavy air.

Heavier, less streamlined birds such as starlings and robins flew easily downwind, but when they had to travel upwind, it was another story. Flapping their wings forcefully, the birds dove under the oncoming wind in much the same way as people walk against incoming surf and, just as a wave hits, dive under it. Sometimes the birds flew above an oncoming wave of air, then "bodysurfed" down over it.

While other birds were flying in the wind, a killdeer spent the windy day walking on the road, feasting on insects that were blowing off the meadow. If it was a female (killdeer sexes look alike), it may also have been swallowing bits of sand and gravel from the road. A nesting bird eats sand and gravel to provide its system with minerals, especially calcium, which is necessary for egg production. The killdeer walked and ran but never took flight: killdeer prefer to fly in direct routes, which today's wind prohibited.

Later in the day, as the belly of the cold front barreled through, the wind reached near gale force. It blew the loose paint off the house and pressed so powerfully against the north wall that the old house beams began to creak and crack. During the worst wind,

I looked outside. No birds were flying. Not even the swallows.

*T*he cove is a bit more sheltered from wind than the trout pond and had no whitecaps, just ripples of waves. A large snapping turtle was resting on a lump of vegetation. Even though I approached slowly and downwind, the turtle spotted me and slid into the water. A second later, it emerged on the leeward side of the mound and watched me from there. From the third of its carapace that was sticking out of the water, I could tell the snapper was a big one, probably as big around as a dinner plate. Its shell was green with algae and had the prehistoric-looking lumps and crevices that are characteristic of snapping-turtle shells. Its head was dark brown and as big as my fist.

When the turtle dipped underwater, I decided to wait and see if it would surface again.

The snapping turtles in the cove are the things legends are made of. They are big, and they'll eat anything they can lock their jaws onto. Snapping turtles can grow to forty-five or fifty pounds, and one of the snappers in the cove is nearly that big.

The cove's snappers mate in May in the shallow weedy water. The females bury their fertilized eggs in the soft sand along the banks, in the cinders of the railroad bed, even as far away as the cornfield. Many of the eggs around the cove are dug out and eaten by raccoons.

A few years ago, I had the chance to watch a pair of snapping turtles in the throes of mating. I watched them in the weedy shallows across the cove through binoculars. It looked like some kind of tank war, each turtle trying to push the other over. Even at a distance of fifty yards, I could hear their shells knocking together and their bodies splashing in the water. The male kept trying to climb onto the female's shell. But each time he got close to mounting the female, she knocked him into the water onto his back. When this happened, his yellow, pink, and red bottom shell, called the plastron, stood out brightly against the roiled water. Once, after she'd knocked him onto his back, the female climbed halfway onto the male and held him upside down underwater. The male's tail and legs stuck up comically. Then the female began to push him over and over in the weedy water. He finally righted himself and pushed her off and over onto her back. He then climbed onto her until they were together plastron to plastron. The turtles stayed in that position for a long time, the female upside down and completely underwater with the male on top of her. The male's tail stiffened and slowly arched upward. Finally the female pushed him off and righted herself in the water. There the two continued to fight and push for more than an hour.

When you're watching turtles, you have to allow plenty of time. Almost everything they do is done deliberately, in slow turtle motion. Everything, that is, except striking out to catch prey or bite an enemy. Then turtles can move with snakelike speed.

I was still waiting for the snapping turtle near the mound of vegetation to emerge when the wind suddenly died. At the water's edge, a green frog made a loud plunk that sounded like a banjo string being plucked. Blue-backed dragonflies appeared and disappeared on shoreline boulders and stones. Birds began to chirp and sing. Two in particular, a pair of song sparrows, carried on a long conversation. A hairy woodpecker rapped loudly on a shagbark hickory. And a female red-winged blackbird scolded me from her perch on the tip of a tall green stem.

The still air was heavily perfumed with honeysuckle. Both pink- and white-blossomed honeysuckle grow around the cove; the white smell more pungent, the pink more sweet.

A pair of swallows flew over the cove at dizzying speeds. When one dipped down to take an insect off the water, it hardly disturbed the surface at all. When a swallow did create a water ring, the bird diving was taking water, not insects, into its beak.

After a while the wind picked up again. The swallows left the cove. The smell of honeysuckle was carried away. All sounds, except for the sound of wind, became muted. I'd been waiting for the turtle for about forty-five minutes when, a few feet from the mound, the snapper finally popped its head up out of the water. It held its nostrils high to sniff the air. I was close but still downwind; the turtle couldn't possibly smell me. After we'd both had a long look—the turtle at the surrounding cove, me at the turtle—the snapper disappeared underwater again.

*T*he next day we were in the tail end of the cold front and the wind was still terrific, blowing constant and strong. I took to watering the plants in the garden to keep them from being blow-dried to death. On the mown lawn, I watched a large bumblebee take refuge from the buffeting wind. It climbed down into the short-cut grass and rested near the windless ground, rubbing its head and back and stroking and straightening its wings. Then it climbed up to the top of a grass blade and, taking flight, was blown on its way.

Toward sunset the wind diminished. Everything—trees, grass, water, even the air itself—seemed to sigh with relief. The cove was calm, reflecting the clearing sky. The setting sun brightened the tops of trees and brush. The two song sparrows spoke to each other in fluent strings of whistles, warbles, calls, and whole songs. The male perched on the top twig of a leafy waterside bush. The dark brown identifying spot on the sparrow's breast glowed reddish brown in the sunlight. When it lifted its beak to sing, its white throat patch shone. The sparrow barely opened its mouth to warble; but to sing high, sustained notes, it threw back its head and opened its beak wide, the way young birds do when they want

Song sparrow

149

to be fed. The song sent a thrill through me. I felt I knew what it was about—a song of joy for the return of calm. If I'd known the lyrics, I would have sung along.

The wind had blown down many branches, and whole trees lay across the railroad bed.

I scanned the cove looking for muskrats but saw none. I looked for the snapping turtle on the mound of vegetation. It wasn't there—it was right in front of me on the bank! Its legs were folded under its shell, and its head was pulled in up to its eyeballs. It may have been a female, stopping on its way to the railroad bed to bury its eggs when I blocked its way. The turtle was about as big as I had earlier estimated it, twelve inches in diameter. It must have been out of the water for some time, because the algae on its shell had dried to an olive brown crust. The turtle saw me before I saw it. Since it couldn't dive to safety, it did its best to look like a boulder with eyes fixed in my direction.

I've learned that while it's possible to watch most wild animals without their being aware of your presence, with turtles you can rarely watch them without being watched back. Turtles have excellent eyesight. Other animals are more adept at seeing movement than at recognizing shapes, but turtles, I believe, do recognize and react to still figures. I suppose this is natural, since they spend so much time being still themselves.

The snapper on the bank followed me with its eyes, looking up when I stood, down when I squatted, right and left when I shifted my weight from one leg to the other. When it had finally had enough of staring at me and of me staring at it, it stuck out its powerful legs, lifted its heavy body, made an about-face, and clambered over branches, stems, and debris, down the bank to the water.

In the spot where the turtle had been resting, the vegetation was severely depressed. Wild strawberry plants, yarrow fronds, green grasses, dry brown grasses, honeysuckle sprouts, dandelion leaves, and some small white wildflowers had all been flattened by the weight of the turtle's body.

Near the turtle's spot, I found fresh otter droppings. On the riverbank, directly across the railroad bed, there were more. They were so fresh that the area stank. I held my nose, vaguely remembering reading something about airborne parasites that can be contracted from fresh feces. Apparently a number of otters, probably a mother and her young, have been dividing their hunting between the river and the cove. The cinders on the railroad bed were streaked with lines made by the otters' dragging tails. I was wondering if the otters and the snapping turtles had together cleaned out the cove's muskrat population, since it had been a while since I'd seen a muskrat there, when I happened to glance across the cove. On the far side, in the weediest section of water, a muskrat was swimming. I looked at the sky and marked the time. It was nearing sundown.

On my way home, excited about seeing the muskrat, I tripped in the woods, getting myself tangled in some old, rusty barbed wire. Though the barbs had barely scratched my flesh, I drove into town and subjected myself to a tetanus shot, just to be safe.

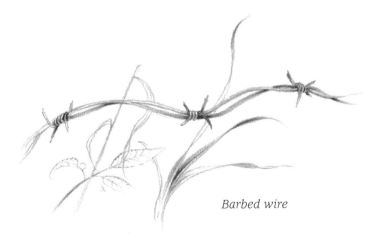

Barbed wire

Large painted turtle

Fifteen

Turtle Days

June began with three days of frost. Then it turned hot and unusually dry. The pea vines are toughing out the dry weather and keeping green, but they haven't shown much new growth, nor have they produced any flowers. The heat-loving beans have continued to grow, but slowly. The rest of the garden we've kept alive by watering, but for any more substantial growth, the garden needs rain. Only rain can saturate the ground enough for the plant roots to draw not only water but also dissolved vitamins and minerals.

The pasture grass has stopped growing, and the sheep are grazing the same spots they grazed only a day or two ago. I saw one old ewe down on her front ankles to graze. She was having to nip the sparse grasses down to the nubs. This isn't good for either the pasture or the sheep. The grass will suffer from such close cropping. The sheep, consuming more dirt than usual, increase their chances of becoming infested with parasites that lay their eggs in the soil. There's little we can do about the sheep aside from feeding them grain and hay. As for the pasture, we can only hope for rain.

Our lawn is dry and browning. Earthworms, dry-skinned from being in dry ground, emerge only to find the ground surface even drier. Worms attempting to migrate overland are being fried in the hot sun.

Only the woods and meadows look June lush: they can shade themselves, keeping soil, roots, stems, and leaves cool and somewhat moist.

For the past three days the temperature has risen into the nineties. Surface water is rapidly evaporating. The trout pond is down a half foot. The river is also low. This evening I saw a river trout swimming downstream to deeper, cooler water. No doubt many of the river fish are doing the same.

But amid all this dryness, the cove is brimming. Three beavers—a big blackish one, a medium-sized cinnamon-colored beaver, and a smaller dark brown beaver—have all adopted the cove and, working together, have fully restored the old dam to a solid, leakless mass. For building materials, they've been using mostly mud and grasses. Yesterday I noticed a clump of tall shoreline grasses being jerked around: a beaver was cutting the grass stems at their bases. By this evening, those grasses had been woven into the dam. The beavers haven't cut any of the small brush that grows along the water's edge. There are hundreds of honeysuckle stems, but the beavers have ignored them. Bush honeysuckle grows from a multistemmed base with all the stems branching up into a triangle at the top. A beaver would have trouble manipulating it. And, too, honeysuckle bark is dry and flaky—not very appetizing. Beavers prefer to eat soft bark and green, wet inner wood. The other small trees and brush growing around the cove are probably just as distasteful. Hawthorn branches would poke and stab any beaver that tried to chew them, as would the thickets of prickly berry stems. There are poplars and birch saplings nearby, but to get at them the beavers would have to leave the water and cross overland, which is something they are never eager to do.

This hot afternoon, I watched the cinnamon beaver adding fresh mud to the dam, diving and clawing the black mud from the cove bottom. It looked like refreshingly cool work.

After working for long intervals underwater, the beaver's fur was saturated. The fur on its head was disheveled and the fur on its back was parted down the middle in a most unbeaverlike way. Its normally dry underfur looked wet too. Some serious grooming and oiling were in order. But with the weather so hot and dry, maybe the beaver felt good being soaked to the skin.

Tree swallows were cooling off by bathing in the cove, belly flopping into the water, sometimes twice in a row. I picked one swallow to watch closely through my binoculars. It glided over the water until it was about three feet above the surface, then dropped down into a belly-flopping plunge. Then it flapped its wings rapidly to regain a few feet of altitude so that it could splash into the water again. After that, the swallow flew high and fast, drying out in the air.

I stopped a wood turtle on its way to the woods and squatted down beside it to have a long, close look. The turtle's dark eyes were big and round, and I could see myself reflected in them. An ant crawled over one eyelid, but the turtle didn't blink. It kept its eye open and on me. A small, sky blue butterfly alighted first on the turtle's rough shell and then on its right hind foot. The scales on the turtle's feet and legs were orange. Its mouth was the same color, and when the turtle opened it a crack, I thought I saw pinkish flesh inside. I wondered, Do turtles have tongues? I'm sure they must, but I've never really noticed one. I leaned forward for a closer look, but as I moved, the turtle closed its mouth and pulled its head in right up to its unblinking eyes, which remained on me.

Turtle tracks on loose sand

Lately the railroad bed is marked by the tracks of turtles, large and small, all apparently seeking nesting sites. Turtle tracks are unmistakable. On soft ground, you can see the claw scrapings of each laborious step, arched grooves where edges of the turtle's shell cut into the ground, and if the ground is soft enough, the drag marks of its tail. Except for the heat, I should think this dry weather is ideal for egg-laying turtles. Dry, loose dirt is easy to dig and to push back in order to bury the eggs. Also, dry dirt doesn't hold the turtle's scent as well as moist soil does, so more eggs can incubate undiscovered by egg-eating predators.

Turtle eggs are incubated by the warmth in the soil. Right now the soil is well warmed, and it will remain warm long after the weather turns cooler and wetter.

In the cindery area of the railroad bed, I found two fresh turtle digs. The turtles had dug below the cinders, into the sandy soil below. After they'd deposited their eggs, they pushed the dirt back, mixing the dark cinders with the light sand. The buried nests were conspicuous light spots in the black cinder roadway.

There was a fresh path broken through the vegetation where the snapping turtle had crawled up the cove bank. On its way up the incline, it had paused to rest a number of times, and there the vegetation was crushed and flattened down. The snapper had climbed onto the railroad bed and followed it north for a hundred yards or more. In a soft, sandy mound where the railroad bed runs up against the fox field, it had dug one hole and covered it, walked a few feet away, then dug another hole and covered it.

A snapping turtle can lay anywhere from eight to eighty eggs but, on average, lays about twenty-five. A turtle nest hole need be only a little bigger than the turtle's body, so perhaps this snapper had more eggs than would fit in one hole.

After nesting, the turtle had headed back down the railroad bed to where she had first crawled up. Along her way back, she had dug another nest and covered it over. After that, the turtle was finished with her eggs. She won't return to the nest spots.

*T*he turtles have been on the move for a week. Every day I find fresh turtle tracks from cove and river to nesting places. Yesterday I encountered a small painted turtle coming up the cove bank. Its shell was dark and shiny. Its red legs and green-and-yellow neck were clean and bright. It walked onto the railroad bed, which lately has become a turtle highway, and began its search for a nesting sight.

A couple of paces away, a large wood turtle was heading back to the cove. Its shell was covered with dry soil and its hind legs were dull and dirty from digging.

A turtle digs with its hind legs, pushing the dirt away with sideways swipes of its hind feet. It digs down at about a forty-five-degree angle, making a hole about the same size and shape as its body and backing into it. When the turtle has dug deep enough that only its head and front legs are sticking up out of the ground, it stops and climbs up. Then, with its hind end still in the hole, the turtle lays its eggs, guiding each one down carefully with one of its hind feet. Whenever I've watched turtles laying, I've been impressed by how carefully they manipulate each egg, cupping it in a webbed hind foot and lowering it into the nest as if they were placing a baby in a cradle.

Turtle eggs dug up and eaten by raccoon

If a turtle nest is dug up by an egg-eating predator, the size and shape of the excavated nest hole is a clue to the type of turtle eggs that have been destroyed. Raccoons have sniffed out and dug up some of the turtle eggs that are buried around the cove. As far as I could tell from the emptied nest holes, they've destroyed two that were made by wood turtles and one that belonged to a snapping turtle. White, leathery eggshells lay scattered around each one. It looked like the wood-turtle nest holes held under a dozen eggs each. The snapper's held more than two dozen.

The turtles have buried many more eggs than the raccoons will find. Most of them will hatch, and many of the hatchlings will safely make the journey from nest to water. There will be enough turtles.

Index 🌰